# ESSAYS AND LETTERS

BY

## LEO TOLSTOY

TRANSLATED BY
AYLMER MAUDE

LONDON
GRANT RICHARDS
LEICESTER SQUARE
1903

PRINTED BY
BILLING AND SONS, LIMITED,
GUILDFORD, ENGLAND

10731
14.12.49

XLVI.

# THE WORKS
OF
# LEO TOLSTOY.—I.

## ESSAYS AND LETTERS

# PREFACE

THE articles in this volume of *Essays and Letters* all belong to one period of Tolstoy's career (the years 1888-1903). The subjects with which they deal are religion and moral duty : what man should believe and do, and what he should not believe and not do.

Some of the letters are of the nature of rough essays or drafts of essays, but if less carefully finished than the longer essays, they have the special merit of showing Tolstoy's opinions in application to certain people and to certain definite conditions. They thus help to bridge the gulf between theory and practice.

Some of the articles in this book are now published, in English, for the first time ; and most of the articles are newly translated. During their preparation I have had the great advantage of receiving repeated assistance from Leo Tolstoy, as well as kind encouragement.

Footnotes that occur in the original are marked L. T. For those not so marked I am responsible.

AYLMER MAUDE.

GREAT BADDOW,
CHELMSFORD.

# CONTENTS

The articles marked in the above Table of Contents with an asterisk (*) are not included in the Moscow editions of Tolstoy's works; being, for the most part, prohibited in Russia.

# ESSAYS AND LETTERS

## I

### INDUSTRY AND IDLENESS

'In the sweat of thy face shalt thou eat bread, till thou return unto the ground; for out of it wast thou taken.'—GEN. iii. 19.

THE above are the title and the epigraph of a book by Timothy Miháylovitch Bóndaref* which I have read in manuscript.

That book seems to me very remarkable for its strength, its clearness, and the beauty of its language, as well as for a sincerity of conviction that is apparent in every line, but above all for the importance, truth, and depth of its fundamental thought.

---

* T. M. Bóndaref was born a serf in 1820. In 1858 he was sent to serve for twenty-five years in the army, but joining the sect of 'Sabbatarians' (who accept the Old Testament as authoritative, and follow the Jewish faith in many things), he was banished in 1867 to Údina in Siberia. There, as a ploughman of great energy, he built up for himself a fairly comfortable peasant home, but again impoverished himself by efforts to spread his doctrine of 'bread-labour.' His book could not be published in Russia, but has been translated into French and other languages. Another title Bóndaref gave to his book is 'The Agriculturist's Triumph.'

A

The fundamental thought of the book is the following : In all the affairs of life the important thing is to know, not what is good and necessary, but what of all the good and necessary things in existence comes first in importance, what second, what third, and so on.

If that is important in worldly affairs, yet more is it important in matters of faith, which define man's duties.

Tatian, a teacher of the early Church, says that men's sufferings come not so much from their not knowing God, as from their acknowledging a false god and esteeming as God that which is not God. The same thought applies to the duties men acknowledge. Misfortune and evil come, not so much from men not knowing their duties, as from the fact that they acknowledge false duties and esteem as duties things that are not really such, while they do not recognise as a duty that which is really their first duty. Bóndaref declares that the misfortunes and evil in men's lives come from regarding many empty and harmful regulations as religious duties, while forgetting, and hiding from themselves and others, that chief, primary, undoubted duty announced at the beginning of the Holy Scriptures : ' In the sweat of thy face shalt thou eat bread.'

For those who believe in the sanctity and infallibility of the word of God as expressed in the Bible, the command there given by God Himself, and nowhere revoked, is sufficient proof of its own validity. But for those who do not acknowledge the Holy Scriptures, the importance and validity of this commandment (if only it be considered without prejudice as a simple, not supernatural, expression of human wisdom) may be proved by a consideration of the conditions of human life, as is done by Bóndaref in his book.

An obstacle to such consideration unfortunately exists in the fact that many of us are so accustomed to hear from theologians perverted and senseless interpretations of the words of Holy Scripture, that the mere reminder that a certain principle coincides with the teachings of Scripture, is enough to cause some people to distrust that principle.

'What do I care for the Holy Scriptures? We know that anything you like can be deduced from them, and that they are all rubbish.'

But this is unreasonable. Surely the Holy Scriptures are not to blame because people interpret them falsely; and a man who says what is true, is not to blame because the truth he utters is contained in the Holy Scriptures.

One must not forget that, if it be granted that what are called the Scriptures are human productions, it has still to be explained why just these human writings, and not some others, have come to be regarded by men as the words of God Himself. There must be some reason for it.

And the reason is clear.

Superstitious people called the Scriptures Divine because they were superior to anything else that people knew; and that is also the reason why these Scriptures, though always rejected by some men, have survived and are still considered Divine. These Scriptures are called Divine and have come down to us because they contain the highest human wisdom. And, in many of its parts, such is really the character of the Scriptures called the Bible.

And such, among these Scriptures, is that forgotten, neglected, and misunderstood saying which Bóndaref has explained and set at the head of the corner.

That saying, and the whole story of Paradise, are commonly taken in a literal sense, as though everything actually happened as described; whereas the meaning of the whole narrative is, that it figuratively represents the conflicting tendencies which exist in human nature.

Man fears death, but is subject to it. Man seems happier while ignorant of good and evil, yet strives irresistibly to reach that knowledge. Man loves idleness, and wishes to satisfy his desires without suffering, yet only by labour and suffering can he or his race have life.

The sentence Bóndaref quotes is important, not

because it is supposed to have been said by God to Adam, but because it is true; it states one of the indubitable laws of human life. The law of gravity is not true because it was stated by Newton ; but I know of Newton, and am grateful to him, because he showed an eternal law which explains to me a whole series of facts.

It is the same with the law: ' In the sweat of thy face shalt thou eat bread.' That is a law which explains to me a whole series of facts. And having once known it, I cannot forget it, and am grateful to him who revealed it to me.

This law seems very simple and familiar, but that is only apparently so; and to convince one's self of that fact we need only look around us. Not only do people not acknowledge this law, but they acknowledge the very reverse of it. People's belief leads them (from King to beggar) to strive, not to fulfil that law but to avoid fulfilling it. Bóndaref's book is devoted to explaining the permanence and immutability of that law, and the inevitable sufferings that flow from its neglect.

Bóndaref calls that law the 'first-born' and chief of all laws.

Bóndaref demonstrates that sins—*i.e.*, mistakes, false actions—result solely from the violation of this law. Of all the definite duties of man, Bóndaref considers that the chief, primary, and most immutable for every man, is to earn his bread with his own hands, understanding by bread-labour all heavy rough work necessary to save man from death by hunger and cold, and by ' bread ' food, drink, clothes, shelter, and fuel.

Bóndaref's fundamental thought is that this law— that to live man must work—heretofore acknowledged as inevitable, should be acknowledged as being a benefi-cent law of life, obligatory on everyone.

This law should be acknowledged as a religious law, like keeping the Sabbath or being circumcised among the Jews, like receiving the Sacrament or fasting among Church Christians, like praying five times a day among the Mohammedans. Bóndaref says, in one place, that if people but recognised bread-labour as a religious obligation, no private or special occupations could prevent their doing it, any more than special occupations prevent Church-people from keeping their holidays. There are about eighty holidays in the year,* but to perform 'bread-labour,' according to Bóndaref's calculation, only forty days are needed.

However strange it may seem at first that such a simple method, intelligible to everyone, and involving nothing cunning or profound, can save humanity from its innumerable ills, yet more strange, when one comes to think of it, must it seem that we, having at hand so clear, simple, and long familiar a method, can, while neglecting it, seek a cure for our ills in various subtleties and profundities. Yet consider the matter well and you will see that such is the case.

A man omitting to fix a bottom to his tub, and then devising all sorts of cunning means to keep the water from running away, would typify all our efforts to heal existing ills.

Indeed, from what do all the ills of life arise, if we except those that people cause to one another directly, by murders, executions, imprisonments, fights, and the many cruelties in which men sin by using violence? All the ills of humanity—except those produced by direct violence—come from hunger, from want of all kinds, from being overworked, or, on the other hand, from excess and idleness, and the vices they produce. What more sacred duty can man have than to co-operate in the destruction of this inequality—this want, on the one hand, and this temptation of riches on the other? And how can man co-operate in the destruction of these evils but by taking part in work which supplies human needs, and by liberating himself from superfluities and idleness productive of temptations and vices

* Saints' days are numerous in Russia, but on the other hand, no Saturday or other weekly half-holiday is customary, so that the total time allowed for holidays comes to much the same in Russia as in England.

—how, that is, but by each man doing bread-labour to feed himself with his own hands, as Bóndaref expresses it?

We have become so entangled, have involved ourselves in so many laws—religious, social, and family—have accepted so many precepts—as Isaiah says, precept upon precept, here a precept and there a precept—that we have completely lost the perception of what is good and what is bad.

One man performs Mass, another collects an army or the taxes to pay for it, a third acts as judge, a fourth studies books, a fifth heals people, a sixth instructs them, and freeing themselves from bread-labour under these pretexts, they thrust it on to others, and forget that men are dying of exhaustion, labour, and hunger; and that, in order that there may be people to sing Mass to, to defend with an army, to judge, to doctor, or to instruct, it is necessary, first of all, that they should not die of hunger. We forget that there may be many duties, but that among them all there is a first and a last, and that one must not fulfil the last before fulfilling the first, just as one must not harrow before ploughing.

And it is to this first, undoubted duty in the sphere of practical activity, that Bóndaref's teaching brings us back. Bóndaref shows that the performance of this duty hinders nothing and presents no obstacles, yet saves men from the misery of want and temptation Above all, the performance of this duty would destroy that terrible separation of mankind into two classes which hate each other and hide their mutual hatred by cajolery. Bread-labour, says Bóndaref, equalizes all and clips the wings of luxury and lust.

One cannot plough or dig wells dressed in fine clothes, with clean hands, and nourishing one's self on delicate food. Work at one sacred occupation, common to all, will draw men together. Bread-labour, Bóndaref says, will restore reason to those who have lost it by standing aside from the life natural to man, and will give happiness and content to those engaged in work undoubtedly useful, and appointed by God Himself and by the laws of Nature.

Bread-labour, says Bóndaref, is a medicine to save mankind. If men acknowledged this first-born law as an unalterable law of God—if each one admitted bread-labour (to feed himself by the work of his own hands) to be his inexorable duty—all men would unite in belief in one God and in love one to another, and the sufferings which now weigh us down would be destroyed.

We are so accustomed to a way of life which assumes the opposite of this—namely, assumes that riches (means to avoid bread-labour) represent either a blessing from God or a higher social status—that, without analysing Bóndaref's proposition, we wish to consider it narrow, one-sided, empty, and stupid. But we must examine his position carefully, and consider whether it be just or not.

We weigh all kinds of religious and political theories. Let us weigh Bóndaref's also as a theory. Let us consider what the result will be if, in accord with his thought, the influence of religious teaching is directed to the elucidation of this commandment, and all men are brought to admit this sacred, first-born law of labour.

All will then work, and eat the fruit of their own labours. Corn and articles of primary necessity will cease to be objects of purchase or sale.

What will be the result?

The result will be that men will not perish from want. If from unfortunate circumstances one man fails to grow enough food for himself and his family, someone else, who from fortunate circumstances has grown too much, will supply the lack ; and will do so the more readily because there is no other use for his corn, it being no longer an article of commerce. Then men will not be tempted by want to get their bread by cunning or by violence. And not being so tempted, they will not use cunning or violence ; the need that now compels them will no longer exist.

If a man then still uses cunning or violence, it will

be because he loves such ways, and not because they are necessary to him—as at present.

Nor will it be necessary for the weak—those who, for some reason, are unable to earn their bread, or who have lost it in any way—to sell themselves, their labour, or sometimes even their souls, for bread.

There will not be the present general striving to free one's self from bread-labour and to put it on to others —a striving to crush the weak with overwork and to free the strong from all work.

There will not be that tendency which now directs the greatest efforts of men's minds, not towards lightening the labour of the workers, but towards lightening and embellishing the idleness of the idlers. The participation of all in bread-labour, and its recognition as first among human affairs, will accomplish what would be achieved by taking a cart, which stupid people were hauling along upside down, and turning it over on to its wheels. The cart would be saved from breaking, and would move easily.

And our life, with its contempt for, and rejection of, bread-labour, and our attempts at reforming that false life, are like a cart drawn along with its wheels in the air. All our reforms are useless till we turn the cart over and stand it right way up.

Such is Bóndaref's thought, with which I fully agree. The matter presents itself to me again as follows. There was a time when people ate one another. The consciousness of unity among men developed until that became impossible, and they ceased to eat each other. Then came a time when people seized the fruits of labour by violence from their fellows, and made slaves of men. But consciousness developed till that also became impossible. Violence, though still practised in hidden ways, has been destroyed in its grosser forms : men no longer openly seize the fruits of one another's labour. In our day the form of violence practised is, that some people take advantage of the needs of others to exploit them In Bóndaref's opinion the time is near when there will be such a perception of human unity that men will feel it impossible to take advantage of the need, the hunger, and the cold of others to exploit them ; and when men, acknowledging the law of bread-labour as binding on everyone, will recognise it as their bounden duty, without selling articles of prime necessity, to feed, clothe, and warm one another in case of need.

Approaching the matter from another side, I look at this problem of Bóndaref's thus : We often hear reflections on the insufficiency of merely negative laws or commandments—*i.e.*, of rules telling us what not to do. People say, We need positive laws or commandments— rules telling us what to do. The five commandments of Christ—(1) to consider no one insignificant or insane, and to be angry with no one ; (2) not to consider sexual intercourse as a matter of pleasure, nor to leave the wife or husband with whom one has once united ; (3) to take no oaths to anyone, and not to give away one's freedom ; (4) to endure injuries and violence, and not to resist them by violence ; and (5) to consider no man an enemy, but to love enemies as friends—it is said that these five commandments of Christ all tell only what should not be done, but that there are no commandments or laws telling what should be done.

And, indeed, it may seem strange that in Christ's teaching there are no equally definite commandments telling us what we ought to do. But this seems strange only to those who do not believe Christ's real teaching, which is contained, not in five commandments, but in the teaching of truth itself.

The teaching of truth expressed by Christ is not contained in laws and commandments, but in one thing only—the meaning given to life. And that meaning is, that life and the blessing of life are not to be found in personal happiness, as people generally suppose, but in the service of God and man. And this is not a command which must be obeyed to gain a reward, nor is it a mystical expression of something mysterious and unintelligible, but it is the elucidation of a law of life previously concealed ; it is the indication of the fact that life can be a blessing only when this truth is understood. And, therefore, the whole positive teaching of Christ is expressed in this one thing : Love God, and thy neighbour as thyself.    And no expositions of that precept are possible.    It is one, because it contains all.    The law and commandments of Christ, like the Jewish and Buddhist laws and commandments, are but indications of cases in which the snares of the world turn men aside from a true understanding of life.    And that is why there may be many laws and many commandments, but the positive teaching of life—of what should be done—must and can be only one.

The life of each man is a movement somewhere : whether he will or not, he moves, he lives.    Christ shows man the road, and at the same time indicates the paths leading from the right road—paths which lead astray.    Of such indications there may be many—they are the commandments.

Christ gives five such commandments, and those He gave are such that up to the present not one can with advantage be added or spared.    But only one direction showing the road is given, for there can be but one straight line showing a certain direction.

Therefore the idea that in Christ's teaching there are only negative commands and no positive ones seems true only to those who do not know, or do not believe, in the teaching of truth itself—the direction of the true path of life indicated by Christ.    Believers in the truth of the path of life shown by Jesus will not seek for positive commandments in His teaching.    All positive activity flowing from the teaching of the true path of life—most diverse as that activity may be—is always clearly and indubitably defined for them.

Believers in that path of life are, in Christ's simile, like an abundant spring of living water.    All their activity is like the course of water, which flows everywhere regardless of obstacles.    A man believing in the teaching of Christ can as little ask what positive commands he is to obey as a stream of water, bursting from the ground, could ask the question.    It flows, watering the earth, grass, trees, birds, animals, and men. And a man who believes Christ's teaching of life does likewise.

A believer in the teaching of Jesus will not ask what he is to do. Love, which becomes the motive-force of his life, will surely and inevitably show him where to act, and what to do first and what afterwards.

Not to speak of indications Christ's teaching is full of, showing that the first and most necessary activity of love is to feed the hungry, give drink to the thirsty, clothe the naked, and help the poor and the prisoners, —our reason, conscience, and feelings all impel us (before undertaking any other service of love to living men) first to sustain life in our brethren by saving them from sufferings and death that threaten them in their too arduous struggles with Nature. That is to say, we are called on to share the labour needful for the life of man—the primary, rough, heavy labour on the land.

As a spring cannot question where its waters are to flow—upwards, splashing the grass and the leaves of the trees, or downwards to the roots of the grass and trees—so a believer in the teaching of truth cannot ask what he must do first—whether to teach people, defend them, amuse them, supply them with the pleasures of life, or save them from perishing of want. And just as water from a spring flows along the surface and fills ponds and gives drink to animals and men, only after it has soaked the ground, so a believer in the teaching of truth can serve less urgent human demands only after he has satisfied the primary demand : has helped to feed men, and to save them from perishing in their struggle against want. A man following the teaching of truth and love, not in words but in deeds, cannot mistake where first to direct his efforts. A man who sees the meaning of his life in service to others can never make such a blunder as to begin to serve hungry and naked humanity by forging cannon, manufacturing elegant ornaments, or playing the violin or the piano.

Love cannot be stupid.

As love for one man would not let us read novels to

him who was starving, or hang costly earrings on him
who was naked, so love for mankind will not let us
serve it by amusing the well-fed while we leave the cold
and hungry to die of want.

True love, love not merely in words but in deeds,
cannot be stupid—it is the one thing giving true perception and wisdom.

And, therefore, a man penetrated by love will not
make a mistake, but will be sure to do first what love
of man first requires : he will do what maintains the
life of the hungry, the cold, and the heavy-laden, and
*that* is all done by a direct struggle with Nature.

Only he who wishes to deceive himself and others,
can, while men are in danger, struggling against want,
stand aside from helping them, and, while he adds to
their burden, assure himself and those who perish
before his eyes, that he is occupied, or is devising
means to save them.

No sincere man who sees that the purpose of his life
is to serve others will say that.  Or if he says it, he
will find in his conscience no confirmation of his delusion, but will have to seek it in the insidious doctrine
of the division of labour.  In all expressions of true
human wisdom, from Confucius to Mohammed, he will
find one and the same truth (and will find it most
forcibly in the Gospels)—a summons to serve man not
according to the theory of the division of labour, but
in the simplest, most natural, and only necessary way :
he will find a demand to serve the sick, the prisoners,
the hungry, and the naked.  And help to the sick, the
prisoners, the hungry, and the naked, can be rendered
only by one's own immediate direct labour—for the
sick, hungry, and naked do not wait, but die of hunger
and cold.

His own life, which consists of service to others,
will guide a man confessing the teaching of truth, to
that primary law expressed at the commencement of
Genesis, 'In the sweat of thy face shalt thou eat
bread,' which Bóndaref calls ' first-born ' and puts
forward as a positive command.

And positive that law really is, for those who do not acknowledge the meaning of life which Christ disclosed. Such it was for men before Christ, and such it remains for those who do not acknowledge Christ's teaching. It demands that everyone should—according to the law of God expressed in the Bible and in our reason—feed himself by his own labour. That law was positive, and such it remains till the meaning of life is revealed to man by the teaching of truth.

But from the plane of the higher consciousness of life disclosed by Christ, the law of bread-labour, remaining true as before, fits into Christ's one positive teaching of service to man ; and must be regarded no longer as positive, but as negative. That law, from the Christian point of view, merely indicates an ancient snare, and tells men what they should avoid in order not to stray from the path of true life.

For a follower of the Old Testament who does not acknowledge this teaching of truth, this law means: 'Produce thy bread by the labour of thine own hands.' But for a Christian its meaning is negative. To him this law says : ' Do not suppose it possible to serve men while you consume what others labour to produce, and do not produce your own maintenance with your own hands.'

This law, for a Christian, is an indication of one of the most ancient and terrible of the temptations from which mankind suffers. Against that temptation (terrible in its consequences, and so old that it is hard for us to admit that it is not a natural characteristic of man, but a deception) this teaching of Bondaref is directed—a teaching equally obligatory on a believer in the Old Testament, on a Christian who believes in the Gospels, and on him who disbelieves in the Bible and follows only common-sense.

There is much I could and would write to prove the truth of this position and overthrow the various and complex arguments against it which rise to the lips of us all ; we know we are to blame, and are therefore always ready with justifications. But however much I may write, however well I may write, and however logically exact I may be, I shall not convince my reader, so long as his intellect is pitted against mine and his heart remains cold.

And that is why I ask you, reader, to check for awhile the activity of your intellect, and not to argue nor to demonstrate, but to ask only your heart. Whoever you may be, however gifted, however kind to those about you, however circumstanced, can you sit unmoved over your tea, your dinner, your political, artistic, scientific, medical, or educational affairs, while you hear or see at your door a hungry, cold, sick, suffering man? No. Yet they are always there, if not at the door, then ten yards or ten miles away. They are there, and you know it.

And you cannot be at peace—cannot have pleasure which is not poisoned by this knowledge. Not to see them at your door you have to fence them off, or keep them away by your coldness, or go somewhere where they are not. But they are everywhere.

And if a place be found where you cannot see them, still, you can nowhere escape from the truth. What, then, must be done?

You know these things, and the teaching of truth tells you them.

Go to the bottom—to what seems to you the bottom, but is really the top—take your place beside those who produce food for the hungry and clothes for the naked, and do not be afraid: it will not be worse, but better in all respects. Take your place in the ranks, set to work with your weak, unskilled hands at that primary work which feeds the hungry and clothes the naked: at bread-labour, the struggle with Nature; and you will feel, for the first time, firm ground beneath your feet, will feel that you are at home, that you are free and stand firmly, and have reached the end of your journey. And you will feel those complete, unpoisoned joys which can be found nowhere else—not secured by any doors nor screened by any curtains.

You will know joys you have never known before;

you will, for the first time, know those strong, plain men, your brothers, who from a distance have fed you until now; and to your surprise you will find in them such qualities as you have never known : such modesty, such kindness to yourself as you will feel you have not deserved.

Instead of the contempt or scorn you expected, you will meet with such kindness, such gratitude and respect for having—after living on them and despising them all your life—at last recollected yourself, and with unskilled hands tried to help them.

You will see that what seemed to you like an island on which you were saved from the sea that threatened to engulf you, was a marsh in which you were sinking ; and the sea you feared, was dry land on which you will walk firmly, quietly, and happily ; as must be the case, for from a deception (into which you did not enter of your own wish, but into which you were led) you will escape to the truth, and from the evasion of God's purpose you will pass to its performance.

[1888.]

## II

## WHY DO MEN STUPEFY THEMSELVES?

### I.

WHAT is the explanation of the fact that people use things that stupefy them: vódka, wine, beer, hashish, opium, tobacco, and other things less common: ether, morphia, fly-agaric, etc.? Why did the practice begin? Why has it spread so rapidly, and why is it still spreading among all sorts of people, savage and civilized? How is that where there is no vódka, wine or beer, there we find opium, hashish, fly-agaric, etc., and that tobacco is used everywhere?

Why do people wish to stupefy themselves?

Ask anyone why he began drinking wine and why he now drinks it. He will reply, 'Oh, it's pleasant, and everybody drinks,' and he may add, 'it cheers me up.' Some—those who have never once taken the trouble to consider whether they do well or ill to drink wine—may add that wine is good for the health and adds to one's strength; that is to say, will make a statement long since proved baseless.

Ask a smoker why he began to use tobacco and why he now smokes, and he also will reply: 'To while away time; everybody smokes.'

Similar answers would probably be given by those who use opium, hashish, morphia, or fly-agaric.

'To while away time, to be cheerful; everybody does it.' But it might be excusable to twiddle one's thumbs, to whistle, to hum tunes, to play a fife or to do something of that sort 'to while away time,' 'to be cheerful,' or 'because everybody does it'—that is to say, it might be excusable to do something for which

[ 16 ]

one need not waste Nature's wealth, nor spend what has cost great labour to produce, nor do what brings evident harm to one's self and to others. But to produce tobacco, wine, hashish, and opium, the labour of millions of men is spent, and millions and millions of acres of the best land (often amid a population that is short of land) are employed to grow potatoes, hemp, poppies, vines, and tobacco. Moreover, the use of these evidently harmful things produces terrible evils known and admitted by everyone, and destroys more people than all wars and contagious diseases added together. And people know this, so that it cannot be that they use these things 'to while away time,' 'to be cheerful,' or because 'everybody does it.'

There must be some other reason. Continually and everywhere one meets people who love their children and are ready to make all kinds of sacrifices for them, but who yet spend on vódka, wine and beer, or on opium, hashish, and even on tobacco, as much as would quite suffice to feed their hungry and poverty-stricken children, or at least as much as would suffice to save them from misery. Evidently, if a man who has to choose between the want and sufferings of a family he loves, on the one hand, and abstinence from stupefying things on the other, chooses the former—he must be induced thereto by something more potent than the consideration that 'everybody does it,' or that it is pleasant. Evidently it is done not 'to while away time,' nor merely 'to be cheerful,' but he is actuated by some more powerful cause.

This cause—as far as I have detected it by reading about this subject and by observing other people, and particularly by observing my own case when I used to drink wine and smoke tobacco—this cause, I think, may be explained as follows:

When observing his own life, a man may often notice in himself two different beings: the one is blind and physical, the other sees and is spiritual. The blind animal being eats, drinks, rests, sleeps, propagates, and moves, like a wound-up machine. The seeing, spiritual being that is bound up with the animal does nothing of itself, but only appraises the activity of the animal being ; coinciding with it when approving its activity, and diverging from it when disapproving.

This observing being may be compared to the arrow of a compass, pointing with one end to the north and with the other to the south, but screened along its whole length by something not noticeable so long as it and the arrow both point the same way ; but which becomes obvious as soon as they point different ways.

In the same manner the seeing, spiritual being, whose manifestation we commonly call conscience, always points with one end towards right and with the other towards wrong, and we do not notice it while we follow the course it shows : the course from wrong to right. But one need only do something contrary to the indication of conscience, to become aware of this spiritual being, which then shows how the animal activity has diverged from the direction indicated by conscience. And as a navigator, conscious that he is on the wrong track, cannot continue to work the oars, engine, or sails, till he has adjusted his course to the indications of the compass, or has obliterated his consciousness of this divergence—each man who has felt the duality of his animal activity and his conscience, can continue his activity only by adjusting that activity to the demands of conscience, or by hiding from himself the indications conscience gives him of the wrongness of his animal life.

All human life, we may say, consists solely of these two activities : (1) bringing one's activities into harmony with conscience, or (2) hiding from one's self the indications of conscience in order to be able to continue to live as before.

Some do the first, others the second. To attain the first there is but one means : moral enlightenment— the increase of light in one's self and attention to what it shows ; for the second—to hide from one's self the indications of conscience—there are two means : one external and the other internal. The external means

consists in occupations that divert one's attention from
the indications given by conscience; the internal
method consists in darkening conscience itself.

As a man has two ways of avoiding seeing an object
that is before him: either by diverting his sight to
other, more striking objects, or by obstructing the
sight of his own eyes—just so a man can hide from himself the indications of conscience in two ways: either
by the external method of diverting his attention to
various occupations, cares, amusements, or games;
or by the internal method of obstructing the organ
of attention itself. For people of dull, limited moral
feeling, the external diversions are often quite sufficient to enable them not to perceive the indications
conscience gives of the wrongness of their lives. But
for morally sensitive people those means are often
insufficient.

The external means do not quite divert attention
from the consciousness of discord between one's life
and the demands of conscience. This consciousness
hampers one's life: and people, in order to be able to
go on living as before, have recourse to the reliable, internal method, which is that of darkening conscience
itself by poisoning the brain with stupefying substances.

One is not living as conscience demands, yet lacks
the strength to reshape one's life in accord with its
demands. The diversions which might distract attention from the consciousness of this discord are insufficient, or have become stale, and so—in order to be able
to live on, disregarding the indications conscience
gives of the wrongness of their life—people (by poisoning it temporarily) stop the activity of the organ
through which conscience manifests itself, as a man by
covering his eyes hides from himself what he does not
wish to see.

## II.

Not in the taste, nor in any pleasure, recreation, or
mirth they afford, lies the cause of the world-wide consumption of hashish, opium, wine, and tobacco, but

simply in man's need to hide from himself the demands of conscience.

I was going along the street one day, and passing some cabmen who were talking, I heard one of them say: 'Of course, when one's sober, one's ashamed to do it!'

When one's sober one is ashamed of what seems all right when one is drunk. In these words we have the essential underlying cause, prompting men to resort to stupefiers. People resort to them, either to escape feeling ashamed after having done something contrary to their consciences, or to bring themselves, beforehand, into a state in which they can commit actions contrary to conscience, but to which their animal nature prompts them.

A man when sober is ashamed to go after a prostitute, ashamed to steal, ashamed to kill. Of none of these things is a drunken man ashamed, and therefore if a man wishes to do something his conscience condemns—he stupefies himself.

I remember being struck by the evidence of a man cook who was tried for murdering a relation of mine, an old lady in whose service he lived. He related that when he had sent away his paramour, the servant-girl, and the time had come to act, he wished to go into the bedroom with a knife, but felt that while sober he could not commit the deed he had planned . . . 'when one's sober one's ashamed.' He turned back, drank two tumblers of vódka he had prepared beforehand, and only then felt himself ready, and committed the crime.

Nine-tenths of the crimes are committed in that way: 'Drink to keep up your courage.'

Half the women who fall do so under the influence of wine. Nearly all visits to disorderly houses are paid by men who are intoxicated. People know this capacity of wine to stifle the voice of conscience, and intentionally use it for that purpose.

Not only do people stupefy themselves to stifle their own consciences, but (knowing how wine acts) when they wish to make others commit actions contrary to conscience, they intentionally stupefy them—that is, arrange to stupefy people in order to deprive them of conscience. In war, soldiers are usually intoxicated before a hand-to-hand fight. All the French soldiers in the assaults on Sevastopol were drunk.

When a fortified place has been captured, but the soldiers do not sack it and slay the defenceless old men and children, orders are often given to make them drunk, and then they do what is expected of them.*

Every one knows people who have taken to drink in consequence of some wrong-doing that has tormented their conscience. Any one can notice that those who lead immoral lives are more attracted than others by stupefying substances. Bands of robbers or thieves, and prostitutes, cannot live without intoxicants.

Every one knows and admits that the use of stupefying substances is a consequence of the pangs of conscience, and that in certain immoral ways of life stupefying substances are employed to stifle conscience. Every one knows and admits also that the use of stupefiers does stifle conscience: that a drunken man is capable of deeds of which when sober he would not think for a moment. Every one agrees to this, but, strange to say, when the use of stupefiers does not result in such deeds as thefts, murders, violations and so forth— when stupefiers are taken not after some terrible crimes, but by men following professions which we do not consider criminal, and when the substances are consumed not in large quantities at once but continually in moderate doses—then (for some reason) it is assumed that stupefying substances have no tendency to stifle conscience.

Thus, it is supposed that a well-to-do Russian's glass of vódka before each meal, and tumbler of wine with the meal; or a Frenchman's absinthe; or an Englishman's port wine and porter; or a German's lager-beer;

* See the allusion to Skóbelef's conduct at Geok-Tepe in a preface by Tolstoy, given in Grant Richards' sixpenny edition of 'Sevastopol and other Stories.'

or a well-to-do Chinaman's moderate dose of opium; and the smoking of tobacco with them—is done only for pleasure, and has no effect whatever on these people's consciences.

It is supposed that if after this customary stupefaction no crime is committed: nor theft, nor murder, but only customary bad and stupid actions—then these actions have occurred of themselves and are not evoked by the stupefaction. It is supposed that if these people have not committed offences against the criminal law, they have no need to stifle the voice of conscience, and that the life led by people who habitually stupefy themselves is quite a good life, and would be precisely the same if they did not stupefy themselves. It is supposed that the constant use of stupefiers does not in the least darken their consciences.

Though everybody knows by experience that one's frame of mind is altered by the use of wine or tobacco, that one is not ashamed of things which but for the stimulant one would be ashamed of, that after each twinge of conscience, however slight, one is inclined to have recourse to some stupefier, and that under the influence of stupefiers it is difficult to reflect on one's life and position, and that the constant and regular use of stupefiers produces the same physiological effect as its occasional immoderate use does—yet, in spite of all this, it seems to men who drink and smoke moderately, that they use stupefiers not at all to stifle conscience, but only for the flavour or for pleasure.

But one need only think of the matter seriously and impartially—not trying to excuse one's self—to understand, first, that if the use of stupefiers in large occasional doses stifles man's conscience, their regular use must have a like effect (always first intensifying and then dulling the activity of the brain) whether they are taken in large or small doses. Secondly, that all stupefiers have the quality of stifling conscience, and have this always—both when under their influence murders, robberies, and violations are committed, and when under their influence words are spoken which would not have been spoken, or things are thought and felt which would not have been thought and felt but for them; and, thirdly, that if the use of stupefiers is needed to pacify and stifle the consciences of thieves, robbers, and prostitutes, it is also wanted by people engaged in occupations condemned by their own consciences, even though these occupations may by other people be considered proper and honourable.

In a word, it is impossible to avoid understanding that the use of stupefiers, in large or small amounts, occasionally or regularly, in the higher or lower circles of society, is evoked by one and the same cause, the need to stifle the voice of conscience in order not to be aware of the discord existing between one's way of life and the demands of one's conscience.

### III.

In that alone lies the reason of the widespread use of all stupefying substances, and among the rest of tobacco—probably the most generally used and most harmful.

It is supposed that tobacco cheers one up, clears the thoughts, and attracts one merely like any other habit —without at all producing the deadening of conscience produced by wine. But you need only observe attentively the conditions under which a special desire to smoke arises, and you will be convinced that stupefying with tobacco acts on the conscience as wine does, and that people consciously have recourse to this method of stupefaction just when they require it for that purpose. If tobacco merely cleared the thoughts and cheered one up, there would not be such a passionate craving for it, a craving showing itself just on certain definite occasions. People would not say that they would rather go without bread than without tobacco, and would not often actually prefer tobacco to food.

That man cook who murdered his mistress, said that when he entered the bedroom and had gashed her throat with his knife, and she had fallen with a rattle in her throat and the blood had gushed out in a torrent—he lost his courage. 'I could not finish her off,' he said, 'but I went back from the bedroom to the sitting-room, and there sat down and smoked a cigarette.' Only after stupefying himself with tobacco was he able to return to the bedroom, finish cutting the old lady's throat, and begin examining her things.

Evidently the desire to smoke at that moment was evoked in him, not by a wish to clear his thoughts, or be merry, but by the need to stifle something that prevented him from completing what he had planned to do.

Any smoker may detect in himself the same definite desire to stupefy himself with tobacco at certain, specially difficult, moments. I look back at the days when I used to smoke: when was it that I felt a special need of tobacco? It was always at moments when I did not wish to remember certain things that presented themselves to my recollection, when I wished to forget —not to think. I sit by myself doing nothing and know I ought to set to work, but don't feel inclined to, so I smoke and go on sitting. I have promised to be at some one's house by five o'clock, but I have stayed too long somewhere else; I remember that I have missed the appointment, but I do not like to remember it, so I smoke. I get vexed, and say unpleasant things to some one, and know I am doing wrong, and see that I ought to stop, but I want to give vent to my irritability—so I smoke and continue to be irritable. I play at cards and lose more than I intended to risk—so I smoke. I have placed myself in an awkward position, have acted badly, have made a mistake, and ought to acknowledge the mess I am in and thus escape from it, but I do not like to acknowledge it, so I accuse others—and smoke. I write something and am not quite satisfied with what I have written. I ought to abandon it, but I wish to finish what I have planned to do—so I smoke. I dispute, and see that my opponent and I do not understand, and cannot understand, one another, but I wish to express my opinion, so I continue to talk—and I smoke.

What distinguishes tobacco from most other stupefiers, besides the ease with which one can stupefy one's self with it, and its apparent harmlessness, is its portability and the possibility of applying it to meet small, isolated occurrences that disturb one. Not to mention that the use of opium, wine, and hashish, involves the use of certain appliances not always at hand, while one can always carry tobacco and paper with one; and that the opium-smoker and the drunkard evoke horror, while a tobacco-smoker does not seem at all repulsive—the advantage of tobacco over other stupefiers is, that the stupefaction of opium, hashish, or wine, extends to all the sensations and acts received or produced during a certain somewhat extended period of time—while the stupefaction from tobacco can be directed to any separate occurrence. You wish to do what you ought not to, so you smoke a cigarette and stupefy yourself sufficiently to enable you to do what should not be done, and then you are again fresh, and can think and speak clearly; or you feel you have done what you should not—again you smoke a cigarette and the unpleasant consciousness of the wrong or awkward action is obliterated, and you can occupy yourself with other things and forget it.

But apart from individual cases in which every smoker has recourse to smoking, not to satisfy a habit or while away time, but as a means of stifling his conscience with reference to acts he is about to commit or has already committed, is it not quite evident that there is a strict and definite relation between men's way of life and their passion for smoking?

When do lads begin to smoke? Usually, when they lose their childish innocence. How is it that smokers can abandon smoking when they come among more moral conditions of life, and again start smoking as soon as they fall among a depraved set? Why do gamblers almost all smoke? Why among women do those who lead a regular life smoke least? Why do prostitutes and madmen *all* smoke? Habit is habit; but evidently smoking stands in some definite connection with the craving to stifle conscience, and achieves the end required of it.

One may observe in the case of almost every smoker to what an extent smoking drowns the voice of conscience. Every smoker when yielding to his desire forgets, or sets at naught, the very first demands of social life—demands he expects others to observe, and which he observes in all other cases until his conscience is stifled by tobacco. Every one of average education considers it inadmissible, ill-bred, and inhumane to infringe the peace, comfort, and yet more the health, of others for his own pleasure. No one would allow himself to wet a room in which people are sitting, or to make a noise, shout, let in cold, hot, or ill-smelling air, or commit acts that incommode or harm others. But out of a thousand smokers not one will shrink from producing unwholesome smoke in a room where the air is breathed by non-smoking women and children.

If smokers do usually say to those present: 'You don't object?' every one knows that the customary answer is: 'Not at all' (although it cannot be pleasant to a non-smoker to breathe tainted air, and to find stinking cigar-ends in glasses and cups or on plates and candlesticks, or even in ashpans).* But even if non-smoking adults did not object to tobacco-smoke, it could not be pleasant or good for the children whose consent no one asks. Yet people who are honourable and humane in all other respects, smoke in the presence of children at dinner in small rooms, vitiating the air with tobacco-smoke, without feeling the slightest twinge of conscience.

It is usually said (and I used to say) that smoking

* In the matters alluded to, the Russian customs are worse than the English, partly, perhaps, because in Russia, owing to a drier climate, the smell of stale tobacco in the rooms is less offensive than in England.

facilitates mental work. And that is undoubtedly true if one considers only the quantity of one's mental output. To a man who smokes, and who consequently ceases strictly to appraise and weigh his thoughts, it seems as if he suddenly had many thoughts. But this is not because he really has many thoughts, but only because he has lost control of his thoughts.

When a man works, he is always conscious of two beings in himself: the one works, the other appraises the work. The stricter the appraisement, the slower and the better is the work; and *vice versâ*, when the appraiser is under the influence of something that stupefies him, more work gets done, but its quality is lower.

'If I do not smoke I cannot write. I cannot get on; I begin and cannot continue,' is what is usually said, and what I used to say. What does it really mean? It means either that you have nothing to write, or that what you wish to write has not yet matured in your consciousness, but is only beginning dimly to present itself to you, and the appraising critic within, when not stupefied with tobacco, tells you so. If you did not smoke you would either abandon what you have begun, or you would wait until your thought has cleared itself in your mind; you would try to penetrate into what presents itself dimly to you, would consider the objections that offer themselves, and would turn all your attention to the elucidation of the thought. But you smoke, the critic within you is stupefied, and the hindrance to your work is removed. What to you when not inebriated by tobacco seemed insignificant, again seems important; what seemed obscure, no longer seems so; the objections that presented themselves vanish, and you continue to write, and write much and rapidly.

## IV.

But can such a small—such a trifling—alteration as the slight intoxication produced by the moderate use of wine or tobacco produce important consequences?

'If a man smokes opium or hashish, or intoxicates himself with wine till he falls down and loses his senses, of course the consequences may be very serious ; but for a man merely to come slightly under the influence of hops or tobacco, surely cannot have any serious consequences,' is what is usually said.   It seems to people that a slight stupefaction, a little darkening of the judgment, cannot have any important influence. But to think so, is as if one supposed that it may harm a watch to be struck against a stone, but that a little dirt introduced into it cannot do it any harm.

Remember, however, that the chief work actuating man's whole life is not work done by his hands, feet, or back, but by his consciousness.   For a man to do anything with feet or hands, a certain alteration has first to take place in his consciousness.   And this alteration defines all the subsequent movements of the man. Yet these alterations are always minute and almost imperceptible.

Brulóf* one day corrected a pupil's study.   The pupil, having glanced at the altered drawing, exclaimed : ' Why, you only touched it a tiny bit, but it is quite another thing.'   Brulóf replied :   ' Art begins where the tiny bit begins.'

That saying is strikingly true, not of art alone, but of all life.   One may say that true life begins where the tiny bit begins—where what seem to us minute and infinitely small alterations take place.   True life is not lived where great external changes take place—where people move about, clash, fight, and slay one another— but it is lived only where these tiny, tiny, infinitesimally small changes occur.

Raskólnikoft lived his true life, not when he murdered the old woman or her sister.   When murdering the old woman herself, and especially when murdering her sister, he did not live his true life, but acted like a machine, doing what he could not help doing—dis-

* K. P. Brulóf, a celebrated Russian painter (1799-1852).

† The hero of Dostoyéfsky's novel, ' Crime and Punishment.'

charging the cartridge with which he had long been loaded. One old woman was killed, another stood before him, the axe was in his hand.

Raskólnikof lived his true life, not when he met the old woman's sister, but at the time when he had not yet killed any old woman, nor entered a stranger's lodging with intent to kill, nor held the axe in his hand, nor had the loop in his overcoat by which the axe hung—at the time when he was lying on the sofa in his room, deliberating not at all about the old woman, nor even as to whether it is, or is not, permissible at the will of one man to wipe from the face of the earth another, unnecessary and harmful, man, but was deliberating whether he ought to live in Petersburg or not, whether he ought to accept money from his mother or not, and on other questions not at all relating to the old woman. And then—in that region quite independent of animal activities—the question whether he would or would not kill the old woman was decided. That question was decided—not when he, having killed one old woman, stood before another, axe in hand—but when he was doing nothing and was only thinking: when only his consciousness was active, and in that consciousness tiny, tiny alterations were taking place. It is at such times that one needs the greatest clearness to decide correctly the questions that have arisen, and it is just then that one glass of beer, or one cigarette, may prevent the solution of the question, may postpone the decision, stifle the voice of conscience, prompt a decision of the question in favour of one's lower, animal nature—as was the case with Raskólnikof.

Tiny, tiny alterations—but on them depend the most immense, the most terrible consequences. From what happens when a man has taken a decision and begun to act, many material changes may result : houses, riches, and people's bodies may perish, but nothing more important can happen than what was hidden in the man's consciousness. The limits of what can happen are set by consciousness.

But from most minute alterations occurring in the

domain of consciousness, boundless results of unimaginable importance may follow.

Do not let it be supposed that what I am saying has anything to do with the question of free-will or determinism. Discussion on that question is superfluous for my purpose, or for any other for that matter. Without deciding the question whether a man can, or cannot, act as he wishes to (a question, in my opinion, not correctly stated), I am merely saying that since human activity is conditioned by infinitesimal alterations in consciousness, it follows (no matter whether we admit, or do not admit, the existence of free-will) that we must pay particular attention to the condition in which these minute alterations take place, just as one must be specially attentive to the condition of scales on which other things are to be weighed. We must, as far as it depends on us, try to put ourselves and others in conditions which will not disturb the clearness and delicacy of thought necessary for the correct working of conscience, and must not act in the contrary manner : trying to hinder and confuse the work of conscience by the use of stupefying substances.

For man is a spiritual as well as an animal being. Man may be moved by things that influence his spiritual nature, or may be moved by things that influence his animal nature, as a clock may be moved by its hands or by its main wheel. And just as it is best to regulate the movement of a clock by means of its inner mechanism, so a man—one's self or another—is best regulated by means of his consciousness. And as with a clock one has to take special care of the thing by means of which one can best move the inner mechanism, so with a man, one must attend most of all to the cleanness and clearness of consciousness ; consciousness being the thing that best moves the whole man. To doubt this is impossible ; every one knows it. But a need to deceive one's self arises. People are not as anxious that consciousness should work correctly, as they are that it should seem to them that what they are doing is right, and they knowingly make use of substances that disturb the proper working of their consciousness.

v.

People drink and smoke, not casually, not from dulness, not to cheer themselves up, not because it is pleasant, but in order to drown the voice of conscience in themselves. And if that is so, how terrible must be the consequences! Indeed, think what a building would be like erected by people who did not use a straight plumb-rule to get the walls perpendicular, nor right-angled squares to get the corners correct, but used a soft rule which would bend to suit all irregularities in the walls, and a square that expanded to fit any angle, acute or obtuse.

Yet, thanks to self-stupefaction, that is just what is being done in life. Life does not accord with conscience, so conscience is made to bend to life.

This is done in the life of individuals, and it is done in the life of humanity as a whole, which consists of the lives of individuals.

To grasp the full significance of such stupefying of one's consciousness, let each one carefully recall the spiritual conditions he has passed through at each period of his life. Every one will find that at each period of his life certain moral questions confronted him, which he ought to solve, and on the solution of which the whole welfare of his life depended. For the solution of these questions great concentration of attention was needful. Such concentration of attention is a labour. In every labour, especially at the commencement, there is a time when the work seems difficult and painful, and when human weakness prompts a desire to abandon it. Physical work seems painful at first; mental work seems yet more painful. As Lessing says : people are inclined to cease to think at the point at which thought begins to be difficult ; but it is just there, I would add, that thinking begins to be fruitful. A man feels that to decide the questions confronting him needs labour—often painful labour—and he wishes to evade this. If he had no means of stupefying his faculties he could not expel

from his consciousness the questions that confront
him, and the necessity of solving them would be forced
upon him. But man finds that there exists a means to
drive off these questions whenever they present themselves—and he uses it. As soon as the questions
awaiting solution begin to torment him he has recourse to these means, and avoids the disquietude
evoked by the troublesome questions. Consciousness
ceases to demand their solution, and the unsolved
questions remain unsolved till his next period of enlightenment. But when that period comes, the same
thing is repeated, and the man goes on for months,
years, or even for his whole life, standing before those
same moral questions, and not moving a step towards
their solution. Yet it is in the solution of moral questions that life's whole movement consists.

What occurs is as if a man who needs to see to the
bottom of some muddy water to obtain a precious pearl,
but who dislikes entering the water, should stir it up
each time it begins to settle and become clear. Many
a man continues to stupefy himself all his life long,
and remains immovable at the same, once-accepted,
obscure, self-contradictory view of life—pressing, as
each period of enlightenment approaches, ever at one
and the same wall against which he pressed ten or
twenty years ago, and which he cannot break through
because he intentionally blunts that sharp point of
thought which alone could pierce it.

Let each man remember himself as he has been
during the years of his drinking or smoking, and let him
test the matter in his experience of other people, and
every one will see a definite constant line dividing those
who are addicted to stupefiers from those who are free
from them. The more a man stupefies himself, the
more he is morally immovable.

## VI.

Terrible, as they are described to us, are the consequences of opium and hashish on individuals; terrible,
as we know them, are the consequences of alcohol to

flagrant drunkards; but incomparably more terrible to our whole society are the consequences of what is considered the harmless, moderate use of spirits, wine, beer, and tobacco, to which the majority of men, and especially our so-called cultured classes, are addicted.

The consequences must naturally be terrible, admitting the fact, which must be admitted—that the guiding activities of society: political, official, scientific, literary, and artistic—are carried on, for the most part, by people in an abnormal state: by people who are drunk.

It is generally supposed that a man who, like most people of our well-to-do classes, takes alcoholic drink almost every time he eats, is, next day, during working hours, in a perfectly normal and sober condition. But this is quite an error. A man who drank a bottle of wine, a glass of spirits, or two glasses of ale, yesterday, is now in the usual state of drowsiness or depression which follows excitement, and is therefore in a condition of mental prostration, which is increased by smoking. For a man who habitually smokes and drinks in moderation, to bring his brain into a normal condition would require at least a week or more of abstinence from wine and tobacco. But that hardly ever occurs.*

* But how is it that people who do not drink or smoke are often morally on an incomparably lower plane than others who drink and smoke? And why do people who drink and smoke often manifest the highest qualities both mentally and morally?

The answer is, first, that we do not know the height that those who drink and smoke would have attained had they not drunk and smoked. And, secondly, from the fact that morally gifted people achieve great things in spite of the deteriorating effect of stupefying substances, we can but conclude that they would have produced yet greater things had they not stupefied themselves. It is very probable, as a friend remarked to me, that Kant's works would not have been written in such a curious and bad style had he not smoked so much. Lastly, the lower a man's mental and

c

So that most of what goes on among us, whether done by people who rule and teach others, or by those who are ruled and taught, is done when the doers are not sober.

And let not this be taken as a joke or an exaggeration; the confusion, and, above all, the imbecility, of our lives, arises chiefly from the constant state of intoxication in which most people live. Could people who are not drunk possibly do all that is being done around us—from building the Eiffel Tower to accepting military service?

Without any need whatever, a company is formed, capital collected, men labour, make calculations, and draw plans; millions of working days and thousands of tons of iron are spent to build a tower; and millions of people consider it their duty to climb up it, stop awhile on it, and then climb down again; and the building and visiting of this tower evoke no other reflection than a wish and intention to build other towers, in other places, still bigger. Could sober people act like that? Or take another case. All the European peoples have for dozens of years past been busy devising the very best ways of killing people, and teaching as many young men as possible, as soon as they reach manhood, how to murder. Everyone knows that there can be no invasion by barbarians, but that these preparations made by the different civilized and Christian nations are directed against one another; all know that this is burdensome, painful, inconvenient, ruinous, immoral, impious, and irrational—but all continue to prepare for mutual murder. Some devise political combinations to decide who, with what allies, is to kill whom; others

moral plane, the less does he feel the discord between his conscience and his life, and, therefore, the less does he feel a craving to stupefy himself; and, on the other hand, a parallel reason explains why the most sensitive natures—those which immediately and morbidly feel the discord between life and conscience—so often indulge in narcotics and perish by them.—L. T.

direct those who are being taught to murder; and others, again, yield—against their will, against their conscience, against their reason—to these preparations for murder. Could sober people do these things? Only drunkards who never reach a state of sobriety could do them, and could live on in the horrible state of discord between life and conscience in which, not only in this, but in all other respects, the people of our society are now living.

Never before, I suppose, have people lived with the demands of their conscience so evidently in contradiction to their actions.

Humanity to-day has, as it were, stuck fast. It is as though some external cause hindered it from occupying a position naturally in accord with its perceptions. And the cause—if not the only one, then certainly the greatest—is this physical condition of stupefaction, to which, by wine and tobacco, the great majority of people in our society reduce themselves.

Emancipation from this terrible evil will be an epoch in the life of humanity; and that epoch seems to be at hand. The evil is recognised. An alteration has already taken place in our perception concerning the use of stupefying substances. People have understood the terrible harm of these things, and are beginning to point them out, and this almost unnoticed alteration in perception will inevitably bring about the emancipation of men from the use of stupefying things—will enable them to open their eyes to the demands of their consciences, and they will begin to order their lives in accord with their perceptions.

And this seems to be already beginning. But, as always, it is beginning among the upper classes only after all the lower classes have already been infected.

[June 10, o.s., 1890.]

The above essay was written by Leo Tolstoy as a preface to a book on *Drunkenness* written by my brother-in-law, Dr. P. S. Alexéyef.—A. M.

## AN AFTERWORD TO 'THE KREUTZER SONATA'

MANY letters from strangers have reached and still continue to reach me asking for a clear and simple explanation of what I meant by the story called 'The Kreutzer Sonata.' I will try, to the best of my ability, to do what is asked of me, and explain briefly the essence of what I wished that story to convey, as well as the conclusions which, I think, may be derived from it.

In the first place I wished to say that a strong opinion has taken root in all classes of our society, and is supported by pseudo-science, to the effect that sexual intercourse is indispensable to health, and that, since marriage is sometimes out of the question, sexual intercourse without marriage and without involving the man in any obligation beyond a monetary payment, is perfectly natural, and should therefore be encouraged.

To such an extent has this opinion prevailed and so firmly is it established, that parents on the advice of doctors actually arrange debauchery for their children; while Governments—whose only purpose should be the moral well-being of their citizens—organize debauchery by regulating an entire class of women destined to perish physically and morally for the satisfaction of the supposed needs of men;* and unmarried people,

* The registration and medical examination of prostitutes, which was long practised in our garrisoned towns, is still generally, systematically, and unblushingly carried on in Russian towns, on behalf of the civil as well as the military population.

with untroubled consciences, yield themselves to debauchery.

I intended to say that this is wrong; for it cannot be right that some people should be destroyed body and soul for the health of others, any more than it can be right that some people for their health's sake should drink the blood of others.

The natural conclusion I would draw is that we must not yield to this error and deception. And to withstand it we must refuse to accept immoral doctrines, no matter what false sciences are quoted in their support. And we must, moreover, understand that sexual intercourse in which people either abandon the children who come as a result of their actions, or throw the whole burden of them on to the woman, or prevent the possibility of their birth, is a violation of the plainest claims of morality, and is shameful. And unmarried people who do not wish to act shamefully should refrain from such conduct.

That they may be able to refrain, they must lead a natural life: not drink intoxicants, nor overeat, nor eat flesh-meat, nor shirk labour (not gymnastics or play, but real fatiguing labour). Furthermore, they must not tolerate, even in thought, the possibility of intercourse with strange women, any more than with their own mothers, sisters, near relatives, or the wives of their friends.

That self-restraint is not only possible, but less dangerous or harmful to one's health than incontinence, is a fact of which any man may find hundreds of proofs around him.

That is the first thing I wanted to say.

Next—as a result of the fact that people regard amatory intercourse as both a necessary condition of health and a pleasure, and, more than that, as a poetic and elevating blessing—conjugal infidelity has, in all classes of our society, become extremely common. (Among the peasants conjugal infidelity is specially due to army service.)

And this I consider wrong. And the conclusion to be drawn is—that people should not behave so.

And in order that they may not behave so, it is necessary that this view of sex-love should be altered. Men and women must be trained, both by their parents and by public opinion, to look on falling in love and the accompanying sexual desire—whether before or after marriage—not as the poetic and elevated state it is now considered to be, but as an animal state degrading to a human being. And the breach of the promise of fidelity given at marriage should be dealt with by public opinion at least as severely as a breach of pecuniary obligation, or a business fraud, and should on no account be eulogized, as is now done in novels, poems, songs, operas, etc.

That is my second point.

Thirdly (in consequence, again, of the false opinion held in our society about physical love), child-bearing is not properly regarded, and, instead of being the aim and the justification of marriage, it has become an impediment to the pleasurable continuance of amorous relations, and consequently, both among married and unmarried people (instructed by exponents of medical science), the employment of means to prevent the birth of children has spread ; and a practice has become common which did not exist formerly, and does not now exist in patriarchal peasant families—the continuation of conjugal relations during the months of pregnancy and while the woman is still nursing.

And I think such conduct as that is wrong.

To use means to prevent child-birth is wrong : first, because it frees the parents from the anxiety and care for the children which are the redeeming feature in sexual love, and, secondly, because it is an action very near to that which is most shocking to man's conscience, namely, murder. And incontinence at the time of pregnancy and nursing is wrong, because it wastes the physical, and, above all, the spiritual, strength of the woman.

The deduction which follows from this is, that such things should be avoided. And, in order to avoid them, it should be understood that continence, which is an indispensable condition of human dignity to the unmarried, is still more obligatory on the married.

That is the third point.

Fourthly, in our society—in which children are regarded as an impediment to enjoyment, or as an unlucky accident, or (if only a prearranged number are born) as a special kind of pleasure—what is considered in their training is not their preparation for the duties of life which await them as reasonable and loving beings, but merely the gratification they may afford to their parents. The result is that human children are brought up like the young of animals, and the chief care of the parents (encouraged by false medical science) is, not to prepare them for activities worthy of human beings, but to overfeed them, to increase their size, and to make them clean, white, well-conditioned and handsome. (If this is not the case among the lower classes, it is only because they cannot afford it. They look on the matter just as the upper classes do.)

And in these pampered children (as in all overfed animals) an overpowering sexual sensitiveness shows itself unnaturally early, causing them terrible distress as they approach the age of puberty. All the surroundings of their life : clothes, books, sight-seeing, music, dances, dainty fare—everything, from the pictures on their boxes of bon-bons to the stories, novels, and poems they read—more and more increases this sensitiveness, and, as a result, the most terrible sexual vices and diseases are frequent incidents in the life of children of both sexes, and often retain their hold after maturity is reached.

And I consider that this is wrong. And the conclusion to be drawn is that human children should not be brought up like the young of animals, but in the education of human children other results should be aimed at than producing handsome, well-kept bodies.

That is the fourth point.

Fifthly, in our society, where the falling in love of young men and women (which still has physical attraction as its root) is extolled as though it were the highest and most poetic aim of human endeavour (as all our art and poetry bears witness), young people devote the best part of their lives—the men to spying out, pursuing, and obtaining (whether in marriage or free union), those best suited to attract them; the women and girls to enticing and entrapping men into free unions or marriages.

In this way the best powers of many people run to waste in activity not merely unproductive but injurious. Most of our insensate luxury results from this, as well as most of the idleness of the men and the shamelessness of the women who are not above following fashions admittedly borrowed from depraved women, and exposing parts of the body that excite sensuality.

And this, I think, is wrong.

It is wrong because, however it may be idealized, to obtain connection—in marriage or without marriage—with the object of one's love is an aim as unworthy of a man as is that of securing tasty and abundant food, which seems to many people the highest good.

The conclusion to be drawn from this is that we must cease to consider sex-love as something specially elevated, and must understand that no aim that we count worthy of a man—whether it be the service of humanity, fatherland, science or art (not to speak of the service of God)—can be attained by means of connection with the object of one's love (either with or without a marriage rite). On the contrary, falling in love and connection (however men may seek to prove the contrary in prose and verse) never facilitate, but always impede, the attainment of any aim worthy of man.

That is the fifth point.

That is the substance of what I wanted to say, and thought I had said, by my story; and it seemed to me that one might discuss the question of how to remedy the evils indicated, but that it was impossible not to agree with the considerations advanced. It seemed impossible not to agree: first, because these considerations quite coincide with what we know of the progress of mankind (which has ever advanced from dissoluteness to greater and greater purity), and accord also with the moral perceptions of the community, and with our conscience, which always condemns dissoluteness and esteems chastity.* Secondly, because these propositions are merely unavoidable conclusions from the Gospel teaching, which we either profess or at least (even if unconsciously) admit to lie at the root of our ideas of morality.

But I was mistaken.

No one, it is true, directly disputes the statements that one should not be dissolute either before or after marriage, should not artificially prevent childbirth, should not make toys of one's children, and should not put amatory intercourse above everything else. In short, no one denies that chastity is better than depravity. But it is said : 'If abstinence is better than marriage, people ought certainly to follow the better course. But if they do, then the human race will come to an end, and the ideal for the race cannot be—its own extinction.' But—apart from the fact that the extinction of the human race is not a new idea, but is for religious people one of the dogmas of their faith, and for scientists an inevitable conclusion from observations of the cooling of the sun—there is in that rejoinder a great, wide-spread, and old misunderstanding. It is said : 'If men act up to the ideal of perfect chastity, they will become extinct ; therefore the ideal is false.' But those who speak so, intentionally or unintentionally confuse two different things—a rule or precept, and an ideal.

Chastity is not a rule or precept, but an ideal, or, rather, one condition of the ideal. But an ideal is an ideal only when its accomplishment is only possible in *idea*, in thought, when it appears attainable only in infinity, and when the possibility of approaching towards it is therefore infinite. If the ideal were attained, or if we

* The word is used in the sense of complete purity of mind and body, such as is commonly attributed to Jesus.

could even picture its attainment by mankind, it would cease to be an ideal.

Such was Christ's ideal—the establishment of the kingdom of God on earth—an ideal already foretold by the prophets, of a time when all men will be taught of God, will beat their swords into ploughshares and their spears into pruning-hooks ; when the lion will lie down with the lamb, and all will be united in love. The whole meaning of human life lies in progress towards that ideal ; and therefore the striving towards the Christian ideal in its completeness, and towards chastity as one of its conditions, is far from rendering life impossible. On the contrary, the absence of that ideal would destroy progress, and with it the possibility of real life.

Arguments to the effect that the human race will end if men strive with all their might towards chastity, are like the one (sometimes actually used) to the effect that the race will perish if men try their best to substitute the love of friends, of enemies, and of all that lives, for the prevailing struggle for existence. Such arguments come from not understanding the difference between two methods of moral guidance.

As there are two ways of telling a traveller his road, so there are two methods of moral guidance for seekers after truth. One way consists in pointing out the objects that will be met on the road, by which the traveller can shape his course ; the other way consists in only giving him the direction by a compass he carries, and on which he sees one invariable direction, and consequently is made aware of every divergence from it.

The first method of moral guidance is by externally defined rules : certain definite actions are indicated which a man must, or must not, perform.

'Keep the Sabbath ;' ' Be circumcised ;' ' Do not steal ;' ' Abstain from wine ;' ' Do not destroy life ;' ' Give tithes to the poor ;' ' Wash and pray five times daily ;' ' Baptize ;' ' Receive the Eucharist,' etc. Such are the ordinances of external religious teaching : Brahminical, Buddhist, Mohammedan or Jewish, and of Ecclesiasticism, falsely called Christianity.

The other method consists in indicating a perfection man can never reach, but which he consciously desires. An ideal is set before him by attending to which he can always see to what extent he deviates from the right road.

'Love God with all thy heart, and with all thy soul, and with all thy mind, and thy neighbour as thyself.' 'Be perfect as your heavenly Father is perfect.' Such is the teaching of Christ.

The test of fulfilment of external religious teachings is the conformity of our conduct to the injunctions given, and such conformity is possible.

The test of the fulfilment of Christ's teaching lies in a consciousness of the extent of one's deviation from the ideal perfection. (The degree of one's approach to it is not seen; but the degree of deviation from it is seen.)

A man who accepts an external law is like a man standing in the light thrown by a lantern fixed to a post. He stands in the light of this lantern, and it is light around him, but he has no place towards which to advance. A man who accepts Christ's teaching is like one who carries a lantern before him on a pole: the light is always before him, and by lighting up fresh ground which attracts him, always invites him to advance.

The Pharisee thanks God he has fulfilled the whole law. The rich young man has also from his childhood fulfilled all, and cannot understand what more can be demanded. Nor can they think otherwise: they see nothing ahead of them towards which they might aspire. Tithes have been paid; Sabbaths observed; parents honoured; they have not committed adultery, nor stolen, nor murdered. What more can be required? But for him who follows the Christian teaching, each step gained towards perfection makes plain the need of ascending another, from which he perceives a yet higher, and so on without end. He who follows the law of Christ is always in the position of the Publican—always conscious of imperfection, he does not look behind him at the road he has passed, but sees always before him the road he has still to travel.

In this lies the difference between Christ's teaching
and all other religious teachings ; a difference not in
the demands made, but in the guidance afforded. Jesus
did not lay down rules of life. He established no
institutions, and did not institute marriage. But men
(not understanding the character of Christ's teaching,
and accustomed to external teachings) wished to feel
themselves justified—as the Pharisee felt himself justified—and from the letter of his teaching, but contrary
to its whole spirit, have constructed an external code of
rules called Church doctrine, and with it have sup-
planted Christ's true teaching of the ideal.

This has been done concerning government, law,
war, the Church, and Church worship ; and it has also
been done in relation to marriage.

In spite of the fact that Jesus not only never instituted marriage, but (if we must seek external regulations) rather discountenanced it (' Leave thy wife and
follow me '), the Church doctrine (called Christian) has
established marriage as a Christian institution. That
is to say, it has defined certain external conditions
under which sexual love is supposed to be quite right
and lawful for a Christian.

As, however, the institution of marriage has no basis
whatever in true Christianity, the result has been that
people in our society have quitted one shore, but have
not reached the other. They do not really believe in
the ecclesiastical definitions of marriage, for they feel
that such an institution has no foundation in Christ's
teaching ; yet as they do not perceive Christ's ideal
(which the Church doctrine has hidden)—the ideal of
striving towards complete chastity—they are left, in
relation to marriage, quite without guidance. This
explains the fact (which seems so strange at first
sight) that among Jews, Mohammedans, Lamaists, and
others professing religious doctrines much lower than
the Christian, but having strict external regulations
concerning marriage, the family principle and conjugal
fidelity are far firmer than in so-called Christian
society. Those people have their regular systems of

concubinage, or polygamy, or polyandry, confined
within certain bounds.   Among us wholesale dissoluteness finds place : concubinage, polygamy, and polyandry,
free from all limitations, and concealed by the pretence
of monogamy.

For no better reason than because the clergy, for
money, perform certain ceremonies (called marriage
services) over a certain number of those who unite,
people in our society naïvely or hypocritically imagine
that we are a monogamous people.

There never was, or could be, such a thing as Christian
marriage, any more than Christian worship,* Christian
teachers and Fathers of the Church,† Christian pro-

---

* 'And when ye pray, ye shall not be as the hypocrites :
for they love to stand and pray in congregations and in the
corners of the streets, that they may be seen of men.
Verily I say unto you, they have received their reward.
But thou, when thou prayest, enter into thine inner
chamber, and having shut thy door, pray to thy Father
which is in secret, and thy Father which, seeth in secret,
shall recompense thee.   And in praying use not vain repetitions as the Gentiles do : for they think they shall be
heard for their much speaking.   Be not therefore like unto
them : for your Father knoweth what things ye have need
of, before ye ask him.'—MATT. vi. 5-12.

'Woman, believe me, the hour cometh, when neither in
this mountain, nor in Jerusalem, shall you worship the
Father.   You know not whom you worship, but we worship
him whom we know.   But the hour cometh, and now is,
when the true worshippers shall worship the Father in spirit
and by deeds : for such doth the Father seek to be his
worshippers.   God is a Spirit, and must be worshipped in
spirit and by deeds.'—JOHN iv. 21-24.

† 'But be not ye called teachers : for one is your Teacher,
and all ye are brethren.   And call no man your father on
the earth : for one is your Father, which is in heaven.
Neither be ye called masters : for one is your Master, even
the Christ.'—MATT. xxiii. 8-10.

(Where the Revised Version is not followed, Tolstoy's
*Union and Translation of the Four Gospels* has been
used.)

perty, armies, law-courts, or Governments, and this was understood by Christians who lived in the first centuries.

The Christian ideal is that of love to God and to one's fellow-man: it is the renunciation of one's self for the service of God and one's neighbour; whereas sexual love, marriage, is a service of self, and consequently in any case an obstacle to the service of God and man, and therefore, from a Christian point of view, a fall, a sin.

To get married would not help the service of God and man, though it were done to perpetuate the human race. For that purpose, instead of getting married and producing fresh children, it would be much simpler to save and rear those millions of children who are now perishing around us for lack of food for their bodies, not to mention food for their souls.

Only if he were sure all existing children were provided for could a Christian enter upon marriage without being conscious of a moral fall.

It may be possible to reject Christ's teaching—which permeates our whole life and on which all our morality is founded—but once that teaching is accepted, we cannot but admit that it points to the ideal of complete chastity.

For in the Gospels it is said clearly, and so that there is no possibility of misinterpretation: First, that a married man should not divorce his wife to take another, but should live with her whom he has once taken.* Secondly, that it is wrong (and it is said of men generally, married or unmarried) to look on a

* 'It was said also, Whosoever shall put away his wife, let him give her a writing of divorcement: but I say unto you, that if anyone putteth away his wife, not only is he guilty of wantonness, but he leads her to adultery: and whosoever shall marry her when she is put away committeth adultery.'—MATT. v. 31, 32.

'He saith unto them, Moses for your coarseness let you divorce from your wives: but this from the first was not right.'—MATT. xix. 8.

woman as an object of desire.* And, thirdly, that for
the unmarried it is better not to marry—*i.e.*, it is
better to be quite chaste.†

To most people these thoughts will seem strange, and
even contradictory. And they really are contradictory,
not in themselves but to the whole manner of our lives:
and the question naturally presents itself: 'Which is
right? These thoughts, or the lives lived by millions,
including myself?'

That feeling forced itself upon me most strongly
when I approached the conclusions I now express. I
never anticipated that the development of my thoughts
would bring me to such a conclusion. I was startled
at my conclusions and did not wish to believe them,
but it was impossible not to believe them. And however they may run counter to the whole arrangement of our lives, however they may contradict
what I thought and said previously, I had to admit
them.

'But these are all general considerations, which may
be true, but relate to the teaching of Jesus, and are
binding only on those who profess it. But life is life,
and it will not do merely to point to a distant and
unattainable ideal, and then leave men with no definite
guidance in face of a burning question, which affects
every one and causes terrible sufferings. A young and

---

* 'Every one that looketh on a woman to lust after her
hath committed adultery with her already in his heart.'—
MATT. v. 28.

† 'The disciples say unto him, If the case of a man is so
with his wife, it is not expedient to marry, But he said
unto them, All men cannot receive this saying, but they to
whom it is given. For there are men who are virgin from
lust from their mother's womb; and there are some who
have been deprived of their desire by men, and there are
some who have become pure for the kingdom of heaven's
sake. He that is able to receive it, let him receive it.'—
MATT. xix. 10-12.

Tolstoy's *A Union and Translation of the Four Gospels*
has been followed in these quotations.

passionate man may, at first, be attracted by this ideal, but will not hold to it, and when once he has broken down, not knowing or acknowledging any fixed rules, he will lapse into complete depravity.'

So people generally argue: 'Christ's ideal is unattainable, therefore it cannot serve as a guide in practical life; it may do to talk about, or dream about, but it is not applicable to life, and must therefore be put aside. We do not want an ideal, but a rule—a guidance—suited to our strength and to the average level of the moral forces of our society: honourable Church-marriage; or even a marriage not quite honourable, in which one party (as occurs with men among us) has already known many other women; or, say, marriage with the possibility of divorce, or civil marriage, or even (advancing in the same direction) a marriage, Japanese fashion, for a certain term'—but why not go as far as brothels? They are said to be preferable to street prostitution!

That is where the trouble comes in. Once you let yourself lower the ideal to suit your weakness, there is no finding the line at which to stop.

In reality, this argument is altogether unsound. It is untrue that an ideal of infinite perfection cannot be a guide in life, and that I must either throw it away, saying, 'It is useless to me since I can never reach it,' or must lower it to the level at which it suits my weakness to rest.

To argue so is as though a mariner said to himself: 'Since I cannot keep to the line indicated by the compass, I must either throw the compass overboard and cease to bother with it' (*i.e.*, must discard the ideal); 'or I must fix the needle of the compass in the position which corresponds to the direction my vessel is now following' (*i.e.*, must lower the ideal to suit my own weakness).

The ideal of perfection Jesus gave is not a fancy, or a theme for rhetorical sermons, but is an indispensable and accessible guide to moral life, as the compass is an indispensable and accessible instrument wherewith to guide a ship. But the one must be believed in as implicitly as the other.

In whatever position a man may find himself, the teaching of the ideal that Jesus gave is sufficient to afford him always the best indications as to what he should or should not do. But he must entirely believe this teaching, and this alone, and must not trust to any other—just as a steersman guiding himself by the compass must not look to either side, but must keep his attention fixed on the compass.

One must know how to guide one's self by Christ's teaching as by a compass; and for this the chief thing is to understand one's own position. One must not fear to define clearly one's own deviation from the direction of the ideal. Whatever plane a man may be on, it is always possible for him to move towards the ideal, and in no position can he say he has attained it and can approach no nearer.

Such is the case in regard to man's aspiration towards the Christian ideal in general, and it applies to the question of chastity in particular. If we take men in the most diverse positions that they can occupy, from innocent childhood to marriage without self-restraint, the teaching of Jesus and the ideal it holds up will afford clear and definite guidance as to what should and what should not be done at each stage.

' What should a pure lad or maid do?'

Keep themselves pure and free from snares; and, in order to be able to give all their strength to the service of God and man, strive after greater and greater purity of thought and desire.

' What should a youth or a maid do who has fallen into temptation, is absorbed by vague desire, or by love of some particular person, and who has thereby lost to some extent the power to serve God and man?'

Again the same thing. Not allow themselves to fall (knowing that a fall will not free them from temptation, but will only render it stronger); but go on striving ever towards greater and greater purity, to be able more fully to serve God and man.

D

'What should those do who have not been equal to the struggle and have fallen?'

They must look on their fall, not as on a legitimate enjoyment (as is now done when it is sanctioned by a wedding service), nor as a casual pleasure which may be repeated with someone else, nor as a calamity, when the fall has been with an inferior and without ritual; but they must look on this first fall as the only one, and regard it as the entrance to an actual indissoluble marriage.

This marriage, by the results that follow from it—the birth of children—restricts the married couple to a new and more limited field of service of God and man. Before marriage they could serve God and man directly and in most varied ways; but marriage limits their sphere of activity, and demands from them the rearing and education of children, who may be future servants of God and man.

'What must a married man and woman do, who, by rearing and educating children, are fulfilling the limited service of God and man which corresponds to their position?'

Again the same thing. Together strive to free themselves from temptation, purify themselves, and cease from sin, by substituting for physical love, which hinders both public and private service of God and man, the pure relationship of brother and sister.

And, therefore, it is not true that we cannot guide ourselves by the ideal of Jesus, because it is so high, so perfect, and so inaccessible. If we cannot guide ourselves by it, that is only because we lie to ourselves and deceive ourselves. For if we say we require a rule more accessible than Christ's ideal, or, falling short of Christ's ideal, we shall become dissolute—what we say really amounts to this: not that Christ's ideal is too high for us, but that we do not believe in it and do not wish to appraise our conduct by it.

To say that when once we have fallen we shall have begun a loose life, is really to say that we decide in advance that a fall with an inferior is not a sin, but is an amusement, an infatuation, which we are not bound to rectify by the permanent union called marriage. Whereas, if we realized that a fall is a sin which should and must be redeemed by an inviolate marriage, and by all the activity involved in educating the children born of marriage—then the fall would by no means be a reason for taking to vice.

It is as if a husbandman learning to sow corn did not reckon as sown any field in which the sowing was unsuccessful, but went on sowing a second and a third field, and took into account only the one that succeeded. Evidently such a man would waste much land and much seed, and would not learn to sow properly.

Only acknowledge chastity as the ideal, and regard every fall (of whomsoever with whomsoever) as the one irrevocable life-long marriage, and it will be clear that the guidance given by Jesus is sufficient, and, more than that, is the only possible guidance.

'Man is weak, and his task must accord with his strength,' is what people say. But that is as if one said : 'My hand is weak, and I cannot draw a line that shall be quite straight (the shortest between two points), so, to help matters, I will take as my model a crooked or broken line.' In reality, the weaker my hand, the more I need a perfect model.

Having once recognised the Christian teaching of the ideal, we cannot act as if we were ignorant of it, and replace it by external rules. The Christian teaching of the ideal has been set before us just because it can guide us in our present stage of progress. Humanity has already outgrown the stage of religious, external ordinances, and people believe in them no more.

Christ's teaching of the ideal is the one teaching that can guide mankind. We must not and cannot replace the ideal of Jesus by external regulations ; but we must firmly keep that ideal before us in all its purity, and, above all, we must believe in it.

To the sailor while he kept near the coast one could say : 'Steer by that cliff, that cape, or that tower'; but a time has come when the sailor has left the land behind, and his only guide can and must be the unattainable stars, and the compass showing a direction.

And the one and the other are given us.

[September 26, o.s., 1890.

The above is a new translation, in preparing which I have been allowed to make free use of one that appeared in the *New Age* in 1897.

# IV

## THE FIRST STEP

### I.

If a man is not making a pretence of work, but is working in order to accomplish the matter he has in hand, his actions will necessarily follow one another in a certain sequence determined by the nature of the work. If he postpones to a later time what from the nature of the work should be done first, or if he altogether omits some essential part, he is certainly not working seriously, but only pretending. This rule holds unalterably true whether the work be physical or not. As one cannot seriously wish to bake bread unless one first kneads the flour and then heats the brick-oven, sweeps out the ashes, and so on, so also one cannot seriously wish to lead a good life without adopting a certain order of succession in the attainment of the necessary qualities.

With reference to right living this rule is especially important; for whereas in the case of physical work, such as making bread, it is easy to discover by the result whether a man is seriously engaged in work or is only pretending, with reference to goodness of life no such verification is possible. If people, without kneading the dough or heating the oven, only pretend to make bread—as they do in the theatre—then from the result (the absence of bread) it becomes evident that they were only pretending; but when a man pretends to be leading a good life we have no such direct indications that he is not striving seriously but only pretending, for not only are the results of a good life not always evident and palpable to those around, but very often such results even appear to them harmful. Respect for a man's activity, and the acknowledgment of its utility and pleasantness by his contemporaries, furnish no proof of the real goodness of his life.

Therefore, to distinguish the reality from the mere appearance of a good life, the indication given by a regular order of succession in the acquirement of the essential qualities is especially valuable. And this indication is valuable, not so much to enable us to discover the seriousness of other men's strivings after goodness as to test this sincerity in ourselves, for in this respect we are liable to deceive ourselves even more than we deceive others.

A correct order of succession in the attainment of virtues is an indispensable condition of advance towards a good life, and consequently the teachers of mankind have always prescribed a certain invariable order for their attainment.

All moral teachings set up that ladder which, as the Chinese wisdom has it, reaches from earth to heaven, and the ascent of which can only be accomplished by starting from the lowest step. As in the teaching of the Brahmins, Buddhists, Confucians, so also in the teaching of the Greek sages, steps were fixed, and a superior step could not be attained without the lower one having been previously taken. All the moral teachers of mankind, religious and non-religious alike, have admitted the necessity of a definite order of succession in the attainment of the qualities essential to a righteous life. The necessity for this sequence lies in the very essence of things, and therefore, it would seem, ought to be recognised by everyone.

But, strange to say, from the time Church-Christianity spread widely, the consciousness of this necessary order appears to have been more and more lost, and is now retained only among ascetics and monks. Among worldly Christians it is taken for granted that the higher virtues may be attained not only in the absence of the lower ones, which are a necessary condition of the higher, but even in company with the greatest vices; and consequently the very conception of what it is that constitutes a good life, has reached, in the minds of the majority of worldly people to-day, a state of the greatest confusion.

## II.

In our times people have quite lost the consciousness of the necessity of a sequence in the qualities a man must have to enable him to live a good life, and, as a consequence, they have lost the very conception of what constitutes a good life. This, it seems to me, has come about in the following way.

When Christianity replaced heathenism it put forth moral demands superior to the heathen ones, and at the same time (as was also the case with heathen morality) it necessarily laid down one indispensable order for the attainment of virtues—certain steps to the attainment of a righteous life.

Plato's virtues, beginning with self-control, advanced through courage and wisdom to justice; the Christian virtues, commencing with self-renunciation, rise through devotion to the will of God, to love.

Those who accepted Christianity seriously and strove to live righteous Christian lives, thus understood Christianity, and always began living rightly by renouncing their lusts; which renunciation included the self-control of the pagans.

But let it not be supposed that Christianity in this matter was only echoing the teachings of paganism; let me not be accused of degrading Christianity from its lofty place to the level of heathenism. Such an accusation would be unjust, for I regard the Christian teaching as the highest the world has known, and as quite different from heathenism. Christian teaching replaced pagan teaching simply because the former was different from, and superior to, the latter. But both Christian and pagan teaching alike, lead men toward truth and goodness; and as these are always the same, the way to them must also be the same, and the *first steps* on this way must inevitably be the same for Christian as for heathen.

The difference between the Christian and pagan teaching of goodness lies in this: that the heathen teaching is one of final perfection, while the Christian is one of infinite perfecting. Every heathen, non-Christian, teaching sets before men a model of final perfection; but the Christian teaching sets before them a model of infinite perfection. Plato, for instance, makes justice the model of perfection, whereas Christ's model is the infinite perfection of love. '*Be ye perfect, even as your Father in heaven is perfect.*' In this lies the difference, and from this results the different relation of pagan and Christian teaching toward different grades of virtue. According to the former, the attainment of the highest virtue was possible, and each step toward this attainment had its comparative merit—the higher the step the greater the merit; so that from the pagan point of view men may be divided into moral and immoral, into more or less immoral—whereas, according to the Christian teaching, which sets up the ideal of infinite perfection, this division is impossible. There can be neither higher nor lower grades. In the Christian teaching, which shows the infinity of perfection, all steps are equal in relation to the infinite ideal.

Among the heathens the plane of virtue attained by a man constituted his merit; in Christianity merit consists only in the process of attaining, in the greater or lesser speed of attainment. From the heathen point of view, a man who possessed the virtue of reasonableness stood morally higher than one deficient in that virtue; a man who, in addition to reasonableness, possessed courage stood higher still; a man who to reasonableness and courage added justice stood yet higher. But one Christian cannot be regarded as morally either higher or lower than another. A man is more or less of a Christian only in proportion to the speed with which he advances towards infinite perfection, irrespective of the stage he may have reached at a given moment. Hence the stationary righteousness of the Pharisee was worth less than the progress of the repentant thief on the cross.

Such is the difference between the Christian and the heathen teachings. Consequently the stages of virtue, as, for instance, self-control and courage, which in paganism constitute merit, constitute none whatever in Christianity. In this respect the teachings differ. But with regard to the fact that there can be no advance toward virtue, toward perfection, except by mounting the lowest steps, paganism and Christianity are alike: here there can be no difference.

The Christian, like the heathen, must commence the work of perfecting himself from the beginning—*i.e.*, at the step at which the heathen begins it, namely, self-control; just as a man who wishes to ascend a flight of stairs cannot avoid beginning at the first step. The only difference is that for the pagan, self-control itself constitutes a virtue; whereas for the Christian, it is only part of that self-abnegation which is itself but an indispensable condition of all aspiration after perfection. Therefore the manifestation of true Christianity could not but follow the same path that had been indicated and followed by paganism.

But not all men have understood Christianity as an aspiration towards the perfection of the heavenly Father. The majority of people have regarded it as a teaching about salvation—*i.e.*, deliverance from sin by grace transmitted through the Church, according to Catholics and Greek Orthodox; by faith in the Redemption, according to Protestants, the Reformed Church, and Calvinists; or, according to some, by means of the two combined.

And it is precisely this teaching that has destroyed the sincerity and seriousness of men's relation to the moral teaching of Christianity. However much the representatives of these faiths may preach that these means of salvation do not hinder man in his aspiration after a righteous life, but on the contrary contribute toward it—still, from certain assertions certain deductions necessarily follow, and no arguments can prevent men from making these deductions, when once they have accepted the assertions from which they flow.  If a man believe that he can be saved through grace transmitted by the Church, or through the sacrifice of the Redemption, it is natural for him to think that efforts of his own to live a right life are unnecessary—the more so when he is told that even the hope that his efforts will make him better is a sin.  Consequently a man who believes that there are means other than personal effort by which he may escape sin or its results, cannot strive with the same energy and seriousness as the man who knows no other means.  And not striving with perfect seriousness, and knowing of other means besides personal effort, a man will inevitably neglect the unalterable order of succession for the attainment of the good qualities necessary to a good life.  And this has happened with the majority of those who profess Christianity.

### III.

The doctrine that personal effort is not necessary for the attainment of spiritual perfection by man, but that there are other means for its acquirement, caused a relaxation of efforts to live a good life and a neglect of the consecutiveness indispensable for such a life.

The great mass of those who accepted Christianity, accepting it only externally, took advantage of the substitution of Christianity for paganism to rid themselves of the demands of the heathen virtues—no longer necessary for a Christian—and to free themselves from all conflict with their animal nature.

The same thing happens with those who cease to believe in the teaching of the Church.  They are like the before-mentioned believers, only they put forward —instead of grace, bestowed by the Church or through Redemption—some imaginary good work, approved of

by the majority of men, such as the service of science,
art, or humanity ; and in the name of this imaginary
good work they liberate themselves from the consecutive attainment of the qualities necessary for a good
life, and are satisfied, like men on the stage, with pretending to live a good life.

Those who fell away from paganism without embracing Christianity in its true significance, began to preach
love for God and man apart from self-renunciation,
and justice without self-control ; that is to say, they
preached the higher virtues omitting the lower ones :
*i. e.*, not the virtues themselves, but the semblance.

Some preach love to God and man without self-
renunciation, and others humaneness, the service of
humanity, without self-control.   And as this teaching,
while pretending to introduce man into higher moral
regions, encourages his animal nature by liberating
him from the most elementary demands of morality
—long ago acknowledged by the heathens, and not
only not rejected but strengthened by true Christianity—it was readily accepted both by believers and
unbelievers.

Only the other day the Pope's Encyclical* on
Socialism was published, in which, after a pretended
refutation of the Socialist view of the wrongfulness of
private property, it was plainly said : ' *No one is com-
manded to distribute to others that which is required for
his own necessities and those of his household ; nor even to
give away what is reasonably required to keep up becom-
ingly his condition in life ; for no one ought to live
unbecomingly.*' (This is from St. Thomas Aquinas, who
says, *Nullus enim inconvenienter vivere debet.*) ' *But
when necessity has been fairly supplied, and one's position
fairly considered, it is a duty to give to the indigent out of
that which is over.   That which remaineth give alms.*'

Thus now preaches the head of the most wide-spread
Church.   Thus have preached all the Church teachers,

---

* This refers to the Encyclical of Pope Leo XIII.   In the
passage quoted the official English translation of the Encyclical has been followed.   See the *Tablet*, 1891.

who considered salvation by works as insufficient. And together with this teaching of selfishness, which prescribes that you shall give to your neighbours only what you do not want yourself, they preach love, and recall with pathos the celebrated words of Paul in the thirteenth chapter of the First Epistle to the Corinthians, about love.

Notwithstanding that the Gospels overflow with demands for self-renunciation, with indications that self-renunciation is the first condition of Christian perfection; notwithstanding such clear expressions as: 'Whosoever will not take up his cross . . .' 'Whosoever hath not forsaken father and mother . . .' 'Whosoever shall lose his life . . .'—people assure themselves and others that it is possible to love men without renouncing that to which one is accustomed, or even what one pleases to consider becoming for one's self.

So speak the Church people; and those who reject not only the Church but also the Christian teaching (Freethinkers) think, speak, write, and act, in just the same way. These men assure themselves and others that without in the least diminishing their needs, without overcoming their lusts, they can serve mankind —*i.e.*, lead a good life.

Men have thrown aside the heathen sequence of virtues; but, not assimilating the Christian teaching in its true significance, they have not accepted the Christian sequence, and are left quite without guidance.

### IV.

In olden times, when there was no Christian teaching, all the teachers of life, beginning with Socrates, regarded as the first virtue of life, self-control—ἐγκράτεια or σωφροσύνη; and it was understood that every virtue must begin with and pass through this one. It was clear that a man who had no self-control, who had developed an immense number of desires and had yielded himself up to them, could not lead a good life. It was evident that before a man could even think of disinterestedness, justice—to say nothing of generosity or love—he must learn to exercise control over himself. According to our ideas now, nothing of the sort is necessary. We are convinced that a man who has developed his desires to the climax reached in our society, a man who cannot live without satisfying the hundred unnecessary habits that enslave him, can yet lead an altogether moral and good life. Looked at from any point of view: the lowest, utilitarian; the higher, pagan, which demands justice; but especially from the highest, Christian, which demands love—it should surely be clear to every one that a man who uses for his own pleasure (which he might easily forego) the labour, often the painful labour, of others, behaves wrongly; and that this is the very first wrong he must cease to commit if he wishes to live a good life.

From the utilitarian point of view such conduct is bad, because as long as he forces others to work for him a man is always in an unstable position; he accustoms himself to the satisfaction of his desires and becomes enslaved by them, while those who work for him do so with hatred and envy, and only await an opportunity to free themselves from the necessity of so working. Consequently such a man is always in danger of being left with deeply rooted habits which create demands he cannot satisfy.

From the point of view of justice such conduct is bad, because it is not well to employ for one's own pleasure the labour of other men who themselves cannot afford a hundredth part of the pleasures enjoyed by him for whom they labour.

From the point of view of Christian love it can hardly be necessary to prove that a man who loves others will give them his own labour rather than take from them, for his own pleasure, the fruit of their labour.

But these demands of utility, justice, and love, are altogether ignored by our modern society. With us the effort to limit one's desires is regarded as neither the first, nor even the last, but as an altogether un-necessary, condition of a good life.

On the contrary, according to the prevailing and most widely spread teaching of life to-day, the augmentation of one's wants is regarded as a desirable condition; as a sign of development, civilization, culture, and perfection. So-called educated people regard habits of comfort, that is, of effeminacy, as not only harmless, but even good, indicating a certain moral elevation—as almost a virtue.

It is thought that the more the wants, and the more refined these wants, the better.

Nothing shows this more clearly than the descriptive poetry, and especially the novels, of the last two centuries.

How are the heroes and heroines who represent the ideals of virtue portrayed?

In most cases the men who are meant to represent something noble and lofty—from Childe Harold down to the latest heroes of Feuillet, Trollope, or Maupassant—are simply depraved sluggards, consuming in luxury the labour of thousands, and themselves doing nothing useful for anybody. The heroines are the mistresses who in one way or another afford more or less delight to these men, are as idle as they, and are equally ready to consume the labour of others by their luxury.

I do not refer to the representations of really abstemious and industrious people one occasionally meets with in literature. I am speaking of the usual type that serves as an ideal to the masses: of the character that the majority of men and women are trying to resemble. I remember the difficulty (inexplicable to me at the time) that I experienced when I wrote novels, a difficulty with which I contended and with which I know all novelists now contend who have even the dimmest conception of what constitutes real moral beauty—the difficulty of portraying a type taken from the upper classes as ideally good and kind, and at the same time true to life. To be true to life, a description of a man or woman of the upper, educated classes must show him in his usual surroundings—that is, in luxury, physical idleness, and demanding much.

From a moral point of view such a person is undoubtedly objectionable. But it is necessary to represent this person in such a way that he may appear attractive. And novelists try so to represent him. I also tried. And, strange to say, such a representation, making an immoral fornicator and murderer (duellist or soldier), an utterly useless, idly drifting, fashionable buffoon, appear attractive, does not require much art or effort. The readers of novels are, for the most part, exactly such men, and therefore readily believe that these Childe Harolds, Onégins, Monsieurs de Camors,* etc., are very excellent people.

## v.

Clear proof that the men of our time really do not admit pagan self-control and Christian self-renunciation to be good and desirable qualities, but, on the contrary, regard the augmentation of wants as good and elevated, is to be found in the education given to the vast majority of children in our society. Not only are they not trained to self-control, as among the pagans, or to the self-renunciation proper to Christians, but they are deliberately inoculated with habits of effeminacy, physical idleness, and luxury.

I have long wished to write a fairy-tale of this kind: A woman, wishing to revenge herself on one who has injured her, carries off her enemy's child, and, going to a sorcerer, asks him to teach her how she can most cruelly wreak her vengeance on the stolen infant, the only child of her enemy. The sorcerer bids her carry the child to a place he indicates, and assures her that a most terrible vengeance will result. The wicked woman follows his advice ; but, keeping an eye upon the child, is astonished to see that it is found and adopted by a wealthy, childless man. She goes to the sorcerer and

* Onégin is the hero of a Russian poem by Poúshkin. M. de Camors is the hero of a French novel by Octave Feuillet.

reproaches him, but he bids her wait. The child grows up in luxury and effeminacy. The woman is perplexed, but again the sorcerer bids her wait. And at length the time comes when the wicked woman is not only satisfied, but has even to pity her victim. He grows up in the effeminacy and dissoluteness of wealth, and owing to his good nature is ruined. Then begins a sequence of physical sufferings, poverty, and humiliation, to which he is especially sensitive and against which he knows not how to contend. Aspirations toward a moral life—and the weakness of his effeminate body accustomed to luxury and idleness; vain struggles; lower and still lower decline; drunkenness to drown thought, then crime and insanity or suicide.

And, indeed, one cannot regard without terror the education of the children of the wealthy class in our day. Only the cruellest foe could, one would think, inoculate a child with those defects and vices which are now instilled into him by his parents, especially by mothers. One is awestruck at the sight, and still more at the results of this, if only one knows how to discern what is taking place in the souls of the best of these children, so carefully ruined by their parents. Habits of effeminacy are instilled into them at a time when they do not yet understand their moral significance. Not only is the habit of temperance and self-control neglected, but, contrary to the educational practice of Sparta and of the ancient world in general, this quality is altogether atrophied. Not only is man not trained to work, and to all the qualities essential to fruitful labour—concentration of mind, strenuousness, endurance, enthusiasm for work, ability to repair what is spoiled, familiarity with fatigue, joy in attainment— but he is habituated to idleness, and to contempt for all the products of labour : is taught to spoil, throw away, and again procure for money anything he fancies, without a thought of how things are made. Man is deprived of the power of acquiring the primary virtue of reasonableness, indispensable for the attainment of all the others, and is let loose in a world where people

preach, and praise, the lofty virtues of justice, the
service of man, and love.

It is well if the youth be endowed with a morally
feeble and obtuse nature, which does not detect the
difference between make-believe and genuine goodness
of life, and is satisfied with the prevailing mutual
deception.  If this be the case all goes apparently well,
and such a man will sometimes quietly live on with his
moral consciousness unawakened till death.

But it is not always thus, especially of late, now that
the consciousness of the immorality of such life fills the
air, and penetrates the heart unsought.  Frequently,
and ever more frequently, it happens that there
awakens a demand for real, unfeigned morality; and
then begin a painful inner struggle and suffering which
end but rarely in the triumph of the moral sentiment.

A man feels that his life is bad, that he must reform
it from the very roots, and he tries to do so; but he is
then attacked on all sides by those who have passed
through a similar struggle and have been vanquished.
They endeavour by every means to convince him that
this reform is quite unnecessary: that goodness does
not at all depend upon self-control and self-renunciation, that it is possible, while addicting himself to
gluttony, personal adornment, physical idleness, and
even fornication, to be a perfectly good and useful man.
And the struggle, in most cases, terminates lamentably.
Either the man, overcome by his weakness, yields to
the general opinion, stifles the voice of conscience,
distorts his reason to justify himself, and continues to
lead the old dissipated life, assuring himself that it is
redeemed by faith in the Redemption or the Sacraments, or by service to science, to the State, or to art;
or else he struggles, suffers, and finally becomes insane
or shoots himself.

It seldom happens, amid all the temptations that
surround him, that a man of our society understands
what was thousands of years ago, and still is, an
elementary truth for all reasonable people: namely,
that for the attainment of a good life it is necessary,

E

first of all, to cease to live an evil life; that for the attainment of the higher virtues it is needful, first of all, to acquire the virtue of abstinence or self-control, as the pagans called it, or of self-renunciation, as Christianity has it, and therefore it seldom happens that, by gradual efforts, he succeeds in attaining this primary virtue.

## VI.

I have just been reading the letters of one of our highly educated and advanced men of the 'forties, the exile Ogaryóf, to another yet more highly educated and gifted man, Herzen. In these letters Ogaryóf gives expression to his sincere thoughts and highest aspirations, and one cannot fail to see that—as was natural to a young man—he rather shows off before his friend. He talks of self-perfecting, of sacred friendship, love, the service of science, of humanity, and the like. And at the same time he calmly writes that he often irritates the companion of his life by, as he expresses it, 'returning home in an unsober state, or disappearing for many hours with a fallen, but dear creature. . . .'

Evidently it never even occurred to this remarkably kind-hearted, talented, and well-educated man that there was anything at all objectionable in the fact that he, a married man, awaiting the confinement of his wife (in his next letter he writes that his wife has given birth to a child), returned home intoxicated, and disappeared with dissolute women. It did not enter his head that until he had commenced the struggle, and had, at least to some extent, conquered his inclination to drunkenness and fornication, he could not think of friendship and love, and still less of serving any one or any thing. But he not only did not struggle against these vices—he evidently thought there was something very nice in them, and that they did not in the least hinder the struggle for perfection; and, therefore, instead of hiding them from the friend in whose eyes he wishes to appear in a good light, he exhibits them.

Thus it was half a century ago. I was contemporary with such men. I knew Ogaryóf and Herzen themselves, and others of that stamp, and men educated in the same traditions. There was a remarkable absence of consistency in the lives of all these men. Together with a sincere and ardent wish for good, there was an utter looseness of personal desire, which, they thought, could not hinder the living of a good life, nor the performance of good, and even great, deeds. They put unkneaded loaves into a cold oven, and believed that bread would be baked. And then, when with advancing years they began to remark that the bread did not bake —*i.e.*, that no good came of their lives—they saw in this something peculiarly tragic.

And the tragedy of such lives is indeed terrible. And this same tragedy apparent in the lives of Herzen, Ogaryóf, and others of their time, exists to-day in the lives of very many so-called educated people who hold the same views. A man desires to lead a good life, but the consecutiveness which is indispensable for this is lost in the society in which he lives. As fifty years ago Ogaryóf, Herzen, and others, so also the majority of men of the present day are persuaded that to lead an effeminate life, to eat sweet and fat dishes, to delight one's self in every way and satisfy all one's desires, does not hinder one from living a good life. But as it is evident that a good life in their case does not result, they give themselves up to pessimism, and say, 'Such is the tragedy of human life.'

What is also strange in the case is that these people know that the distribution of pleasures among men is unequal, and regard this inequality as an evil, and wish to correct it, yet do not cease to strive to augment their own pleasures—*i.e.*, to augment inequality in the distribution of pleasures. In acting thus, these people are like men who being the first to enter an orchard hasten to gather all the fruit they can lay their hands on, and yet wish to organize a more equal distribution of the fruit of the orchard between themselves and later comers, while they continue to pluck all the fruit they can reach.

### VII.

The delusion that men while addicting themselves to their desires and regarding this life of desire as good, can yet lead a good, useful, just and loving life, is so astonishing, that men of later generations will, I should think, simply fail to understand what the men of our time meant by the words 'good life,' when they said that the gluttons—the effeminate, lustful sluggards—of our wealthy classes led good lives. Indeed, one need only put aside for a moment the customary view of the life of our wealthy classes, and look at it, I do not say from the Christian point of view, but from the pagan standpoint, from the standpoint of the very lowest demands of justice, to be convinced that, living amidst the violation of the plainest laws of justice or fairness, such as even children in their games think it wrong to violate, we, men of the wealthy classes, have no right even to talk about a good life.

Any man of our society who would, I do not say begin a good life, but even begin to make some little approach towards it, must first of all cease to lead a bad life, must begin to destroy those conditions of an evil life with which he finds himself surrounded.

How often one hears, as an excuse for not reforming our lives, the argument that any act that is contrary to the usual mode of life would be unnatural, ludicrous —would look like a desire to show off, and would therefore not be a good action. This argument seems expressly framed to prevent people from ever changing their evil lives. If all our life were good, just, kind, then and only then would an action in conformity with the usual mode of life be good. If half our life were good and the other half bad, then there would be as much chance of an action not in conformity with the usual mode of life being good as of its being bad. But when life is altogether bad and wrong, as is the case in our upper classes, then a man cannot perform a single good action without disturbing the usual current of life. He can do a bad action without disturbing this current, but not a good one.

A man accustomed to the life of our well-to-do classes cannot lead a righteous life without first coming out of those conditions of evil in which he is immersed—he cannot begin to do good until he has ceased to do evil. It is impossible for a man living in luxury to lead a righteous life. All his efforts after goodness will be in vain until he changes his life, until he performs that work which stands first in sequence before him. A good life according to the pagan view, and still more according to the Christian view, is, and can be, measured in no other way than by the mathematical relation between love for self and love for others. The less there is of love for self with all the ensuing care about self and the selfish demands made upon the labour of others, and the more there is of love for others, with the resultant care for and labour bestowed upon others, the better is the life.

Thus has goodness of life been understood by all the sages of the world and by all true Christians, and in exactly the same way do all plain men understand it now. The more a man gives to others and the less he demands for himself, the better he is : the less he gives to others and the more he demands for himself, the worse he is.

And not only does a man become morally better the more love he has for others and the less for himself, but the less he loves himself the easier it becomes for him to be better, and contrariwise. The more a man loves himself, and, consequently, the more he demands labour from others, the less possibility is there for him to love and to work for others, and less not only in as many times as his love for himself has increased, but in some enormously greater degree less, as happens if we move the fulcrum of a lever from the long end to the short one : this will not only lengthen the long arm, but will also shorten the short one. So, also, if a man, possessing a certain faculty, love, augment his love and care for himself, he will thereby diminish his power of loving and caring for others, not only in proportion to the love he has transferred to himself, but in a much greater degree. Instead of feeding others a man eats too much himself; by so doing he not only diminishes the possibility of giving away the surplus, but, by overeating, he deprives himself of power to help others.

In order to love others in reality and not in word only, one must cease to love one's self also in reality and not merely in word. In most cases it happens thus: we think we love others, we assure ourselves and others that it is so, but we love them only in words, while ourselves we love in reality. Others we forget to feed and put to bed, ourselves—never. Therefore, in order really to love others in deed, we must learn not to love ourselves in deed, learn to forget to feed ourselves and put ourselves to bed, exactly as we forget to do these things for others.

We say of a self-indulgent person accustomed to lead a luxurious life, that he is a 'good man' and 'leads a good life.' But such a person—whether man or woman—although he may possess the most amiable traits of character, meekness, good nature, etc., cannot be good and lead a good life, any more than a knife of the very best workmanship and steel can be sharp and cut well unless it is sharpened. To be good and lead a good life means to give to others more than one takes from them. But a self-indulgent man accustomed to a luxurious life cannot do this, first because he himself is always in want of much (and this not on account of his selfishness, but because he is accustomed to luxury and it is painful for him to be deprived of that to which he is accustomed); and secondly, because by consuming all that he receives from others he weakens himself and renders himself unfit to labour, and therefore unfit to serve others. A self-indulgent man who sleeps long upon a soft bed, eats and drinks abundance of fat, sweet food, who is always dressed cleanly and suitably to the temperature, who has never accustomed himself to the effort of laborious work, can do very little.

We are so accustomed to our own lies and the lies of others, and it is so convenient for us not to see through the lies of others, that they may not see through ours, that we are not in the least astonished at, and do not doubt the truth of, the assertion of the virtuousness, sometimes even the sanctity, of people who are leading a perfectly unrestrained life.

A person, man or woman, sleeps on a spring bed with two mattresses, and two smooth, clean sheets, and feather pillows in pillow-cases. By the bedside is a rug, that the feet may not get cold on stepping out of bed, though slippers also lie near. Here also are the necessary utensils, so that he need not leave the house —whatever uncleanliness he may produce will be carried away and all made tidy. The windows are covered with curtains that the daylight may not awaken him, and he sleeps as long as he is inclined. Besides all this, measures are taken that the room may be warm in winter and cool in summer, and that he may not be disturbed by the noise of flies or other insects. While he sleeps, water, hot and cold, for his ablutions, sometimes baths and preparations for shaving, are provided. Tea and coffee are also prepared, stimulating drinks to be taken immediately upon rising. Boots, shoes, galoshes—several pairs dirtied the previous day—are already being cleaned and made to shine like glass freed from every speck of dust. Similarly are cleaned various garments, soiled on the preceding day, differing in texture to suit not only summer and winter, but also spring, autumn, rainy, damp, and warm weather. Clean linen, washed, starched, and ironed, is being made ready with studs, shirt buttons, button-holes, all carefully inspected by specially appointed people.

If the person be active he rises early—at seven o'clock—*i.e.*, still a couple of hours later than those who are making all these preparations for him. Besides clothes for the day and covering for the night, there is

also a costume and foot-gear for the time of dressing
—dressing-gown and slippers; and now he undertakes
his washing, cleaning, brushing, for which several
kinds of brushes are used, as well as soap and a great
quantity of water. (Many English men and women,
for some reason or other, are specially proud of using
a great deal of soap and pouring a large quantity of
water over themselves.) Then he dresses, brushes his
hair before a special kind of looking-glass (different
from those that hang in almost every room in the
house), takes the things he needs, such as spectacles
or eyeglasses, and then distributes in different pockets
a clean pocket-handkerchief to blow his nose on; a
watch with a chain, though in almost every room he
goes to there will be a clock; money of various kinds,
small change (often in a specially contrived case which
saves him the trouble of looking for the required coin)
and bank-notes; also visiting cards on which his name
is printed (saving him the trouble of saying or writing
it); pocket-book and pencil. In the case of women,
the toilet is still more complicated: corsets, arranging
of long hair, adornments, laces, elastics, ribbons, ties,
hairpins, pins, brooches.

But at last all is complete and the day commences,
generally with eating: tea and coffee are drunk with a
great quantity of sugar; bread made of the finest white
flour is eaten with large quantities of butter, and sometimes the flesh of pigs. The men for the most part
smoke cigars or cigarettes meanwhile, and read fresh
papers, which have just been brought. Then, leaving
to others the task of setting right the soiled and dis-
ordered room, they go to their office or business, or
drive in carriages produced specially to move such
people about. Then comes a luncheon of slain beasts,
birds, and fish, followed by a dinner consisting, if it be
very modest, of three courses, dessert, and coffee.
Then playing at cards and playing music—or the
theatre, reading, and conversation, in soft spring arm-
chairs, by the intensified and shaded light of candles,
gas, or electricity. After this, again tea, again eating

—supper—and again to bed, shaken up and prepared with clean linen, and with washed utensils to be again made foul.

Thus pass the days of a man of modest life, of whom, if he is good-natured and does not possess any habits specially obnoxious to those about him, it is said that he leads a good and virtuous life.

But a good life is the life of a man who does good to others; and can a man accustomed to live thus do good to others? Before he can do good to men he must cease to do evil. Reckon up all the harm such a man, often unconsciously, does to others, and you will see that he is far indeed from doing good; he would have to perform many acts of heroism to redeem the evil he commits, but he is too much enfeebled by his life full of desires to perform any such acts. He might sleep with more advantage, both physical and moral, lying on the floor wrapped in his cloak, as Marcus Aurelius did; and thus he might save all the labour and trouble involved in the manufacture of mattresses, springs, and pillows, as also the daily labour of the laundress—one of the weaker sex burdened by the bearing and nursing of children—who washes linen for this strong man. By going to bed earlier and getting up earlier he might save window-curtains and the evening lamp. He might sleep in the same shirt he wears during the day, might step barefooted upon the floor, and go out into the yard; he might wash at the pump—in a word, he might live like those who work for him, and might thus save all this work that is done for him. He might save all the labour expended upon his clothing, his refined food, his recreations. And he knows under what conditions all these labours are performed: how in performing them men perish, suffer, and often hate those who take advantage of their poverty to force them to do it.

How, then, is such a man to do good to others and lead a righteous life, without abandoning this self-indulgent, luxurious life?

But we need not speak of how other people appear

in our eyes—every one must see and feel this concerning himself.

I cannot but repeat this same thing again and again, notwithstanding the cold and hostile silence with which my words are received. A moral man, living a life of comfort, a man even of the middle class (I will not speak of the upper classes, who daily consume to satisfy their caprices the results of hundreds of working days), cannot live quietly, knowing that all that he is using is produced by the labour and crushed lives of working people, who are dying without hope—ignorant, drunken, dissolute, half-savage creatures employed in mines, factories, and at agricultural labour, producing the articles that he uses.

At the present moment I who am writing this and you who will read it, whoever you may be—both you and I have wholesome, sufficient, perhaps abundant and luxurious food, pure, warm air to breathe, winter and summer clothing, various recreations, and, most important of all, we have leisure by day and undisturbed repose at night. And here, by our side, live the working people, who have neither wholesome food, nor healthy lodgings, nor sufficient clothing, nor recreations, and who, above all, are deprived not only of leisure but even of rest: old men, children, women, worn out by labour, by sleepless nights, by disease, who spend their whole lives providing for us those articles of comfort and luxury which they do not possess, and which are for us not necessaries but super-fluities. Therefore, a moral man, I do not say a Christian, but simply a man professing humane views or merely esteeming justice, cannot but wish to change his life and to cease to use articles of luxury produced under such conditions.

If a man really pities those who manufacture tobacco, then the first thing he will naturally do will be to cease smoking, because by continuing to buy and smoke tobacco he encourages the preparation of tobacco, by which men's health is destroyed. And so with every other article of luxury. If a man can still continue to eat bread notwithstanding the hard work by which it is produced, this is because he cannot forego what is indispensable while waiting for the present conditions of labour to be altered. But with regard to things which are not only unnecessary but are even superfluous, there can be no other conclusion than this: that if I pity men engaged in the manufacture of certain articles, then I must on no account accustom myself to require such articles.

But nowadays men argue otherwise. They invent the most various and intricate arguments, but never say what naturally occurs to every plain man. According to them, it is not at all necessary to abstain from luxuries. One can sympathize with the condition of the working men, deliver speeches and write books on their behalf, and at the same time continue to profit by the labour that one sees to be ruinous to them.

According to one argument, I may profit by labour that is harmful to the workers, because if I do not another will. Which is something like the argument that I must drink wine that is injurious to me, because it has been bought, and if I do not drink it others will do so.

According to another argument, it is even beneficial to the workers to be allowed to produce luxuries, as in this way we provide them with money—*i.e.*, with the means of subsistence: as if we could not provide them with the means of subsistence in any other way than by making them produce articles injurious to them and superfluous to us.

But according to a third argument, now most popular, it seems that, since there is such a thing as division of labour, any work upon which a man is engaged— whether he be a Government official, priest, landowner, manufacturer, or merchant—is so useful that it fully compensates for the labour of the working classes by which he profits. One serves the State, another the Church, a third science, a fourth art, and a fifth serves those who serve the State, science, and art; and all are firmly convinced that what they give to mankind certainly compensates for all they take. And it is astonishing how, while continually augmenting their luxurious requirements without increasing their activity, these people continue to be certain that their activity compensates for all they consume.

Whereas, if you listen to these people's judgment of one another, it appears that each individual is far from being worth what he consumes. Government officials say that the work of the landlords is not worth what they spend, landlords say the same about merchants, and merchants about Government officials, and so on. But this does not disconcert them, and they continue to assure people that they (each of them) profit by the labours of others exactly in proportion to the service they render to others. So that the payment is not determined by the work, but the value of the imaginary work is determined by the payment. Thus they assure one another, but they know perfectly well in the depth of their souls that all their arguments do not justify them; that they are not necessary to the working men, and that they profit by the labour of these men, not on account of any division of labour, but simply because they have the power to do so, and because they are so spoiled that they cannot do without it.

And all this arises from people imagining that it is possible to lead a good life without first acquiring the primary quality necessary for a good life.

And this first quality is self-control.

## VIII.

There never has been, and cannot be, a good life without self-control. Apart from self-control, no good life is imaginable. The attainment of goodness must begin with that.

There is a scale of virtues, and it is necessary, if one would mount the higher steps, to begin with the lowest ; and the first virtue a man must acquire if he wishes to acquire the others, is that which the ancients called ἐγκράτεια or σωφροσύνη — *i.e.*, self-control or moderation.

If, in the Christian teaching, self-control was included in the conception of self-renunciation, still the order of succession remained the same, and the acquirement of no Christian virtue is possible without self-control—and this not because such a rule has been invented by any one, but because such is the essential nature of the case.

But even self-control, the first step in every righteous life, is not attainable all at once, but only by degrees.

Self-control is the liberation of man from desires—their subordination to moderation, σωφροσύνη. But a man's desires are many and various, and in order successfully to contend with them he must begin with the fundamental ones—those upon which the more complex ones have grown up—and not with those complex lusts which have grown up upon the fundamental ones. There are complex lusts, like that of the adornment of the body, sports, amusements, idle talk, inquisitiveness, and many others ; and there are also fundamental lusts—gluttony, idleness, sexual love. And one must begin to contend with these lusts from the beginning : not with the complex, but with the fundamental ones, and that also in a definite order. And this order is determined both by the nature of things and by the tradition of human wisdom.

A man who eats too much cannot strive against laziness, while a gluttonous and idle man will never be able to contend with sexual lust. Therefore, according to all moral teachings, the effort towards self-control commences with a struggle against the lust of gluttony—commences with fasting. In our time, however, every serious relation to the attainment of a good life has been so long and so completely lost, that not only is the very first virtue—self-control—without which the others are unattainable, regarded as superfluous, but the order of succession necessary for the attainment of this first virtue is also disregarded, and fasting is quite forgotten, or is looked upon as a silly superstition, utterly unnecessary.

And yet, just as the first condition of a good life is self-control, so the first condition of a life of self-control is fasting.

One may wish to be good, one may dream of goodness, without fasting; but to *be* good without fasting is as impossible as it is to advance without getting up on to one's feet.

Fasting is an indispensable condition of a good life, whereas gluttony is, and always has been, the first sign of the opposite—a bad life; and, unfortunately, this vice is in the highest degree characteristic of the life of the majority of the men of our time.

Look at the faces and figures of the men of our circle and day—on all those faces with pendent cheeks and chins, those corpulent limbs and prominent stomachs, lies the indelible seal of a dissolute life. Nor can it be otherwise. Consider our life and the actuating motive of the majority of men in our society, and then ask yourself, What is the chief interest of this majority? And, strange as it may appear to us who are accustomed to hide our real interests and to profess false, artificial ones, you will find that the chief interest of their life is the satisfaction of the palate, the pleasure of eating—gluttony. From the poorest to the richest, eating is, I think, the chief aim, the chief pleasure, of our life. Poor working people form an exception, but only inasmuch as want prevents their addicting themselves to this passion. No sooner have they the time and the means, than, in imitation of the higher classes, they procure what is most tasty and sweet, and eat and drink as much as they can. The more they eat, the more do they deem themselves, not only happy, but also strong and healthy. And in this conviction they are encouraged by the upper classes, who regard food in precisely the same way. The educated classes (following the medical men who assure them that the most expensive food, flesh, is the most wholesome) imagine that happiness and health consist in tasty, nourishing, easily digested food—in gorging; though they try to conceal this.

Look at rich people's lives, listen to their conversation. What lofty subjects seem to occupy them: philosophy, science, art, poetry, the distribution of wealth, the welfare of the people, and the education of the young; but all this is, for the immense majority, a sham,—all this occupies them in the intervals of business, real business: between lunch and dinner, while the stomach is full and it is impossible to eat more. The only real living interest of the majority both of men and women, especially after early youth, is eating—How to eat, what to eat, where and when to eat?

No solemnity, no rejoicing, no consecration, no opening of anything, can dispense with eating.

Watch people travelling. In their case the thing is specially evident. 'Museums, libraries, Parliament—how very interesting! But where shall we dine? Where is one best fed?' Look at people when they come together for dinner, dressed up, perfumed, around a table decorated with flowers—how joyfully they rub their hands and smile!

If we could look into the hearts of the majority of people, what should we find they most desire? Appetite for breakfast and for dinner. What is the severest punishment from infancy upwards? To be put on bread and water. What artisans get the highest wages? Cooks. What is the chief interest of the mistress of the house? To what subject does the conversation of middle-class housewives generally tend? If the conversation of the members of the higher classes does not tend in the same direction, it is not because they are better educated or are occupied with higher interests, but simply because they have a house-keeper or a steward who relieves them of all anxiety about their dinner. But once deprive them of this convenience, and you will see what causes them most anxiety. It all comes round to the subject of eating: the price of grouse, the best way of making coffee, of baking sweet cakes, etc. People come together—

whatever the occasion : a christening, a funeral, a wedding, the consecration of a church, the departure or arrival of a friend, the consecration of regimental colours, the celebration of a memorable day, the death or birth of a great scientist, philosopher, or teacher of morality—men come together as if occupied by the most lofty interests. So they say ; but it is only a pretence : they all know that there will be eating— good tasty food—and drinking, and it is chiefly this that brings them together. For several days before, to this end, animals have been slaughtered, baskets of provisions brought from gastronomic shops ; cooks and their helpers, kitchen boys and maids, specially attired in clean, starched frocks and caps, have been ' at work.' Chefs, receiving £50 a month and more, have been occupied in giving directions. Cooks have been chopping, kneading, roasting, arranging, adorning. With like solemnity and importance a master of the ceremonies has been working, calculating, pondering, adjusting with his eye, like an artist. A gardener has been employed upon the flowers. Scullery-maids. . . . An army of men has been at work, the result of thousands of working days are being swallowed up, and all this that people may come together to talk about some great teacher of science or morality, or to recall the memory of a deceased friend, or to greet a young couple just entering upon a new life.

In the middle and lower classes it is perfectly evident that every festivity, every funeral or wedding, means gluttony. There the matter is so understood. To such an extent is gluttony the motive of the assembly that in Greek and in French the same word means both ' wedding ' and ' feast.' But in the upper classes of the rich, especially among the refined, who have long possessed wealth, great skill is used to conceal this, and to make it appear that eating is a secondary matter, necessary only for appearance. And this pretence is easy, as in the majority of cases the guests are satiated in the true sense of the word—they are never hungry.

They pretend that dinner, eating, is not necessary to them, is even a burden; but this a lie. Try giving them—instead of the refined dishes they expect, I do not say bread and water, but—porridge or gruel or something of that kind, and see what a storm it will call forth, and how evident will become the real truth, namely, that the chief interest of the assembly is, not the ostensible one, but—gluttony.

Look at what men sell; go through a town and see what men buy—articles of adornment and things to devour. And indeed this must be so, it cannot be otherwise. It is only possible not to think about eating, to keep this lust under control, when a man does not eat except in obedience to necessity; but if a man *ceases* to eat only in obedience to necessity—*i.e.*, when the stomach is full—then the state of things cannot but be what it actually is. If men love the pleasure of eating, if they allow themselves to love this pleasure, if they find it good (as is the case with the vast majority of men in our time, and with educated men quite as much as with uneducated, although they pretend that it is not so), there is no limit to the augmentation of this pleasure, no limit beyond which it may not grow. The satisfaction of a *need* has limits, but pleasure has none. For the satisfaction of our needs it is necessary and sufficient to eat bread, porridge, or rice; for the augmentation of pleasure there is no end to the possible flavourings and seasonings.

Bread is a necessary and sufficient food. (This is proved by the millions of men who are strong, active, healthy, and hard-working on rye bread alone.) But it is pleasanter to eat bread with some flavouring. It is well to soak the bread in water boiled with meat. Still better to put into this water some vegetable or, better yet, several vegetables. It is well to eat flesh. And flesh is better not stewed, but roasted; and it is better still with butter, and underdone, and choosing out certain special parts of the meat. But add to this vegetables and mustard. And drink wine with it, red wine for preference. One does not need any more, but

F

one can yet eat some fish if it is well flavoured with
sauces and swallowed down with white wine.   It would
seem as if one could get through nothing more, either
rich or tasty, but a sweet dish can still be managed : in
summer ices, in winter stewed fruits, preserves, etc.
And thus we have a dinner, a modest dinner.   The
pleasure of such a dinner can be greatly augmented.
And it is augmented, and there is no limit to this augmentation : stimulating snacks, *hors-d'œuvres* before
dinner, and *entremets* and desserts, and various combinations of tasty things, and flowers and decorations
and music during dinner.

And, strange to say, men who daily overeat themselves at such dinners—in comparison with which the
feast of Belshazzar, that evoked the prophetic warning,
was nothing—are naïvely persuaded that they may yet
be leading a moral life.

IX.

Fasting is an indispensable condition of a good life ;
but in fasting, as in self-control in general, the question arises, with what shall we begin ?—How to fast,
how often to eat, what to eat, what to avoid eating ? And
as we can do no work seriously without regarding the
necessary order of sequence, so also we cannot fast without knowing where to begin—with what to commence
self-control in food.

Fasting !   And even an analysis of how to fast, and
where to begin !   The notion seems ridiculous and wild
to the majority of men.

I remember how, with pride at his originality, an
Evangelical preacher, who was   attacking monastic
asceticism, once said to me, 'Ours is not a Christianity
of fasting and privations, but of beefsteaks.'   Christianity, or virtue in general—and beefsteaks !

During a long period of darkness and lack of all
guidance, Pagan or Christian, so many wild, immoral
ideas have made their way into our life (especially into
that lower region of the first steps toward a good life—
our relation to food, to which no one paid any atten-

tion), that it is difficult for us even to understand the
audacity and senselessness of upholding, in our days,
Christianity or virtue with beefsteaks.

We are not horrified by this association, solely because
a strange thing has befallen us.   We look and see not :
listen and hear not.   There is no bad odour, no sound,
no monstrosity, to which man cannot become so accustomed that he ceases to remark what would strike a
man unaccustomed to it.   Precisely so it is in the moral
region.   Christianity and morality with beefsteaks !

A few days ago I visited the slaughter-house in our
town of Toúla.   It is built on the new and improved
system practised in large towns, with a view to causing
the animals as little suffering as possible.   It was on a
Friday, two days before Trinity Sunday.   There were
many cattle there.

Long before this, when reading that excellent book,
*The Ethics of Diet,* I had wished to visit a slaughter-
house, in order to see with my own eyes the reality of
the question raised when vegetarianism is discussed.
But at first I felt ashamed to do so, as one is always
ashamed of going to look at suffering which one knows
is about to take place, but which one cannot avert ; and
so I kept putting off my visit.

But a little while ago I met on the road a butcher
returning to Toúla after a visit to his home.   He is not
yet an experienced butcher, and his duty is to stab with
a knife.   I asked him whether he did not feel sorry for
the animals that he killed.   He gave me the usual
answer : 'Why should I feel sorry?   It is necessary.'
But when I told him that eating flesh is not necessary,
but is only a luxury, he agreed ; and then he admitted
that he was sorry for the animals.   'But what can I
do ?   I must earn my bread,' he said.   'At first I was
*afraid* to kill.   My father, he never even killed a
chicken in all his life.'   The majority of Russians
cannot kill ; they feel pity, and express the feeling by
the word '*fear*.'   This man had also been 'afraid,' but
he was so no longer.   He told me that most of the

F 2

work was done on Fridays, when it continues until the evening.

Not long ago I also had a talk with a retired soldier, a butcher, and he, too, was surprised at my assertion that it was a pity to kill, and said the usual things about its being ordained ; but afterwards he agreed with me : 'Especially when they are quiet, tame cattle. They come, poor things ! trusting you. It is very pitiful.'

This is dreadful ! Not the suffering and death of the animals, but that man suppresses in himself, unnecessarily, the highest spiritual capacity—that of sympathy and pity toward living creatures like himself—and by violating his own feelings becomes cruel. And how deeply seated in the human heart is the injunction not to take life !

Once, when walking from Moscow,* I was offered a lift by some carters who were going from Sérpouhof to a neighbouring forest to fetch wood. It was the Thursday before Easter. I was seated in the first cart, with a strong, red, coarse carman, who evidently drank. On entering a village we saw a well-fed, naked, pink pig being dragged out of the first yard to be slaughtered. It squealed in a dreadful voice, resembling the shriek of a man. Just as we were passing they began to kill it. A man gashed its throat with a knife. The pig squealed still more loudly and piercingly, broke away from the men, and ran off covered with blood. Being near-sighted I did not see all the details. I saw only the human-looking pink body of the pig and heard its desperate squeal ; but the carter saw all the details and watched closely. They caught the pig, knocked it down, and finished cutting its throat. When its squeals ceased the carter sighed heavily. 'Do men really not have to answer for such things ?' he said.

* When returning to Yásnaya Polyána in spring, after his winter's residence in Moscow, Tolstoy repeatedly chose to walk the distance (something over 130 miles) instead of going by rail. Sérpouhof is a town he had to pass on the way.

So strong is man's aversion to all killing. But by example, by encouraging greediness, by the assertion that God has allowed it, and, above all, by habit, people entirely lose this natural feeling.

On Friday I decided to go to Toúla, and, meeting a meek, kind acquaintance of mine, I invited him to accompany me.

'Yes, I have heard that the arrangements are good, and have been wishing to go and see it; but if they are slaughtering I will not go in.'

'Why not? That's just what I want to see! If we eat flesh it must be killed.'

'No, no, I cannot!'

It is worth remarking that this man is a sportsman and himself kills animals and birds.

So we went to the slaughter-house. Even at the entrance one noticed the heavy, disgusting, fetid smell, as of carpenter's glue, or paint on glue. The nearer we approached, the stronger became the smell. The building is of red brick, very large, with vaults and high chimneys. We entered the gates. To the right was a spacious enclosed yard, three-quarters of an acre in extent—twice a week cattle are driven in here for sale—and adjoining this enclosure was the porter's lodge. To the left were the chambers, as they are called—*i.e.*, rooms with arched entrances, sloping asphalt floors, and contrivances for moving and hanging up the carcasses. On a bench against the wall of the porter's lodge were seated half a dozen butchers, in aprons covered with blood, their tucked-up sleeves disclosing their muscular arms also besmeared with blood. They had finished their work half an hour before, so that day we could only see the empty chambers. Though these chambers were open on both sides, there was an oppressive smell of warm blood; the floor was brown and shining, with congealed black blood in the cavities.

One of the butchers described the process of slaughtering, and showed us the place where it was done. I did not quite understand him, and formed a wrong,

but very horrible, idea of the way the animals are
slaughtered ; and I fancied that, as is often the case,
the reality would very likely produce upon me a
weaker impression than the imagination. But in this
I was mistaken.

The next time I visited the slaughter-house I went
in good time. It was the Friday before Trinity—a
warm day in June. The smell of glue and blood was
even stronger and more penetrating than on my first
visit. The work was at its height. The dusty yard
was full of cattle, and animals had been driven into all
the enclosures beside the chambers.

In the street, before the entrance, stood carts to
which oxen, calves, and cows were tied. Other carts
drawn by good horses and filled with live calves, whose
heads hung down and swayed about, drew up and were
unloaded ; and similar carts containing the carcasses of
oxen, with trembling legs sticking out, with heads and
bright red lungs and brown livers, drove away from
the slaughter-house. By the fence stood the cattle-
dealers' horses. The dealers themselves, in their long
coats, with their whips and knouts in their hands, were
walking about the yard, either marking with tar cattle
belonging to the same owner, or bargaining, or else
guiding oxen and bulls from the great yard into the
enclosures which lead into the chambers. These men
were evidently all preoccupied with money matters and
calculations, and any thought as to whether it was right
or wrong to kill these animals was as far from their
minds as were questions about the chemical composition
of the blood that covered the floor of the chambers.

No butchers were to be seen in the yard ; they were
all in the chambers at work. That day about a hundred
head of cattle were slaughtered. I was on the point
of entering one of the chambers, but stopped short at
the door. I stopped both because the chamber was
crowded with carcasses which were being moved about,
and also because blood was flowing on the floor and
dripping from above. All the butchers present were
besmeared with blood, and had I entered I, too, should

certainly have been covered with it. One suspended carcass was being taken down, another was being moved toward the door, a third, a slaughtered ox, was lying with its white legs raised, while a butcher with strong hand was ripping up its tight-stretched hide.

Through the door opposite the one at which I was standing, a big, red, well-fed ox was led in. Two men were dragging it, and hardly had it entered when I saw a butcher raise a knife above its neck and stab it. The ox, as if all four legs had suddenly given way, fell heavily upon its belly, immediately turned over on one side, and began to work its legs and all its hind-quarters. Another butcher at once threw himself upon the ox from the side opposite to the twitching legs, caught its horns and twisted its head down to the ground, while another butcher cut its throat with a knife. From beneath the head there flowed a stream of blackish-red blood, which a besmeared boy caught in a tin basin. All the time this was going on the ox kept incessantly twitching its head as if trying to get up, and waved its four legs in the air. The basin was quickly filling, but the ox still lived, and, its stomach heaving heavily, both hind and fore legs worked so violently that the butchers held aloof. When one basin was full, the boy carried it away on his head to the albumen factory, while another boy placed a fresh basin, which also soon began to fill up. But still the ox heaved its body and worked its hind legs.

When the blood ceased to flow the butcher raised the animal's head and began to skin it. The ox continued to writhe. The head, stripped of its skin, showed red with white veins, and kept the position given it by the butcher; on both sides hung the skin. Still the animal did not cease to writhe. Then another butcher caught hold of one of the legs, broke it, and cut it off. In the remaining legs and the stomach the convulsions still continued. The other legs were cut off and thrown aside, together with those of other oxen belonging to the same owner. Then the carcass was dragged to the hoist and hung up, and the convulsions were over.

Thus I looked on from the door at the second, third, fourth ox. It was the same with each: the same cutting off of the head with bitten tongue, and the same convulsed members. The only difference was that the butcher did not always strike at once so as to cause the animal's fall. Sometimes he missed his aim, whereupon the ox leaped up, bellowed, and, covered with blood, tried to escape. But then his head was pulled under a bar, struck a second time, and he fell.

I afterwards entered by the door at which the oxen were led in. Here I saw the same thing, only nearer, and therefore more plainly. But chiefly I saw here, what I had not seen before, how the oxen were forced to enter this door. Each time an ox was seized in the enclosure and pulled forward by a rope tied to its horns, the animal, smelling blood, refused to advance, and sometimes bellowed and drew back. It would have been beyond the strength of two men to drag it in by force, so one of the butchers went round each time, grasped the animal's tail and twisted it so violently that the gristle crackled, and the ox advanced.

When they had finished with the cattle of one owner, they brought in those of another. The first animal of this next lot was not an ox, but a bull—a fine, well-bred creature, black, with white spots on its legs, young, muscular, full of energy. He was dragged forward, but he lowered his head and resisted sturdily. Then the butcher who followed behind seized the tail, like an engine-driver grasping the handle of a whistle, twisted it, the gristle crackled, and the bull rushed forward, upsetting the men who held the rope. Then it stopped, looking sideways with its black eyes, the whites of which had filled with blood. But again the tail crackled, and the bull sprang forward and reached the required spot. The striker approached, took aim, and struck. But the blow missed the mark. The bull leaped up, shook his head, bellowed, and, covered with blood, broke free and rushed back. The men at the doorway all sprang aside; but the experienced butchers,

with the dash of men inured to danger, quickly caught
the rope; again the tail operation was repeated, and
again the bull was in the chamber, where he was
dragged under the bar, from which he did not again
escape. The striker quickly took aim at the spot where
the hair divides like a star, and, notwithstanding the
blood, found it, struck, and the fine animal, full of
life, collapsed, its head and legs writhing while it was
bled and the head skinned.

' There, the cursed devil hasn't even fallen the right
way !' grumbled the butcher as he cut the skin from
the head.

Five minutes later the head was stuck up, red instead
of black, without skin; the eyes, that had shone with
such splendid colour five minutes before, fixed and
glassy.

Afterwards I went into the compartment where small
animals are slaughtered—a very large chamber with
asphalt floor, and tables with backs, on which sheep
and calves are killed. Here the work was already
finished; in the long room, impregnated with the
smell of blood, were only two butchers. One was
blowing into the leg of a dead lamb and patting the
swollen stomach with his hand; the other, a young
fellow in an apron besmeared with blood, was smoking
a bent cigarette. There was no one else in the long,
dark chamber, filled with a heavy smell. After me
there entered a man, apparently an ex-soldier, bringing
in a young yearling ram, black with a white mark on
its neck, and its legs tied. This animal he placed upon
one of the tables, as if upon a bed. The old soldier
greeted the butchers, with whom he was evidently
acquainted, and began to ask when their master allowed
them leave. The fellow with the cigarette approached
with a knife, sharpened it on the edge of the table, and
answered that they were free on holidays. The live
ram was lying as quietly as the dead inflated one,
except that it was briskly wagging its short little tail
and its sides were heaving more quickly than usual.
The soldier pressed down its uplifted head gently,

without effort; the butcher, still continuing the conversation, grasped with his left hand the head of
the ram and cut its throat. The ram quivered, and
the little tail stiffened and ceased to wave. The
fellow, while waiting for the blood to flow, began to
relight his cigarette, which had gone out. The blood
flowed and the ram began to writhe. The conversation
continued without the slightest interruption. It was
horribly revolting.

*        *        *        *        *

And how about those hens and chickens which daily,
in thousands of kitchens, with heads cut off and stream-
ing with blood, comically, dreadfully, flop about, jerking
their wings?

And see, a kind, refined lady will devour the carcasses of these animals with full assurance that she is
doing right, at the same time asserting two contradictory propositions:

First, that she is, as her doctor assures her, so delicate that she cannot be sustained by vegetable food
alone, and that for her feeble organism flesh is indispensable; and, secondly, that she is so sensitive that
she is unable, not only herself to inflict suffering on
animals, but even to bear the sight of suffering.

Whereas the poor lady is weak precisely because she
has been taught to live upon food unnatural to man;
and she cannot avoid causing suffering to animals—for
she eats them.

x.

We cannot pretend that we do not know this. We
are not ostriches, and cannot believe that if we refuse
to look at what we do not wish to see, it will not exist.
This is especially the case when what we do not wish to
see is what we wish to eat. If it were really indispensable, or, if not indispensable, at least in some way
useful! But it is quite unnecessary,* and only serves

---

* Let those who doubt this read the numerous books upon
the subject, written by scientists and doctors—such as
Dr. A. Haig's little book, *Diet and Food*, or his larger

to develop animal feelings, to excite desire, and to promote fornication and drunkenness. And this is continually being confirmed by the fact that young, kind, undepraved people—especially women and girls —without knowing how it logically follows, feel that virtue is incompatible with beefsteaks, and, as soon as they wish to be good, give up eating flesh.

What, then, do I wish to say? That in order to be moral people must cease to eat meat? Not at all.

I only wish to say that for a good life a certain order of good actions is indispensable; that if a man's aspirations toward right living be serious they will inevitably follow one definite sequence; and that in this sequence the first virtue a man will strive after will be self-control, self-restraint. And in seeking for self-control a man will inevitably follow one definite sequence, and in this sequence the first thing will be self-control in food—fasting. And in fasting, if he be really and seriously seeking to live a good life, the first thing from which he will abstain will always be the use of animal food, because, to say nothing of the excitation of the passions caused by such food, its use is simply immoral, as it involves the performance of an act which is contrary to the moral feeling—killing; and is called forth only by greediness and the desire for tasty food.

The precise reason why abstinence from animal food

---

scientific work on *Uric Acid as a Factor in the Causation of Disease*—in which it is proved that flesh is not necessary for the nourishment of man. And let them not listen to these old-fashioned doctors who defend the assertion that flesh is necessary, merely because it has long been so regarded by their predecessors and by themselves; and who defend their opinion with tenacity and malevolence, as all that is old and traditional always is defended.—L. T.

While this volume was in preparation, a letter was received from Tolstoy with instructions to include the above reference to Dr. Haig's works, which had not been mentioned in previous editions of this essay.

will be the first act of fasting and of a moral life is
admirably explained in the book, *The Ethics of Diet* ;
and not by one man only, but by all mankind in the
persons of its best representatives during all the conscious life of humanity.

But why, if the wrongfulness — *i.e.,* the immorality—
of animal food was known to humanity so long ago,
have people not yet come to acknowledge this law?
will be asked by those who are accustomed to be led by
public opinion rather than by reason.

The answer to this question is, that the moral progress of humanity—which is the foundation of every
other kind of progress—is always slow ; but that the
sign of true, not casual, progress is its uninterrupted-
ness and its continual acceleration.

And the progress of vegetarianism is of this kind.
That progress, is expressed both in the words of the
writers cited in the above-mentioned book and in the
actual life of mankind, which from many causes is
involuntarily passing more and more from carniv-
orous habits to vegetable food, and is also deliberately following the same path in a movement which
shows evident strength, and which is growing larger
and larger—viz., vegetarianism. That movement has
during the last ten years advanced more and more
rapidly. More and more books and periodicals on this
subject appear every year ; one meets more and more
people who have given up meat ; and abroad, especially
in Germany, England, and America, the number of
vegetarian hotels and restaurants increases year by
year.

This movement should cause especial joy to those
whose life lies in the effort to bring about the kingdom
of God on earth, not because vegetarianism is in itself
an important step towards that kingdom (all true steps
are both important and unimportant), but because it is
a sign that the aspiration of mankind toward moral
perfection is serious and sincere, for it has taken the one
unalterable order of succession natural to it, beginning
with the first step.

One cannot fail to rejoice at this, as people could not fail to rejoice who, after striving to reach the upper story of a house by trying vainly and at random to climb the walls from different points, should at last assemble at the first step of the staircase and crowd towards it, convinced that there can be no way up except by mounting this first step of the stairs.

[1892.]

The above essay was written as Preface to a Russian translation of Howard William's *The Ethics of Diet*.

# V

## NON-ACTING

### I.

THE editor of a Paris review, thinking that the opinions of two celebrated writers on the state of mind that is common to-day would interest me, has sent me two extracts from French newspapers—one containing Zola's speech delivered at the banquet of the General Association of Students, the other containing a letter from Dumas to the editor of the *Gaulois*.

These documents interested me profoundly, both on account of their timeliness and the fame of their authors, and also because it would be difficult in present-day literature to find in such concise, vigorous, and brilliant form, an expression of the two fundamental forces the sum of which moves humanity. The one is the force of routine, tending to keep humanity in its accustomed path ; the other is the force of reason and love, drawing humanity towards the light.

The following is Zola's speech *in extenso :*

GENTLEMEN,

You have paid me a great honour, and conferred on me a great pleasure, by choosing me to preside at this Annual Banquet. There is no better or more charming society than that of the young. There is no audience more sympathetic, or before whom one's heart opens more freely with the wish to be loved and listened to.

I, alas ! have reached an age at which we begin to regret our departed youth, and to pay attention to the efforts of

the rising generation that is climbing up behind us.   It is
they who will both judge us and carry on our work.   In
them I feel the future coming to birth, and at times I ask
myself, not without some anxiety, What of all our efforts
will they reject, and what will they retain?   What will
happen to our work when it has passed into their hands?
For it cannot last except through them, and it will disappear unless they accept it, to enlarge it and bring it to
completion.

That is why I eagerly watch the movement of ideas
among the youth of to-day, and read the advanced papers
and reviews, endeavouring to keep in touch with the new
spirit that animates our schools, and striving vainly to
know whither you are all wending your way—you, who
represent the intelligence and the will of to-morrow.

Certainly, gentlemen, egotism plays its part in the
matter ; I do not hide it.   I am somewhat like a workman
who, finishing a house which he hopes will shelter his old
age, is anxious concerning the weather he has to expect.
Will the rain damage his walls?   May not a sudden wind
from the north tear the roof off?   Above all, has he built
strongly enough to resist the storm?   Has he spared neither
durable material nor irksome labour?   It is not that I think
our work eternal or final.   The greatest must resign themselves to the thought that they represent but a moment in
the ever-continuing development of the human spirit ; it
will be more than sufficient to have been for one hour the
mouthpiece of a generation !   And since one cannot keep a
literature stationary, but all things continually evolve and
recommence, one must expect to see younger men born and
grow up, who will, perhaps, in their turn cause you to be
forgotten.   I do not say that the old warrior in me does
not at times desire to resist, when he feels his work attacked.
But, in truth, I face the approaching century with more of
curiosity than of revolt, and more of ardent sympathy than
of personal anxiety ; let me perish, and let all my generation
perish with me, if, indeed, we are good for nothing but to fill
up the ditch for those who follow us in the march towards
the light.

Gentlemen, I constantly hear it said that Positivism is at
its last gasp, that Naturalism is dead, that Science has
reached the point of bankruptcy, having failed to supply
either the moral peace or the human happiness it promised.

You will well understand that I do not here undertake to solve the great problems raised by these questions. I am an ignoramus, and have no authority to speak in the name of science or philosophy. I am, if you please, simply a novelist, a writer who has at times seen a little way into the heart of things, and whose competence consists only in having observed much and worked much. And it is only as a witness that I allow myself to speak of what my generation—the men who are now fifty years old, and whom your generation will soon regard as ancestors—has been, or at least has wished to be.

I was much struck, a few days ago, at the opening of the *Salon du Champ-de-Mars*, by the characteristic appearance of the rooms. It is thought that the pictures are always much the same. That is an error. The evolution is slow ; but how astonished one would be to-day were it possible to revert to the *Salons* of some former years ! For my part, I well remember the last academic and romantic exhibitions, about 1863. Work in the open air (*le plein air*) had not yet triumphed ; there was a general tone of bitumen, a dirtying of canvas, a prevalence of burnt colours, the semi-darkness of studios. Then, some fifteen years later, after the victorious and much-contested influence of Manet, I can recall quite other exhibitions, where the clear tone of full sunlight shone ; it was, as it were, an inundation of light, a care for truth which made each picture-frame a window opened upon Nature bathed in light. And yesterday, after another fifteen years, I could discern, amid the fresh limpidity of the productions, the rising of a kind of mystic fog. There was the same care for clear painting, but the reality was changing, the figures were more elongated, the need of originality and novelty carried the artists over into the land of dreams.

If I have dwelt on these three stages of contemporary painting, I have done so because it seems to me that they correspond very strikingly to the contemporary movements of thought. My generation, indeed, following illustrious predecessors of whom we were but the successors, strove to open the windows wide to Nature, in order to see all and to say all. In our generation, even among those least conscious of it, the long efforts of positive philosophy and of analytical and experimental science came to fruition. Our fealty was to Science, which surrounded us on all sides ; in her we lived, breathing the air of the epoch. I am free to confess that, personally, I was even a sectarian, who lived to transport the rigid methods of Science into the domain of Literature. But where can the man be found who, in the stress of strife, does not exceed what is necessary, and is content to conquer without compromising his victory? On the whole I have nothing to regret, and I continue to believe in the passion which wills and acts. What enthusiasm, what hope, were ours! To know all, to prevail in all, and to conquer all! By means of truth to make humanity more noble and more happy!

And it is at this point, gentlemen, that you, the young, appear upon the scene. I say the young, but the term is vague, distant, and deep as the sea, for where are the young? What will it—the young generation—really become? Who has a right to speak in its name? I must of necessity deal with the ideas attributed to it, but if these ideas are not at all those held by many of you, I ask pardon in advance, and refer you to the men who have misled us by untrustworthy information, more in accord, no doubt, with their own wishes than with reality.

At any rate, gentlemen, we are assured that your generation is parting company with ours, that you will no longer put all your hope in Science, that you have perceived so great a social and moral danger in trusting fully to her, that you are determined to throw yourselves back upon the past, in order to construct, from the débris of dead faiths, a living faith.

Of course, there is no question of a complete divorce from Science; it is understood that you accept her latest conquests and mean to extend them. It is agreed that you will admit demonstrated truths, and efforts are even being made to fit them to ancient dogmas. But, at bottom, Science is to stand out of the road of faith—it is thrust back to its ancient rank as a simple exercise of the intelligence, an inquiry permitted so long as it does not infringe on the supernatural and the hereafter. It is said that the experiment has been made, and that Science can neither repeople the heavens she has emptied nor restore happiness to souls whose naïve peace she has destroyed. The day of her mendacious triumph is over; she must be modest since she cannot immediately know everything, enrich everything, heal everything. And if they dare not yet bid intelligent

youth to throw away its books and desert its masters, there
are already saints and prophets to be found going about to
exalt the virtue of ignorance, the serenity of simplicity, and
to proclaim the need a too-learned and decrepit humanity
should experience of recuperating itself in the depths of a
prehistoric village, among ancestors hardly detached from
the earth, anteceding all society and all knowledge.

I do not at all deny the crisis we are passing through—
this lassitude and revolt at the end of the century, after
such feverish and colossal labour, whose ambition it was to
know all and to say all. It seemed that Science, which had
just overthrown the old order, would promptly reconstruct
it in accord with our ideal of justice and of happiness.
Twenty, fifty, even a hundred years passed. And then,
when it was seen that justice did not reign, that happiness did not come, many people yielded to a growing
impatience, falling into despair, and denying that by knowledge one can ever reach the happy land. It is a common
occurrence ; there can be no action without reaction, and
we are witnessing the fatigue inevitably incidental to long
journeys : people sit down by the roadside—seeing the inter-
minable plain of another century stretch before them, they
despair of ever reaching their destination, and they finish
by even doubting the road they have travelled, and
regretting not to have reposed in a field, to sleep for ever
under the stars. What is the good of advancing, if the
goal is ever further removed ? What is the use of knowing, if one may not know everything ? As well let us
keep our unsullied simplicity, the ignorant happiness of a
child.

And thus it seemed that Science, which was supposed to
have promised happiness, had reached bankruptcy.

But did Science promise happiness ? I do not believe it.
She promised truth, and the question is, whether one will
ever reach happiness by way of truth. In order to content
one's self with what truth gives, much stoicism will certainly
be needed : absolute self-abnegation and a serenity of the
satisfied intelligence which seems to be discoverable only
among the chosen few. But, meanwhile, what a cry of
despair rises from suffering humanity ! How can life be
lived without lies and illusions ? If there is no other world
—where justice reigns, where the wicked are punished and
the good are recompensed—how are we to live through this

abominable human life without revolting ? Nature is unjust and cruel, Science seems to lead us to the monstrous law of the strongest—so that all morality crumbles away and every society makes for despotism. And in the reaction which results—in that lassitude from too much knowledge of which I have spoken—there comes a recoil from the truth which is as yet but poorly explained, and seems cruel to our feeble eyes that are unable to penetrate into and to seize all its laws. No, no! Lead us back to the peaceful slumber of ignorance! Reality is a school of perversion which must be killed and denied, since it will lead to nothing but ugliness and crime. So one plunges into dreamland as the only salvation, the only way to escape from the earth, to feel confidence in the hereafter and hope that there, at last, we shall find happiness and the satisfaction of our desire for fraternity and justice.

That is the despairing cry for happiness which we hear to-day. It touches me exceedingly. And notice that it rises from all sides like a cry of lamentation amid the re-echoing of advancing Science, who checks not the march of her waggons and her engines. Enough of truth; give us chimeras! We shall find rest only in dreams of the Non-existent, only by losing ourselves in the Unknown. There only, bloom the mystic flowers whose perfume lulls our sufferings to sleep. Music has already responded to the call, literature strives to satisfy this new thirst, and painting follows the same way. I have spoken to you of the exhibition at the Champ-de-Mars; there you may see the bloom of all this flora of our ancient windows—lank, emaciated virgins, apparitions in twilight tints, stiff figures with the rigid gestures of the Primitivists. It is a reaction against Naturalism, which we are told is dead and buried. In any case the movement is undeniable, for it manifests itself in all modes of expression, and one must pay great attention to the study and the explanation of it, if one does not wish to despair of to-morrow.

For my part, gentlemen, I, who am an old and hardened Positivist, see in it but an inevitable halt in the forward march. It is not really even a halt, for our libraries, our laboratories, our lecture-halls and our schools, are not deserted. What also reassures me is that the social soil has undergone no change; it is still the democratic soil from which our century sprang. That a new art should flourish,

G 2

or a new faith change the direction in which humanity is travelling—that faith would need a new soil which would allow it to germinate and grow : for there can be no new society without a new soil. Faith does not rise from the dead, and one can make nothing but mythologies out of dead religions. Therefore the coming century will but continue our own in the democratic and scientific rush forward which has swept us along, and which still continues. What I can concede is, that in literature we limited our horizon too much. Personally, I have already regretted that I was a sectarian, in that I wished art to confine itself to proven verities. Later comers have extended the horizon by reconquering the region of the unknown and the mysterious ; and they have done well. Between the truths fixed by science, which are henceforth immovable, and the truths Science will to-morrow seize from the region of the unknown to fix in their turn, there lies an undefined borderland of doubt and inquiry, which, it seems to me, belongs to literature as much as to science. It is there we may go as pioneers, doing our work as forerunners, and interpreting according to our characters and minds the action of unknown forces. The ideal—what is it but the unexplained : those forces of the infinite world in which we are plunged without knowing them ? But if it be permissible to invent solutions of what is unknown, dare we, therefore, call in question ascertained laws, imagining them other than they are, and thereby denying them ? As science advances it is certain that the ideal recedes : and it seems to me that the only meaning of life, the only joy we ought to attribute to life, lies in this gradual conquest, even if one has the melancholy assurance that we never shall know everything.

In the unquiet times in which we live, gentlemen,—in our day so satiated and so irresolute—shepherds of the soul have arisen who are troubled in mind and ardently offer a faith to the rising generation. The offer is generous, but, unfortunately, the faith changes and deteriorates according to the personality of the prophet who supplies it. There are several kinds, but none of them appear to me to be very clear, or very well defined.

You are asked to believe, but are not told precisely in what you should believe. Perhaps it cannot be told, or perhaps they dare not tell it.

You are to believe for the pleasure of believing, and,

especially, that you may learn to believe. The advice is not bad in itself; it is certainly a great happiness to rest in the certainty of a faith—no matter what it may be; but the worst of it is that one is not master of this virtue: it bloweth where it listeth.

I, therefore, am also going to finish by proposing to you a faith, and by beseeching you to have faith in work. Work, young people! I well know how trivial such advice appears: no speech-day passes at which it is not repeated amid the general indifference of the scholars. But I ask you to reflect on it, and I—who have been nothing but a worker—will permit myself to speak of all the benefit I have derived from the long task that has filled my life. I had no easy start in life; I have known want and despair. Later on I lived in strife, and I live in it still—discussed, denied, covered with abuse. Well, I have had but one faith, one strength—work! What has sustained me was the enormous labour I set myself. Before me stood always in the distance the goal toward which I was marching, and that sufficed to set me on my feet and to give me courage to advance in spite of all, when life's hardships had cast me down. The work of which I speak to you is the regular work, the daily task, the duty one has undertaken, to advance one step each day toward the fulfilment of one's engagement. How often in the morning have I sat down to my table—my head in confusion—a bitter taste in my mouth—tortured by some great sorrow, physical or moral! And each time—in spite of the revolt my suffering has caused—after the first moments of agony my task has been to me an alleviation and a comfort. I have always come from my daily task consoled—with a broken heart, perhaps, but erect and able to live on till the morrow.

Work! Remember, gentlemen, that it is the sole law of the world, the regulator bringing organic matter to its unknown goal! Life has no other meaning, no other *raison d'être*; we, each of us, appear but to perform our allotted task and to disappear. One cannot define life otherwise than by the movement it receives and bequeaths, and which is, in reality, nothing but work, work at the final achievement accomplished by all the ages. And, therefore, how can we be other than modest, how can we do other than accept the individual task given to each of us, and accept it without rebellion and without yielding to the pride of one's personal

'I,' which considers itself a centre and does not wish to take its place in the ranks ?

From the time one accepts that task, and from the time one begins to fulfil it, it seems to me tranquillity should come even to those most tormented. I know that there are minds tortured by thoughts of the Infinite, minds that suffer from the presence of mystery, and it is to them I address myself as a brother, advising them to occupy their lives with some immense labour, of which it were even well that they should never see the completion. It will be the balance enabling them to march straight ; it will be a continual diversion—grain thrown to their intelligence, that it may grind and convert it into daily bread, with the satisfaction that comes of duty accomplished.

It is true this solves no metaphysical problems ; it is but an empirical recipe enabling one to live one's life honestly and more or less tranquilly ; but is it a small thing to obtain a sound state of moral and physical health, and to escape the danger of dreams, while solving by work the question of finding the greatest happiness possible on this earth ?

I have always, I admit, distrusted chimeras. Nothing is less wholesome for men and nations than illusion ; it stifles effort, it blinds, it is the vanity of the weak. To repose on legends, to be mistaken about all realities, to believe that it is enough to dream of force in order to be strong—we have seen well enough to what terrible disasters such things lead. The people are told to look on high, to believe in a Higher Power, and to exalt themselves to the ideal. No, no ! That is language which at times seems to me impious. The only strong people are those who work, and it is only work that gives courage and faith. To conquer it is necessary that the arsenals should be full, that one should have the strongest and the most perfect armament, that the army should be trained, should have confidence in its chiefs and in itself. All this can be acquired ; it needs but the will and the right method. You may be well assured that the coming century and the illimitable future belong to work. And, in the rising force of Socialism, does one not already see the rough sketch of the social law of to-morrow, the law of work for all—liberating and pacifying work ?

Young men, young men, take up your duties ! Let each one accept his task, a task which should fill his life. It may be very humble; it will not be the less useful. Never mind what it is, so long as it exists and keeps you erect! When you have regulated it, without excess—just the quantity you are able to accomplish each day—it will cause you to live in health and in joy: it will save you from the torments of the Infinite. What a healthy and great society that will be—a society each member of which will bear his reasonable share of work! A man who works is always kind. So I am convinced that the only faith that can save us is a belief in the efficacy of accomplished toil. Certainly it is pleasant to dream of eternity. But for an honest man it is enough to have lived his life, doing his work.

ÉMILE ZOLA.

M. Zola does not approve of this faith in something vague and ill-defined, which is recommended to French youth by its new guides; yet he himself advises belief in something which is neither clearer nor better defined —namely, in science and in work.

A little-known Chinese philosopher, named Lao-Tsze, who founded a religion (the first and best translation of his book, 'Of the Way of Virtue,' is that by Stanislas Julien), takes as the foundation of his doctrine the *Tao*—a word that is translated as 'reason, way, and virtue.' If men follow the law of *Tao* they will be happy. But the *Tao*, according to M. Julien's translation, can only be reached by *non-acting*.

The ills of humanity arise, according to Lao-Tsze, not because men neglect to do things that are necessary, but because they do things that are unnecessary. If men would, as he says, but practise *non-acting*, they would not merely be relieved from their personal calamities, but also from those inherent in all forms of government, which is the subject specially dealt with by the Chinese philosopher.

M. Zola tells us that all should work persistently; work will make their life healthy and joyous, and will save them from the torment of the Infinite. Work! But what are we to work at? The manufacturers of, and the dealers in, opium, or tobacco, or brandy—all the speculators on the Stock Exchange, the inventors and manufacturers of weapons of destruction, all the military, the gaolers and executioners—all work : but it is obvious that mankind would be better off were these workers to cease working.

But perhaps M. Zola's advice refers only to those whose work is inspired by science. The greater part of his speech is, in fact, designed to uphold science, which he thinks is being attacked. Well, it so happens that I am continually receiving from various unappreciated authors—pamphlets, manuscripts, treatises, and printed books—the outcome of their scientific labours.

One of them has finally solved, so he says, the question of Christian gnosiology; another has written a book on the cosmic ether; a third has settled the social question; a fifth is editing a theosophical review; a sixth (in a thick volume) has solved the problem of the Knight's tour at chess.

All these people work assiduously, and work in the name of science, but I do not think I am mistaken in saying that my correspondents' time and work, and the time and work of many other such people, have been spent in a way not merely useless, but even harmful ; for thousands of men are engaged making the paper, casting the type, and manufacturing the presses needed to print their books, and to feed, clothe, and house all these scientific workers.

Work for science ? But the word 'science' has so large and so ill-defined a meaning that what some consider science others consider futile folly ; and this is so, not merely among the profane, but even among men who are themselves priests of science. While one set of the learned esteem jurisprudence, philosophy, and even theology, to be the most necessary and important of sciences, the Positivists consider just those very sciences to be childish twaddle devoid of scientific value. And, *vice versâ*, what the Positivists hold to be the science of sciences, sociology, is regarded by the theologians, the philosophers, and the spiritualists, as a collection of arbitrary and useless observations and assertions. More than this, even in one and the same branch, whether it be philosophy or natural science, each system has its ardent defenders and opponents, just as ardent, equally competent, though maintaining diametrically opposite views.

Lastly, does not each year produce its new scientific discoveries, which, after astonishing the boobies of the whole world, and bringing fame and fortune to the inventors, are eventually admitted to be ridiculous mistakes, even by those who promulgated them?

We all know that what the Romans valued as the greatest science and the most important occupation—that which distinguished them from the barbarians—was rhetoric, which now does not even rank as a science at all. Equally difficult is it to-day to understand the state of mind of the learned men of the Middle Ages, who were fully convinced that all science was concentrated in scholasticism.

Unless, then, our century forms an exception (which is a supposition we have no right to make), it needs no great boldness to conclude, by analogy, that among the kinds of knowledge occupying the attention of our learned men, and called science, there must necessarily be some which will be regarded by our descendants much as we now regard the rhetoric of the ancients and the scholasticism of the Middle Ages.

## II.

M. Zola's speech is chiefly directed against certain leaders who are persuading the young generation to return to religious beliefs; for M. Zola, as champion of science, considers himself an adversary of theirs. Really he is nothing of the sort, for his reasoning rests on the same basis as that of his opponents, namely (as he himself admits), on faith.

It is a generally accepted opinion that religion and science are opposed to one another. And they really are so, but only in point of time; that is to say, that what is considered science by one generation often becomes religion for their descendants. What is usually spoken of as religion is generally the science of the past, while what is called science is, to a great extent, the religion of the present.

We say that the assertions of the Hebrews that the world was created in six days; that sons would be punished for their father's sins; that certain diseases could be cured by the sight of a serpent, were religious statements; while the assertions of our contemporaries that the world created itself by turning round a centre which is everywhere, that all the different species arose from the struggle for existence, that criminals are the product of heredity, that micro-organisms, shaped like commas, exist, which cause certain diseases—we call scientific statements. By reverting in imagination to the state of mind of an ancient Hebrew, it becomes easy to see that for him the creation of the world in six days, the serpent that cured diseases, etc., were statements of science in accord with its highest stage of development, just as the Darwinian law, Koch's commas, heredity, etc., are for a man of our day.

And just as the Hebrew believed not so much in the creation of the world in six days, in the serpent that healed certain diseases, etc., as in the infallibility of his priests, and, therefore, in all that they told him— so to-day the great majority of cultured people believe, not in the formation of the world by rotation, nor in heredity, nor in the comma bacilli, but in the infallibility of the secular priests, called scientists, who, with an assurance equal to that of the Hebrew priests, assert whatever they pretend to know.

I will even go so far as to say that if the ancient priests, controlled by none but their own colleagues, allowed themselves at times to diverge from the path of truth merely for the pleasure of astonishing and mystifying their public, our modern priests of science do much the same thing, and do it with equal effrontery.

The greater part of what is called religion is simply the superstition of past ages; the greater part of what is called science is nothing but the superstition of to-day. And I suppose that the proportion of error and of truth is much about the same in the one as in the other. Consequently, to work in the name of a faith, whether religious or scientific, is not merely a doubtful method of helping humanity, but is a dangerous method which may do more harm than good.

To consecrate one's life to the fulfilment of duties imposed by religion—prayers, communions, alms—or, on the other hand, to devote it, as M. Zola advises, to some scientific work, is to run too great a risk: for on the brink of death one may find that the religious or scientific principle to whose service one has consecrated one's whole life was all a ridiculous error !

Even before reading the speech in which M. Zola extols work of any kind as a merit, I was always surprised by the opinion, especially prevalent in Western Europe, that work is a kind of virtue. It always seemed to me that only an irrational being, such as the ant of the fable, could be excused for exalting work to the rank of a virtue, and boasting of it. M. Zola assures us that work makes men kind ; I have always observed the contrary. Not to speak of selfish work, aiming at the profit or fame of the worker, which is always bad ; self-conscious work, the pride of work, makes not only ants, but men, cruel. Who does not know those men, inaccessible to truth or to kindliness, who are always so busy that they never have time either to do good or even to ask themselves whether their work is not harmful ? You say to such people, 'Your work is useless, perhaps even harmful. Here are the reasons ; pause awhile ; let us examine the matter.' They will not listen to you, but scornfully reply, ' It's all very well for you, who have nothing to do, to argue, but have I time for discussions ? I have worked all my life, and work does not wait ; I have to edit a daily paper, with half a million subscribers ; I have to organize the army ; I have to build the Eiffel Tower, to arrange the Chicago Exhibition, to pierce the Isthmus of Panama, to investigate the problem of heredity, or of telepathy, or of how many times this classical author has used such and such words.'

The most cruel of men—the Neros, the Peter the Greats—were constantly occupied, never remaining for a moment at their own disposal without activity or amusement.

Even if work be not a vice, it can from no point of view be considered a virtue.

Work can no more be considered a virtue than nutrition. Work is a necessity, to be deprived of which involves suffering, and to raise it to the rank of a merit is as monstrous as it would be to do the same for nutrition. The strange value our society attaches to work can only be explained as a reaction from the view held by our ancestors, who thought idleness an attribute of nobility, and almost a merit, as indeed it is still regarded by some rich and uneducated people to-day.

Work, the exercise of our organs, cannot be a merit, because it is a necessity for every man and every animal —as is shown alike by the capers of a tethered calf and by the silly exercises to which rich and well-fed people among ourselves are addicted, who find no more reasonable or useful employment for their mental faculties than reading newspapers and novels, or playing chess or cards, nor for their muscles than gymnastics, fencing, lawn-tennis, and racing.

In my opinion, not only is work not a virtue, but in our ill-organized society it is often a moral anæsthetic, like tobacco, wine, and other means of stupefying and blinding one's self to the disorder and emptiness of our lives ; and it is just as such that M. Zola recommends it to young people.

Dumas says something quite different.

### III.

The following is the letter he sent to the editor of the *Gaulois* :

DEAR SIR,

You ask my opinion of the aspirations which seem to be arising among the students in the schools, and of the polemics which preceded and followed the incidents at the Sorbonne.

I should prefer not to express my opinion further on any matter whatever. Those who were of our opinion will continue to be so for some time yet; those who held other views will cling to them more and more tenaciously. It would be better to have no discussions. 'Opinions are like nails,' said a moralist, a friend of mine: 'the more one hits them the more one drives them in.'

It is not that I have no opinion on what one calls the great questions of life, and on the diverse forms in which the mind of man momentarily clothes the subjects of which it treats. Rather, that opinion is so correct and absolute, that I prefer to keep it for my own guidance, having no ambition to create anything, or to destroy anything. I should have to go back to great political, social, philosophical and religious problems, and that would take us too far, were I to follow you in the study you are commencing of the small exterior occurrences they have lately aroused, and that they arouse in each new generation. Each new generation, indeed, comes with ideas and passions old as life itself, which each generation believes no one has ever had before, for it, for the first time, finds itself subject to their influence, and is convinced it is about to change the aspect of everything.

Humanity for thousands of years has been trying to solve that great problem of cause and effect, which will, perhaps, take thousands of years yet to settle, if, indeed (as I think it should be), it is ever settled. Of this problem children of twenty declare that they have an irrefutable solution in their quite young heads. And as a first argument, at the first discussion, one sees them hitting those who do not share their opinions. Are we to conclude that this is a sign that a whole society is readopting the religious ideal, which has been temporarily obscured and abandoned? Or is it not, with all these young apostles, simply a physiological question of warm blood and vigorous muscles, such as threw the young generation of twenty years ago into the opposite movement? I incline to the latter supposition.

He would indeed be foolish, who in these manifestations of an exuberant period of life found proof of development that was final, or even durable. There is in it nothing more than an attack of growing fever. Whatever the ideas may be, for the sake of which these young people have been hitting one another, we may safely wager that they will

resist them at some future day, if their own children reproduce them. Age and experience will have come by that
time.

Sooner or later many of these combatants and adversaries
of to-day will meet on the cross-roads of life, somewhat
wearied, somewhat dispirited by their struggle with realities,
and hand-in-hand will find their way back to the main road,
regretfully acknowledging that, in spite of all their early
convictions, the world remains round, and continues always
turning in one and the same direction, and that the same
horizons ever reappear under the same infinite and fixed
sky. After having disputed and fought to their hearts'
content, some in the name of faith, others in the name of
science, both to prove there is a God, and to prove there is
no God (two propositions about which one might fight for
ever should it be decided not to disarm till the case was
proven), they will finally discover that the one knows no
more about it than the other, but that what they may all
be sure of is, that man needs hope as much if not more than
he needs knowledge—that he suffers abominably from the
uncertainty he is in concerning the things of most interest
to him, that he is ever in quest of a better state than that
in which he now exists, and that he should be left at full
liberty, especially in the realms of philosophy, to seek this
happier condition.

He sees around him a universe which existed before he
did, and will last after he is gone ; he feels and knows it
to be eternal, and in its duration he would like to share.
From the moment he was called to life he demanded his
share of the permanent life that surrounds him, raises him,
mocks him, and destroys him. Now that he has begun he
does not wish to end. He loudly demands, and in low tones
pleads for, a certainty which ever evades him—fortunately,
since certain knowledge would mean for him immobility
and death, for the most powerful motor of human energy is
uncertainty. And as he cannot reach certainty, he wanders
to and fro in the vague ideal ; and whatever excursions he
may make into scepticism and negation, whether from pride,
curiosity, anger, or for fashion's sake, he ever returns to the
hope he certainly cannot forego. Like lovers' quarrels,
it is not for long.

So there are, at times, obscurations, but never any complete obliteration of the human ideal. Philosophical mists

pass over it, like clouds that pass before the moon; but the
white orb, continuing its course, suddenly reappears from
behind them intact and shining. Man's irresistible need of
an ideal explains why he has accepted with such confidence,
such rapture, and without reason's control, the various
religious formulas which, while promising him the Infinite,
have presented it to him conformably with his nature,
enclosing it in the limits always necessary even to the ideal.

But for centuries past, and especially during the last
hundred years, at each new stage, new men, more and more
numerous, emerge from the darkness, and in the name of
reason, science, or observation, dispute the old truths,
declare them to be relative, and wish to destroy the formulas
which contain them.

Who is in the right in this dispute? All are right while
they seek; none are right when they begin to threaten.
Between truth, which is the aim, and free inquiry, to which
all have a right, force is quite out of place, notwithstanding
celebrated examples to the contrary. Force merely drives
further back that at which we aim. It is not merely cruel,
it is also useless, and that is the worst of faults in all that
concerns civilization. No blows, however forcibly delivered,
will ever prove the existence or the non-existence of God.

To conclude, or, rather, to come to an end,—seeing that
the Power, whatever it be, that created the world (which, I
think, certainly cannot have created itself) has, for the
present, while using us as its instruments, reserved to itself
the privilege of knowing why it has made us and whither it
is leading us—seeing that this Power (in spite of all inten-
tions attributed to it, in spite of all the demands made upon
it) appears ever more and more determined to guard its own
secret—I believe, if I may say all I think, that mankind is
beginning to cease to try to penetrate that eternal mystery.
Mankind went to religions, which proved nothing, for they
differed among themselves; it went to philosophies, which
revealed no more, for they contradicted one another; and it
will now try to find its way out of the difficulty by itself,
trusting to its own instinct and its own simple good sense;
and since mankind finds itself here on earth without knowing
why or how, it is going to try to be as happy as it can with
just those means the earth supplies.

Zola recently, in a remarkable address to students, recommended to them work as a remedy, and even as a panacea,

for all the ills of life. *Labor improbus omnia vincit.* The remedy is familiar, nor is it less good on that account; but it is not, never has been, and never will be, sufficient. Whether he works with limbs or brain, man must have some other aim than that of gaining his bread, making a fortune, or becoming famous. Those who confine themselves to such aims feel, even when they have gained their object, that something is still lacking, for no matter what we may say, or what we may be told, man has not only a body to be nourished, an intelligence to be cultivated and developed, but also, assuredly, a soul to be satisfied. That soul, too, is incessantly at work, ever evolving toward light and truth. And so long as it has not reached full light and conquered the whole truth, it will continue to torment man.

Well! The soul never so harassed man, never so dominated him, as it does to-day. It is as though it were in the air we all breathe. The few isolated souls that had separately desired the regeneration of society have, little by little, sought one another out, beckoned one another, drawn nearer, united, comprehended one another, and formed a group, a centre of attraction, toward which others now fly from the four quarters of the globe, like larks toward a mirror. They have, as it were, formed one collective soul, so that men, in future, may realize together, consciously and irresistibly, the approaching union and steady progress of nations that were but recently hostile one to another. This new soul I find and recognise in events seemingly most calculated to deny it.

These armaments of all nations, these threats their representatives address to one another, this recrudescence of race persecutions, these hostilities among compatriots, and even these youthful escapades at the Sorbonne, are all things of evil aspect, but not of evil augury. They are the last convulsions of that which is about to disappear. The social body is like the human body. Disease is but a violent effort of the organism to throw off a morbid and harmful element.

Those who have profited, and expect for long or for ever to continue to profit by the mistakes of the past, are uniting to prevent any modification of existing conditions. Hence these armaments, and threats, and persecutions; but look carefully and you will see that all this is quite superficial. It is colossal, but hollow. There is no longer any soul in it—the soul has gone elsewhere; these millions of armed men who are daily drilled to prepare for a general war of extermination, no longer hate the men they are expected to fight, and none of their leaders dares to proclaim this war. As for the appeals, and even the threatening claims, that rise from the suffering and the oppressed—a great and sincere pity, recognising their justice, begins at last to respond from above.

Agreement is inevitable, and will come at an appointed time, nearer than is expected. I know not if it be because I shall soon leave this earth and the rays that are already reaching me from below the horizon have disturbed my sight, but I believe our world is about to begin to realize the words, 'Love one another,' without, however, being concerned whether a man or a God uttered them.

The spiritual movement one recognises on all sides, and which so many naïve and ambitious men expect to be able to direct, will be absolutely humanitarian. Mankind, which does nothing moderately, is about to be seized with a frenzy, a madness, of love. This will not, of course, happen smoothly or all at once; it will involve misunderstandings—even sanguinary ones perchance—so trained and so accustomed have we been to hatred, even by those, sometimes, whose mission it was to teach us to love one another. But it is evident that this great law of brotherhood must be accomplished some day, and I am convinced that the time is commencing when our desire for its accomplishment will become irresistible.

A. DUMAS.

*June* 1, 1893.

There is a great difference between Dumas' letter and Zola's speech, not to mention the external fact that Zola seems to court the approval of the youths he addresses, whereas Dumas' letter does not flatter them, nor tell them they are important people and that everything depends on them (which they should never believe if they wish to be good for anything); on the contrary, it points out to them their habitual faults: their presumption and their levity. The chief difference between these two writings consists in the fact that Zola's speech aims at keeping men in the path they are

H

travelling, by making them believe that what they know is just what they need to know, and that what they are doing is just what they ought to be doing—whereas Dumas' letter shows them that they ignore what it is essential for them to know, and do *not* live as they ought to live.

The more fully men believe that humanity can be led, in spite of itself, by some external, self-acting, force (whether religion or science) to a beneficial change in its existence—and that they need only work in the established order of things—the more difficult will it be to accomplish any beneficial change, and it is in this respect chiefly that Zola's speech errs.

On the contrary, the more fully men believe that it depends on themselves to modify their mutual relations, and that they can do this when they like, by loving each other instead of tearing one another to pieces as they do at present—the more will a change become possible. The more fully men let themselves be influenced by this suggestion, the more will they be drawn to realize Dumas' prediction. That is the great merit of his letter.

Dumas belongs to no party and to no religion : he has as little faith in the superstitions of the past as in those of to-day, and that is why he observes and thinks, and sees not only the present but also the future—as those did who in ancient times were called *seers*. It will seem strange to those who in reading a writer's works see only the contents of the book, and not the soul of the writer, that Dumas—the author of *La Dame aux Camélias,* and of *L'Affaire Clémenceau*—that this same Dumas should see into the future and should prophesy. But, however strange it may seem, prophecy making itself heard—not in the desert or on the banks of the Jordan, from the mouth of a hermit clothed in skins of beasts—but published in a daily paper on the banks of the Seine, remains none the less prophecy.

And the words of Dumas have all the characteristics of prophecy : First, like all prophecy, it runs quite counter to the general disposition of the people among whom it makes itself heard; secondly, those who hear it feel its truth, they know not why; and thirdly, and chiefly, it moves men to the realization of what it foretells.

Dumas predicts that, after having tried everything else, men will seriously apply to life the law of brotherly love, and that this change will take place much sooner than we expect. One may question the nearness of this change, or even its possibility; but it is plain that should it take place it will solve all contradictions and all difficulties, and will divert all the evils with which the end of the century sees us threatened.

The only objection, or rather the only question, one can put to Dumas is this: 'If the love of one's neighbour is possible, and is inherent in human nature, why have so many thousand years elapsed (for the command to love God and one's neighbour did not begin with Christ, but had been given already by Moses) without men, who knew this means of happiness, having practised it? What prevents the manifestation of a sentiment so natural and so helpful to humanity? It is evidently not enough to say, 'Love one another.' That has been said for three thousand years past: it is incessantly repeated from all pulpits, religious or even secular; yet men continue none the less exterminating instead of loving one another as they have been bidden to do for so many centuries. In our day no one any longer doubts that if, instead of tearing one another to pieces (each seeking his own welfare, that of his family, or that of his country), men would help one another: if they would replace egotism by love, if they would organize their life on collectivist instead of on individualist principles (as the Socialists express it in their wretched jargon), if they loved one another as they love themselves, or if, at least, they did not do to others what they do not wish to have done to themselves, as has been well expressed for two thousand years past— the share of personal happiness gained by each man would be greater, and human life in general would be reasonable and happy instead of being, what it now is, a succession of contradictions and sufferings.

H 2

No one doubts that if men continue to snatch from one another the ownership of the soil and the products of their labour, the revenge of those who are deprived of the right to till the soil will not much longer be delayed, but the oppressed will retake with violence and vengeance all that of which they have been robbed. No one doubts that the arming of the nations will lead to terrible massacres, and to the ruin and degeneration of all the peoples enchained in the circle of armaments. No one doubts that the present order of things, if it continues for some dozens of years longer, will lead to a general breakdown. We have but to open our eyes, to see the abyss toward which we are advancing. But the prophecy cited by Jesus seems realized among the men of to-day : they have ears that hear not, eyes that see not, and an intelligence that does not understand.

Men of our day continue to live as they have lived, and do not cease to do things that must inevitably lead to their destruction. Moreover, men of our world recognise, if not the religious law of love, at least the moral rule of that Christian principle : not to do to others what one does not wish done to one's self; but they do not practise it. Evidently some greater reason exists preventing their doing what is to their advantage, what would save them from menacing dangers, and what is dictated by the law of their God and by their conscience. Must it be said that love applied to life is a chimera ? If so, how is it that for so many centuries men have allowed themselves to be deceived by this unrealizable dream ? It were time to see through it. But mankind can neither decide to follow the law of love in daily life, nor to abandon the idea. How is this to be explained ? What is the reason of this contradiction lasting through centuries ? It is not that the men of our time neither wish nor are able to do what is dictated alike by their good sense, by the dangers of their situation, and above all by the law of him whom they call God and by their conscience—but it is because they act just as M. Zola advises : they are busy, they

all labour at some work commenced long ago and in
which it is impossible to pause to concentrate their
thoughts, or to consider what they ought to be.    All
the great revolutions in men's lives are made in thought.
When a change takes place in man's thought, action
follows the direction of thought as inevitably as a ship
follows the direction given by its rudder.

IV.

When he first preached, Jesus did not say, 'Love
one another' (he taught love later on to his disciples :
to men who had understood his teaching), but he said
what John the Baptist had preached before : repentance,
μετάνοια—that is to say, a change in the conception of life.
Μετανοεῖτε—change your view of life, or you will all
perish, said he.    The meaning of your life cannot consist in the pursuit of your personal well-being, or in
that of your family or of your nation, for such happiness can be obtained only at the expense of others.
Realize that the meaning of your life can consist only
in accomplishing the will of him that sent you into this
life, and who demands of you, not the pursuit of your
personal interests, but the accomplishment of his aims
—the establishment of the Kingdom of Heaven, as
Jesus said.

Μετανοεῖτε—change your way of understanding life, or
you will all perish, said he, 1,800 years ago ; and he
continues to repeat the same to-day, by all the contradictions and woes of our time, which all come from the
fact that men have not listened to him, and have not
accepted the understanding of life he offered them.
Μετανοεῖτε, said he, or you will all perish.    The alterna-
tive remains the same to-day.    The only difference is,
that now it is more pressing.    If it were possible 2,000
years ago, in the time of the Roman Empire, in the
days of Charles V., or even before the Revolution and
the Napoleonic wars, not to see the vanity—I will even
say the absurdity—of attempts made to obtain personal happiness, family happiness, or national happi-

ness, by struggling against all those who sought the same personal, family, or national happiness—that illusion has become quite impossible in our time for anyone who will pause—were it but for a moment—from his occupations, and will reflect on what he is, on what the world around him is, and on what he ought to be. So that were I called on to give one single piece of advice—the one I considered most useful for men of our century—I should say but this to them: 'For God's sake, pause a moment, cease your work, look around you, think of what you are, and of what you ought to be—think of the ideal.'

M. Zola says that people should not look on high, nor believe in a Higher Power, nor exalt themselves to the ideal. Probably M. Zola understands by the word 'ideal' either the supernatural—that is to say, the theological rubbish about the Trinity, the Church, the Pope, etc.—or else the *unexplained*, as he calls the forces of the vast world in which we are plunged. And in that case men would do well to follow M. Zola's advice. But the fact is that the ideal is neither supernatural nor 'unexplained.' The ideal, on the contrary, is the most natural of things; I will not say it is the most explained, but it is that of which man is most sure.

An ideal in geometry is the perfectly straight line or the circle whose radii are all equal; in science it is exact truth; in morals it is perfect virtue. Though these things—the straight line, exact truth, and perfect virtue—have never existed, they are not only more natural to us, more known and more explicable than all our other knowledge, but they are the only things we know truly and with complete certainty.

It is commonly said that reality is that which exists; or, that only what exists is real. Just the contrary is the case: true reality, that which we really know, is what has never existed. The ideal is the only thing we know with certainty, and it has never existed. It is only thanks to the ideal that we know anything at all; and that is why the ideal alone can guide us in our lives, either individually or collectively. The Christian ideal has stood before us for eighteen centuries; it shines, to-day, with such intensity that it needs great effort to avoid seeing that all our woes arise from the fact that we do not accept its guidance. But the more difficult it becomes to avoid seeing this, the more some people increase their efforts to persuade us to do as they do: to close our eyes in order not to see. To be quite sure to reach port one must, above all, throw the compass overboard, say they, and forge ahead. Men of our Christian world are like people who strain themselves with efforts to get rid of some object that spoils life for them, but who, in their hurry, have no time to agree, and all pull in different directions. It would be enough for man to-day to pause in his activity and to reflect—comparing the demands of his reason and of his heart with the actual conditions of life—in order to perceive that his whole life and all his actions are in incessant and glaring contradiction to his reason and his heart. Ask each man of our time separately what are the moral bases of his conduct, and they will almost all tell you that they are the principles of Christianity, or at least those of justice. And in saying this they will be sincere. According to their consciences, all men should live as Christians; but see how they behave: they behave like wild beasts. So that for the great majority of men in our Christian world, the organization of their life corresponds, not to their way of perceiving or feeling, but to certain forms once necessary for other people with quite different perceptions of life, but existing now merely because the constant bustle men live in allows them no time for reflection.

### v.

If in former times (when the evils produced by pagan life were not so evident, and especially when Christian principles were not yet so generally accepted) men were able conscientiously to uphold the servitude of the workers, the oppression of man by man, penal law, and, above all, war—it has now become quite impossible to explain the *raison d'être* of such institutions. In our time men may continue to live a pagan life, but they cannot excuse it.

That men may change their way of living and feeling, they must first of all change their way of thinking ; and that such a change may take place, they must pause, and attend to the things they ought to understand. To hear what is shouted to them by those who wish to save them, men who run singing towards a precipice must cease their clamour and must stop.

Let men of our Christian world but stop their work and reflect for a moment on their condition, and they will involuntarily be led to accept the conception of life given by Christianity—a conception so natural, so simple, and responding so completely to the needs of the mind and the heart of humanity that it will arise, almost of itself, in the understanding of anyone who has freed himself, were it but for a moment, from the entanglements in which he is held by the complications of work —his own and that of others.

The feast has been ready for eighteen centuries ; but one will not come because he has just bought some land, another because he has married, a third because he has to try his oxen, a fourth because he is building a railway, a factory, is engaged on missionary service, is busy in Parliament, in a bank, or on some scientific, artistic, or literary work. During 2,000 years no one has had leisure to do what Jesus advised at the beginning of his ministry : to look round him, think of the results of his work, and ask himself : What am I ? For what do I exist ? Is it possible that the power that has produced me, with my reason and my desire to love and be loved, has done this only to deceive me, —so that, having imagined the aim of life to be my personal well-being—that my life belonged to me, and I had the right to dispose of it as well as of the lives of others, as seemed best to me—I come at last to the conviction that this well-being (personal, family, or national) that I aimed at, cannot be attained, and that the more I strive to reach it, the more I find myself in conflict with my reason and with my wish to love and be loved, and the more I experience disenchantment and suffering?

Is it not more probable that, not having come into the world by my own will, but by the will of him who sent me, my reason and my wish to love and be loved were given to guide me in doing that will?

Once this μετάνοια is accomplished in men's thought, and the pagan and egotistic conception of life has been replaced by the Christian conception, the love of one's neighbour will become more natural than struggle and egotism now are. And once the love of one's neighbour becomes natural to man, the new conditions of Christian life will come about spontaneously, just as, in a liquid saturated with salt, the crystals begin to form as soon as one ceases to stir it.

And in order that this may result, and that men may organize their life in conformity with their consciences, they need expend no positive effort; they need only pause in efforts they are now making. If men spent but a hundredth part of the energy they now devote to material activities—disapproved of by their own consciences—to elucidating as completely as possible the demands of that conscience, expressing them clearly, spreading them abroad, and, above all, putting them in practice, the change which M. Dumas and all the prophets have foretold would be accomplished among us much sooner and more easily than we suppose, and men would acquire the good that Jesus promised them in his glad tidings : ' Seek the Kingdom of Heaven, and all these things shall be added unto you.'

[August 9, o.s., 1895.]


This essay was written first in Russian, and then (after a misleading translation had appeared in France) in French, also, by Tolstoy. The second version differed in arrangement from the first, and has, at Tolstoy's own request, been relied upon in preparing the present translation. In a few places, however—and especially by including

Zola's speech and Dumas' letter in full—the earlier version has been followed.

Grateful acknowledgment is due to the *Gaulois* for permission to reproduce Dumas' letter ; to M. E. Fasquelle, of the Bibliothèque Charpentier, for permission to reproduce Zola's speech ; and to Mr. E. J. W. Warren for allowing his excellent translation of Tolstoy's French essay to be followed in a number of passages in the present translation.

## VI

## AN AFTERWORD TO AN ACCOUNT RENDERED OF RELIEF SUPPLIED TO THE FAMINE-STRICKEN, IN THE GOVERNMENT OF TOÚLA, IN 1891 AND 1892

OUR two years' experience in distributing among a suffering population contributions that passed through our hands, have quite confirmed our long-established conviction that most of the want and destitution—and the suffering and grief that go with them—which we, almost in vain, have tried to counteract by external means in one small corner of Russia, has arisen, not from some exceptional, temporary cause independent of us, but from general permanent causes quite dependent on us, and consisting entirely in the antichristian, unbrotherly relations maintained by us educated people towards the poor, simple labourers who constantly endure distress and want and the accompanying bitterness and suffering—things that have merely been more conspicuous than usual during the past two years. If this year we do not hear of want, cold, and hunger—of the dying-off, by hundreds of thousands, of adults worn out with overwork and of underfed old people and children—this is not because these things will not occur, but only because we shall not see them—shall forget about them, shall assure ourselves that they do not exist, or that, if they do, they are inevitable and cannot be helped.

But such assurances are untrue : not only is it possible for these things not to exist—but they ought not to exist, and the time is coming when they will not exist—and that time is near.

However well the wine cup may seem to us to be hidden from the labouring classes—however artful, ancient, and generally accepted may be the excuses wherewith we justify our life of luxury amid a working folk who, crushed with toil and underfed, supply our luxury—the light is penetrating more and more into our relations with the people, and we shall soon appear in the shameful and dangerous position of a criminal whom the unexpected dawn of day exposes on the scene of his crime. If a dealer disposing of harmful or worthless goods among the working folk, and trying to charge as much as possible—or disposing even of good and needful bread, but bread which he had bought cheap and was selling dear—could formerly have said he was serving the needs of the people by honest trade ; or if a manufacturer of cotton prints, looking-glasses, cigarettes, spirits, or beer, could say that he was feeding his workmen by giving them employment ; or if an official, receiving hundreds of pounds a year salary collected in taxes from the people's last pence, could assure himself that he was serving for the people's good ; or (a thing specially noticeable these last years in the famine-stricken districts) if formerly a landlord could say—to peasants who worked his land for less pay than would buy them bread, or to those who hired land of him at rack-rents—that by introducing improved methods of agriculture he was promoting the prosperity of the rural population : if all this were formerly possible, now, at least, when people are dying of hunger for lack of bread, amid wide acres belonging to landlords and planted with potatoes intended for distilling spirits or making starch—these things can no longer be said. It has become impossible, surrounded by people who are dying-out for want of food and from excess of work, not to see that all we consume of the product of their work, on the one hand deprives them of what they need for food, and on the other hand increases the work which already taxes their strength to the utmost.

Not to speak of the insensate luxury of parks, conservatories and hunting, every glass of wine, every bit of sugar, butter, or meat, is so much food taken from the people, and so much labour added to their task.

We Russians are specially well situated for seeing our position clearly. I remember, long before these famine years, how a young and morally sensitive savant from Prague, who visited me in the country in winter—on coming out of the hut of a comparatively well-to-do peasant at which we had called, and in which, as everywhere, there was an overworked, prematurely aged woman in rags, a sick child who had ruptured itself while screaming, and, as everywhere in spring, a tethered calf and a ewe that had lambed, and dirt and damp, and foul air, and a dejected, careworn peasant—I remember how, on coming out of the hut, my young acquaintance began to say something to me, when suddenly his voice broke and he wept. For the first time, after some months spent in Moscow and Petersburg—where he had walked along asphalted pavements, past luxurious shops, from one rich house to another, and from one rich museum, library, or palace, to other similar grand buildings—he saw for the first time those whose labour supplies all that luxury, and he was amazed and horrified. To him, in rich and educated Bohemia (as to every man of Western Europe, especially to a Swede, a Swiss, or a Belgian), it might seem (though incorrectly) that where comparative liberty exists—where education is general, where everyone has a chance to enter the ranks of the educated—luxury is a legitimate reward of labour, and does not destroy human life. He might manage to forget the successive generations of men who mine the coal by the use of which most of the articles of our luxury are produced, he might forget—since they are out of sight—the men of other races in the colonies, who die out, working to satisfy our whims; but we Russians cannot share such thoughts: the connection between our luxury and the sufferings and deprivations of men of the same race as ourselves is too evident. We cannot avoid seeing the price paid in human lives for our comfort and our luxury.

For us the sun has risen, and we cannot hide what is obvious. We can no longer hide behind Government, behind the necessity of ruling the people, behind science, or art—said to be necessary for the people—or behind the sacred rights of property, or the necessity of upholding the traditions of our forefathers, etc. The sun has risen, and these transparent veils no longer hide anything from anyone. Everyone sees and knows that those who serve the Government do it, not for the welfare of the people (who never asked them to serve), but simply because they want their salaries; and that people engaged on science and art are so engaged, not to enlighten the people, but for pay and pensions: and that those who withhold land from the people, and raise its price, do this not to maintain any sacred rights, but to increase the incomes they require to satisfy their own caprices. To hide this and to lie is no longer possible.

Only two paths are open to the governing classes— the rich and the non-workers: one way is to repudiate not only Christianity in its true meaning, but humanitarianism, justice, and everything like them, and to say: 'I hold these privileges and advantages, and, come what may, I mean to keep them. Whoever wishes to take them from me will have me to reckon with. The power is in my hands: the soldiers, the gallows, the prisons, the scourge, and the courts.'

The other way is to confess our fault, to cease to lie, to repent, and to go to the assistance of the people, not with words only, nor—as has been done during these last two years—with pence that have first been wrung from the people at the cost of pain and suffering, but by breaking down the artificial barrier existing between us and the working people, and not in words but in deeds acknowledging them to be our brothers: altering our way of life, renouncing the advantages and privileges we possess, and, having renounced them, standing on an equal footing with the people, and

together with them obtaining those blessings of
government, science, and civilization, which we now,
without consulting their wish, seek to supply them
with from outside.

We stand at the parting of the ways, and a choice
must be made.

The first path involves condemning one's self to perpetual falsehood, to continual fear that our lies may be
exposed, and to the consciousness that, sooner or later,
we shall inevitably be ousted from the position to which
we have so obstinately clung.

The second path involves the voluntary acceptance
and practice of what we already profess and of what
is demanded by our heart and our reason—of what
sooner or later will be accomplished, if not by us,
then by others—for in this renunciation of their power
by the powerful lies the only possible escape from the
ills our pseudo-Christian world is enduring. Escape
lies only through the renunciation of a false and the
confession of a true Christianity.

[October 28, o.s., 1893.]

This *Afterword*, written by Tolstoy as a conclusion to
his *Account* relating to the famine of 1891 and 1892, was
suppressed in Russia, and is not contained in the Moscow
editions of his works, where the rest of the *Account* is
given.

# VII

## RELIGION AND MORALITY*

You ask me : (1) What I understand by the word *religion*, and, (2) Is it possible to have a morality independent of *religion*, in the sense in which I understand that word ?

I will do my best to answer these most important and excellently-put questions.

Three different meanings are commonly given to the word *religion*.

The first is, that religion is a special and true revelation given by God to man, and is a worship of God in accord with that revelation. This meaning is given to religion by people who believe in one or other of the existing religions, and who consequently consider *that* particular religion to be the only true one.

The second meaning is, that religion is a collection of certain superstitious beliefs, as well as a superstitious form of worship that accords with such beliefs. This is the meaning given to religion by unbelievers in general, or by such as do not accept the particular religion they are defining.

The third meaning is, that religion is a collection of propositions and laws devised by wise men, and needed to console the common people, to restrain their passions, and to make the masses manageable. This meaning is given to religion by those who are indifferent to religion as religion, but consider it a useful instrument for Governments.

* A reply to questions put to Tolstoy by a German Ethical Society.

Religion according to the first definition is a sure and certain truth, which it is desirable and even necessary for human welfare to promulgate by all possible means.

According to the second definition, religion is a collection of superstitions, from which it is desirable and even necessary for human welfare that man should be emancipated by all possible means.

According to the third definition, religion is a certain useful appliance, not necessary for men of high culture, but indispensable for the consolation and control of the common people, and which must therefore be maintained.

The first is like the definition a man might give of music, who said that music is a particular tune—the one he knows best and is fondest of; and that it ought to be taught to as many people as possible.

The second is like a definition given by a man who does not understand, and consequently dislikes, music, and who says that music is the production of sounds with one's throat or mouth, or by applying one's hands to certain instruments; and that it is a useless and even harmful occupation from which people ought to be weaned as quickly as possible.

The third is like the definition of music by a man who says it is a thing useful for the purpose of teaching dancing, and also for marching; and that it should be maintained for those purposes.

The diversity and incompleteness of all these definitions arise from the fact that they fail to grasp the essential character of music, and only define some of its traits, from the definer's point of view. The same is true of the three definitions given of religion.

According to the first of them, religion is something in which the definer rightly believes.

According to the second, it is something in which, according to the definer's observation, other people mistakenly believe.

According to the third, it is something the definer thinks it useful to get other people to believe in.

I

In all three cases the thing defined is not the real essence of religion, but something people believe in and consider to be religion.

The first definition substitutes for the conception of religion a faith held by the definer ; the second definition substitutes a faith held by other people : something they take to be religion—while the third definition substitutes people's faith in something supplied to them as religion.

But what is faith?    And why do people hold the faith they do hold?    What is faith, and how did it arise?

Among the great mass of the cultured crowd of to-day it is considered a settled question that the essence of every religion consists in superstitious fear, aroused by the not-understood phenomena of Nature, and in the personification and deification of these natural forces, and the worship of them.

This opinion is credulously accepted, without criticism, by the cultured crowd of to-day ; and not only is it not refuted by the scientists, but among them it generally finds its strongest supporters.    If voices are now and then heard (such as that of Max Müller and others) attributing to religion another origin and meaning, they pass almost unheard and unnoticed among the common and unanimous acknowledgment of religion in general as a manifestation of ignorance and superstition.    Not long ago, at the commencement of the nineteenth century, the most advanced men—if (like the Encyclopædists of the later part of the eighteenth century) they rejected Catholicism, Protestantism, and Russo-Greek Orthodoxy—never denied that religion in general has been, and is, an indispensable condition of life for every man.    Not to mention the Deists (such as Bernardin de Saint-Pierre, Diderot, and Rousseau), Voltaire erected a monument to God, and Robespierre instituted a fête of the Supreme Being.    But in our time—thanks to the frivolous and superficial teaching of Auguste Comte (who, like most Frenchmen, really believed Christianity to be the same thing as Catholicism, and saw in Catholicism the complete realization of Christianity)—it has been decided and taken for granted by the cultured crowd (always eager and prompt to accept the lowest view) that religion is only one special, long-outlived phase in the development of humanity, and a hindrance to its further progress. It is taken for granted that humanity has passed through two stages, the religious and the metaphysical, and has now entered on a third and highest one—the scientific; and that all religious manifestations among men are mere survivals of humanity's spiritual organ, which, like the fifth toe-nail of the horse, has long lost all meaning or importance.

It is taken for granted that the essence of religion lies in fear evoked by the unknown forces of Nature, in belief in imaginary beings, and in worship of them, as in ancient times Democritus supposed, and as the latest philosophers and historians of religion assert.

But, apart from the consideration that belief in invisible, supernatural beings, or in one such being, does not always proceed from fear of the unknown forces of nature—as we see in the case of hundreds of the most advanced and highly-educated men of former times (Socrates, Descartes, Newton) as well as of our own day, whose recognition of the existence of a supreme, supernatural being, certainly did not proceed from fear of the unknown forces of Nature—the assertion that religion arose from men's superstitious fear of the mysterious forces of Nature really affords no answer to the main question, 'What was it in men that gave them the conception of unseen, supernatural beings?'

If men feared thunder and lightning, they feared them as thunder and lightning; but why should they invent some invisible, supernatural being, Jupiter, who lives somewhere or other, and sometimes throws arrows at people?

Men struck by the sight of death would fear death; but why should they invent souls of the dead with whom they entered into imaginary intercourse? From thunder men might hide. Fear of death might make

I 2

them try to escape death. But if they invented an eternal and powerful being on whom they supposed themselves to depend, and if they invented live souls for dead people, they did this not simply from fear, but for some other reasons. And in those reasons, evidently, lay the essence of the thing we call religion.

Moreover, every man who has ever, even in childhood, experienced religious feeling, knows by personal experience that it was evoked in him, not by external, terrifying, material phenomena, but by an inner consciousness, which had nothing to do with fear of the unknown forces of Nature—a consciousness of his own insignificance, loneliness, and guilt. And therefore, both by external observation and by personal experience, man may know that religion is not the worship of gods, evoked by superstitious fear of the invisible forces of Nature, proper to men only at a certain period of their development ; but is something quite independent either of fear or of their degree of education —a something that cannot be destroyed by any development of culture. For man's consciousness of his finiteness amid an infinite universe, and of his sinfulness (*i.e.*, of his not having done all he might and should have done) has always existed and will exist as long as man remains man.

Indeed, everyone on emerging from the animal conditions of infancy and earliest childhood, when he lives guided only by the demands of his animal nature— everyone on awakening to rational consciousness, cannot but notice that all around him lives, renewing itself, undestroyed, and infallibly conforming to one, definite, eternal law : and that he alone, recognising himself as a being separate from the rest of the universe, is sentenced to die, to disappear into infinite space and endless time, and to suffer the tormenting consciousness of responsibility for his actions—*i.e.*, the consciousness that, having acted badly, he could have done better. And understanding this, no reasonable man can help pausing to ask himself, ' What is the meaning of my momentary, uncertain, and unstable

existence, amid this eternal, firmly defined and unend-
ing universe?' Entering on truly human life, a man
cannot evade that question.

That question faces every man, and, in one way or
other, every man answers it. And in the reply to that
question lies the essence of every religion. The essence
of religion consists solely in the answer to the question,
' Why do I live, and what is my relation to the infinite
universe* around me ?'

All the metaphysics of religion, all the doctrines
about deities, and about the origin of the world, and
all external worship—which are usually supposed to be
religion—are but indications (differing according to
geographical, ethnographical, and historical circumstances) of the existence of religion. There is no
religion, from the most elevated to the coarsest, that
has not at its root this establishing of man's relation
to the surrounding universe or to its first cause. There
is no religious rite, however coarse, nor any cult, however refined, that has not this at its root. Every religious teaching is the expression which the founder of
that religion has given, of the relation he considered
himself as a man (and consequently all other people
also) to occupy towards the universe and its origin and
first cause.

The expressions of these relations are very numerous,
corresponding to the different ethnographical and historical conditions of the founders of these religions,
and the nations that adopted them. Moreover, all
these expressions are variously interpreted and perverted by the followers of teachers who were usually
hundreds, and sometimes thousands, of years ahead of
the comprehension of the masses. And so these relations of man to the universe—*i.e.*, to religion—appear
to be very numerous, though, in reality, there are only
three fundamental relations in which men stand towards
the universe and its author. They are : (1) The primi-

* ' Universe ' is used here and elsewhere in its primary
significance, embracing the totality of existing things,
spiritual or material.

tive, personal relation ; (2) the pagan, social, or family-State relation ; (3) the Christian or divine relation.

Strictly speaking there are only two fundamental relations in which man can stand towards the world : the *Personal*, which sees the meaning of life in personal well-being, obtained separately, or in union with other individuals ; and the *Christian*, which sees the meaning of life to consist in service of him who sent man into the world. The second of the three divisions mentioned in the first classification—the social—is really only an extension of the first.

The first of these perceptions, the oldest—now found among people on the lowest plane of moral development—consists in man considering himself to be a self-motived being, living in the world to obtain the greatest possible personal happiness, regardless of the suffering such attainment may cause to others.

From this very primitive relation to the world (a relation in which every infant lives on first entering the world ; in which humanity lived during the first, pagan, period of its development ; and in which many of the morally-coarsest individuals and savage tribes still live) flowed the ancient pagan religions, as well as the lowest forms of the later religions : Buddhism,* Taoism, Mohammedanism, and Christianity, in their perverted forms. From this relation to the world comes also modern Spiritualism, which has, at its root, a desire for the preservation and well-being of one's personality. All the pagan cults : divinations ; the deification of beings who enjoy themselves like man ; Saints who intercede for man ; all sacrifices and prayers offered

* Buddhism, though demanding from its followers the renunciation of worldly blessings, and even of life itself, is based on the same relation of a self-motived personality (predestined to personal well-being) to the surrounding universe ; but with this difference—that simple paganism considers man to have a right to happiness, while Buddhism considers that the world ought to disappear because it produces suffering to the personality. Buddhism is negative paganism.

for man's earthly welfare, and for deliverance from calamities—come from this conception of life.

The second form of the pagan relation of man to the world, the social, which he adopts at the next stage of development—a relation natural chiefly to adults—consists in seeing the meaning of life, not in the welfare of one separate individual, but in the welfare of a group of individuals: a family, clan, nation, empire, or even of all humanity (as in the Positivist's attempt to found a religion).

In this relation of man to the world, the meaning of life is transferred from the individual to a family, clan, nation, or empire—to a certain association of individuals, whose welfare is considered to be the aim of existence. From this view come all religions of a certain type—the patriarchal and social: the Chinese and Japanese religions; the religions of a 'chosen people'—the Jewish, the Roman State-religion, our Church and State religion (improperly called Christian, but degraded to this level by Augustine), and the proposed Positivist religion of Humanity.

All the ceremonies of ancestor-worship in China and Japan; the worship of Emperors in Rome; the multitudinous Jewish ceremonials aiming at the preservation of an agreement between the chosen people and God; all family, social, and Church-Christian prayers for the welfare of the State, or for success in war—rest on that understanding of man's relation to the universe.

The third conception of this relation, the Christian—of which all old men are involuntarily conscious, and into which, in my opinion, humanity is now entering—consists in the meaning of life no longer appearing to lie in the attainment of personal aims, or the aims of any association of individuals, but solely in serving that Will which has produced man and the entire universe, not for man's aims but for its own.

From this relation to the world comes the highest religious teaching known to us, germs of which existed already among the Pythagoreans, Therapeutæ, Essenes, and among the Egyptians, Persians, the Brahmins,

Buddhists, and Taoists, in their best representatives, but which received its complete and final expression only in Christianity, in its true and unperverted meaning. All the ritual of those ancient religions that proceeded from this understanding of life, and, in our time, all the external forms of worship among the Unitarians, Universalists, Quakers, Servian Nazarenes, Russian Doukhobórs, and all the so-called rationalistic sects : their sermons, hymns, conferences and books, are religious manifestations of this relation of man to the universe.

All possible religions of whatever kind can, by the nature of the case, be classed according to these three ways of regarding the universe.

Every man who has emerged from the animal state inevitably adopts the first, or the second, or the third, of these relations, and that is what constitutes each man's true religion, no matter to what faith he may nominally belong.

Every man necessarily conceives some relation between himself and the universe, for an intelligent being cannot live in the universe that surrounds him, without having some relation to it. And since man has as yet devised but three relations that we know of to the universe—it follows that every man inevitably holds one of these three, and, whether he wishes to or not, belongs to one of the three fundamental religions among which the human race is divided.

Therefore the assertion, very common among the cultured crowd of Christendom, that they have risen to such a height of development that they no longer need, or possess, any religion, only amounts to this— that repudiating the Christian religion, which is the only one natural to our time, they hold to the lower, social, family, State religion, or to the primitive pagan religion, without being aware of the fact. A man without a religion—*i.e.*, without any relation to the universe—is as impossible as a man without a heart. He may not know he has a religion, just as a man may not know he has a heart, but he can no more exist without a religion than without a heart.

Religion is the relation in which a man acknowledges himself to stand towards the infinite universe around him, or towards its source and first cause ; and a rational man must have some relation to them.

But you will, perhaps, say that to define man's relation to the universe is not the affair of religion, but of philosophy, or of science in general, if one includes philosophy as part of science. I do not think so. On the contrary, I think that the supposition that science in its widest sense, including philosophy as part of it, can define man's relation to the universe is quite erroneous, and is the chief cause of the confusion concerning religion, science, and morality, which prevails among the cultured classes of our society.

Science, including philosophy, cannot define man's relation to the infinite universe or its source, were it only for this reason—that before any philosophy or science could arise, *that* must already have existed without which no activity of thought, nor relation of any kind between man and the universe, is possible.

As a man cannot by any possible motion discover in which direction he ought to move, yet every movement is necessarily performed in some direction, so also is it impossible by mental effort at philosophy or science to discover the direction in which such efforts should be performed ; but all mental effort is necessarily performed in some direction that has been predetermined for it. And it is religion that always indicates this direction for all mental work. All known philosophers, from Plato to Schopenhauer, have always and inevitably followed a direction given them by religion. The philosophy of Plato and his followers was a pagan philosophy, which examined the means of obtaining the greatest possible well-being for separate individuals, and for an association of individuals in a State. The Church-Christian philosophy of the Middle Ages, proceeding from a similar pagan conception of life, investigated ways of obtaining salvation for the individual—that is, ways of obtaining the greatest personal welfare in a future life ; and only in its theocratic attempts did it treat of arrangements for the welfare of society.

Modern philosophy, both Hegel's and Comte's, has at its root the State-social religious conception of life. The pessimistic philosophy of Schopenhauer and Hartmann, wishing to free itself from Judæo-religious cosmology, involuntarily adopted the religious basis of Buddhism.

Philosophy has always been, and will always be, simply the investigation of the consequences that result from the relation religion establishes between man and the universe, for until that relation is settled there is nothing on which philosophy can work.

So also with positive science, in the restricted meaning of the word. Such science has always been, and will always be, merely the investigation and study of all such objects and phenomena, as in consequence of a certain relation religion has set up between man and the universe, appear to demand investigation.

Science always has been, and will be, not the study of ' everything,' as scientists now naïvely suppose (that is impossible, for there are an incalculable quantity of objects that might be studied), but only of such things as religion selects in due order and according to their degree of importance, from among the incalculable quantity of objects, phenomena, and conditions, awaiting examination. And, therefore, science is not one and indivisible, but there are as many sciences as there are religions. Each religion selects a range of objects for investigation, and therefore the science of each different time and people inevitably bears the character of the religion from whose point of view it sees its objects.

Thus pagan science, re-established at the Renaissance and now flourishing in our society under the title of Christian, always was, and continues to be, merely an investigation of all those conditions from which man may obtain the greatest welfare, and of all such phenomena as can be made to promote that end. Brahman and Buddhist philosophic science was always merely the investigation of those conditions under which man escapes from the sufferings that oppress him. Hebrew science (the Talmud) was always merely the study and explanation of the conditions which man had to observe in order to fulfil his contract with God, and to keep the chosen people at the height of their vocation. Church-Christian science has been, and is, an investigation of the conditions under which salvation can be obtained by man. True Christian science, such as is only now being born, is an investigation of the conditions enabling man to know the demands of the Supreme Will from whence he came, and how to apply those demands to life.

Neither philosophy nor science can establish man's relation to the universe, for that relation must be established before any philosophy or science can begin. They cannot do it for this further reason—that science, including philosophy as part of it, investigates phenomena intellectually — independently of the investigator's position or the feelings he experiences. But man's relation to the world is defined not by intellect alone, but also by feeling, and by the whole combination of his spiritual forces. However much you may assure a man, and explain to him, that all that truly exists is only idea—or that everything consists of atoms—or that the essence of life is substance, or will—or that heat, light, movement and electricity are different manifestations of one and the same energy—to a being that feels, suffers, rejoices, fears and hopes, it will all fail to explain his place in the universe.

That place, and consequently his relation to the universe, is shown to him by religion, which says to him : 'The world exists for you, therefore take from life all you can get from it,' or : 'You are a member of a chosen nation loved by God, therefore serve that nation, do all that God has demanded, and you together with your nation will receive the greatest welfare obtainable,' or : 'You are an instrument of the Supreme Will, which has sent you into the world to perform an appointed task ; learn that Will and fulfil

it, and you will do for yourself the best it is possible
for you to do.'

To understand the statements of philosophy and
science, preparation and study are necessary, but for
religious comprehension they are not necessary : it is
given to everyone, even to the most limited and ignorant
of men.

For a man to know his relation to the world around
him or to its source, he needs neither philosophic nor
scientific knowledge (an abundance of knowledge bur-
dening the consciousness is rather a hindrance), but he
needs, if but for a time, to renounce the cares of the
world, to have a consciousness of his material insignificance, and to have sincerity—conditions most often
met with (as is said in the Gospels) among children and
among the plainest, unlearned folk. That is why we often
see that the plainest, least-learned, and least-educated
people quite clearly, consciously, and easily, assimilate
the highest Christian understanding of life, while very
learned and cultured men continue to stagnate in crude
paganism.   So, for instance, there are most refined and
highly educated people who see the meaning of life in
personal enjoyment or in avoidance of suffering, as did
the very wise and highly educated Schopenhauer, or in
the salvation of the soul by Sacraments and means of
grace, as highly educated Bishops have done ; while
an almost illiterate Russian peasant sectarian sees the
meaning of life, without any mental effort, as it was
seen by the greatest sages of the world (Epictetus,
Marcus Aurelius, Seneca)—in acknowledging one's self
an instrument of God's will, a son of God.

But you will ask me : 'What is the essence of this
non-philosophic, non-scientific kind of knowledge ?  If
it is neither philosophic nor scientific, what is it ?  How
is it definable?'  To these questions I can only reply
that, as religious knowledge is that on which all other
knowledge rests, and as it precedes all other knowledge, we cannot define it, for we have no means
enabling us to do so.  In theological language this
knowledge is called revelation, and, if one does not

attach a mystic meaning to the word 'revelation,' that term is quite correct; for this knowledge is not obtained by study, nor by the efforts of one man or of many men, but only by one man or many men accepting that manifestation of infinite wisdom, which is gradually revealing itself to mankind.

Why, 10,000 years ago, were people unable to understand that the meaning of life is not limited to the welfare of one's personality, and why did a time come when a higher understanding of life—the family, social, national, State understanding of life—was revealed to them? Why, within historic memory, was the Christian view of life disclosed to men? And why was it disclosed to this man or that people in particular; and why precisely, at such a time, in one and not in another form? To try to answer these questions by seeking for reasons in the historic conditions of the time, life, and character and special qualities of those who first made this view of life their own, and first expressed it, is like trying to answer the question, 'Why does the rising sun light up some objects before reaching others?' The sun of truth, rising higher and higher over the world, lights up more and more of it, and is reflected first by those objects which are first reached by its illuminating rays, and which are best fitted to reflect them. But the qualities which make some men more suited to receive the rising truth are not any special, active qualities of mind, but, on the contrary, are passive qualities of heart, rarely coinciding with great and inquisitive intellect: renunciation of the cares of the world, consciousness of one's own material insignificance, and great sincerity, as we see exemplified by all the founders of religion, who were never remarkable either for philosophic or scientific erudition.

In my opinion the chief mistake, and the one which more than any other hinders the true progress of our Christian branch of humanity, lies in the fact that the scientists (who now occupy the seat of Moses)—guiding themselves by the pagan view of life re-established at the time of the Renaissance, and accepting as the essence of Christianity something that is really a rude perversion of it—have decided that Christianity is a condition humanity has outlived, and that the ancient, pagan, State-social view of life held by them (one that is really worn out) is the very highest understanding of life, and the one humanity should persistently cling to. Holding this view, they not only do not understand Christianity—that highest view of life humanity is approaching—but they do not even try to understand it.

The chief source of this misunderstanding lies in the fact that the scientists, parting company with Christianity and recognising that their science does not accord with it, have decided that the fault lies with Christianity and not with their science. That is to say, they are pleased to believe, not what is really the case, that their science is 1,800 years behind Christianity, which already influences a large part of contemporary society, but that Christianity has lagged 1,800 years behind science.

From this reversal of rôles come the astonishing fact, that no people have a more confused conception of the essence and true importance of religion, of morality, or of life, than scientists ; and the yet more astonishing fact that the science of to-day—while accomplishing really great success in investigating the phenomena of the material world—turns out to be of no use for the direction of human life, or even does actual harm.

And, therefore, I think that certainly it is neither philosophy nor science that determines man's relation to the universe, but it is *always religion*.

So to your first question, 'What do I understand by the word *religion*,' I reply : *Religion is a relation man sets up between himself and the endless and infinite universe, or, its source and first cause.*

From this answer to the first question, the answer to the second follows naturally.

If religion is a relation man establishes towards the universe—a relation which determines the meaning of life—then *morality* is the indication and explanation of such human activity as naturally results from men holding this or that relation towards the universe. And as only two such fundamental relations are known to us, if we consider the pagan, social relation as an enlargement of the personal ; or three, if we count the social, pagan relation as a separate one—it follows that but three moral teachings exist : the primitive, savage, personal ; the pagan, family, State, or social ; and the Christian or divine teaching, of service to man or to God.

From the first of these relations of man to the universe flows the teaching of morality common to all pagan religions that have at their base the striving after welfare for the separate individual, and that therefore define all the conditions yielding most welfare to the individual, and indicate means to obtain such welfare.    From this relation to the world flow the pagan teachings : the Epicurean in its lowest form ; the Mohammedan teaching of morality, which promises coarse, personal welfare in this and the next world ; the Church-Christian teaching of morality, aiming at salvation—that is, at the welfare of one's personality, especially in the other world ; and also the worldly utilitarian morality, aiming at the welfare of the individual only in this world.

From the same teaching, which places the aim of life in personal welfare, and, therefore, in freedom from personal suffering, flow the moral teaching of Buddhism in its crude form, and the worldly doctrine of the pessimist.

From the second, pagan relation of man to the universe, which sees the aim of life in securing welfare for a group of individuals, flow the moral teachings which demand that man should serve the group whose welfare is regarded as the aim of life.    According to that teaching, personal welfare is only allowable to the extent to which it can be obtained for the whole group of people who form the religious basis of life.    From that relation to the universe flow the well-known Roman and Greek moral teachings, in which personality always sacrifices itself for society, and also the Chinese morality. From this relation flows also the Jewish morality—the subordination of one's own welfare to that of the chosen people—and also the Church and State morality of our own times, which demands the sacrifice of the individual for the good of the State. From this relation to the universe flows also the morality of most women, who sacrifice their whole personality for the benefit of their family, and especially for their children.

All ancient history, and to some extent medieval and modern history, teems with descriptions of deeds of just this family, social, or State morality. And the majority of people to-day—though they think their morality is Christian because they profess Christianity—really hold this family, State, pagan morality, and hold it up as an ideal when educating the young generation.

From the third, the Christian, relation to the universe—which consists in man's considering himself to be an instrument of the Supreme Will, for the accomplishment of its ends—flow the moral teachings which correspond to that understanding of life, elucidating man's dependence on the Supreme Will, and defining its demands. From that relation of man to the universe flow all the highest moral teachings known to man : the Pythagorean, the Stoic, the Buddhist, the Brahminical, and the Taoist, in their highest manifestations, and the Christian teaching in its real meaning, demanding renunciation of one's personal will—and not only of one's own welfare, but even of that of one's family, society, and country—for the sake of fulfilling the will of him who sent us into life—a will revealed by our conscience. From the first, the second, or the third of these relations to the infinite universe or to its source, flows each man's real, unfeigned morality, no matter what he may profess or preach as morality, or in what light he may wish to appear.

So that a man who considers the reality of his relation to the universe to lie in obtaining the greatest welfare for himself—however much he may say he considers it moral to live for his family, for society, for the State, for humanity, or for the performance of God's will—and however artfully he may pretend and may deceive men, will still always have as his real motive of action simply his individual welfare; so that, when a choice has to be made, he will not sacrifice his own personality for his family or State, nor to do the will of God, but will sacrifice them all for his own sake. Since he sees the meaning of life only in personal welfare, he cannot do otherwise until such time as he alters his relation to the universe.

And, similarly, one whose relation to life consists in the service of his own family (as is the case with most women), or of his clan or nation (as among members of the oppressed nationalities, and among men politically active in times of strife)—no matter how much he may declare himself to be a Christian—his morality will always be family or national, but not Christian, and when any inevitable conflict arises between family or social welfare on one side, and that of his personality, or the fulfilment of the will of God, on the other, he will inevitably choose the service of the group for whom, in his view of life, he exists: for only in such service does he see the meaning of his life. And in the same way a man who regards his relation to the world as consisting in fulfilling the will of Him who sent him hither—however much you may impress upon him that he should (in accord with the demands of his personality, or of his family, his nation, empire, or all humanity) commit acts contrary to the Supreme Will of which the operation of the reason and love wherewith he is endowed makes him aware—will always sacrifice all human ties rather than fail to comply with the Will that has sent him here: for only in such compliance does he discern a meaning for his life.

Morality cannot be independent of religion, for not only is it a consequence of religion—that is, a consequence of the relation in which a man feels that he stands towards the universe—but it is implied (*im-*

*pliquée,* as the French say) in religion. Every religion is an answer to the question : 'What is the meaning of my life?' And the religious answer involves a certain moral demand, which may follow or may precede the explanation of the meaning of life. To the question, 'What is the meaning of life?' the reply may be : 'The meaning of life lies in the welfare of the individual, therefore make use of all the advantages within your reach'; or, 'The meaning of life lies in the welfare of a certain group of people, therefore serve that group with all your strength'; or, 'The meaning of life lies in fulfilling the will of Him that sent you, therefore try with all your strength to know that will and to fulfil it.' Or the same question may be answered in this way : 'The meaning of your life lies in your personal enjoyment, for that is the object of man's existence'; or, 'The meaning of your life lies in serving the group of which you consider yourself a member, for that is your destiny'; or, 'The meaning of your life lies in the service of God, for that is your destiny.'

Morality is included in the explanation of the meaning of life that religion gives, and can therefore in no way be separated from religion. This truth is particularly evident in the attempts of non-Christian philosophers to deduce a doctrine of the highest morality from their philosophy. Such philosophers see that Christian morality is indispensable, that we cannot live without it ; they even see that it is an already existing fact, and they want to find some way to attach it to their non-Christian philosophy, and even to put things in such a way that Christian morality may seem to result from their pagan social philosophy. That is what they attempt, but their very efforts show, more clearly than anything else, that Christian morality is not merely independent of pagan philosophy, but that it stands in complete contradiction to that philosophy of individual welfare, or of liberation from individual suffering, or of social welfare.

The Christian ethics, which, in accord with our religious conception of life, we acknowledge, demand not only the sacrifice of one's personality for the group, but the renunciation alike of one's personality and of one's group for the service of God; but pagan philosophy only investigates means of obtaining the greatest welfare for the individual, or for the group of individuals, and therefore a contrast is inevitable. And there is only one way of hiding this contrast—viz., by piling up abstract conditional conceptions one on the top of another, and keeping to the misty domain of metaphysics.

That is what most of the post-Renaissance philosophers have done, and to this circumstance—the impossibility of making the demands of Christian morality (which have been admitted in advance) accord with a philosophy built on pagan foundations—must be attributed the terrible unreality, obscurity, unintelligibility, and estrangement from life, that characterizes modern philosophy. With the exception of Spinoza (whose philosophy, in spite of the fact that he did not consider himself a Christian, develops from truly Christian roots) and Kant (a man of genius, who admittedly treated his system of ethics as not dependent on his metaphysics), all the other philosophers, even the brilliant Schopenhauer, evidently devised artificial connections between their ethics and their metaphysics.

It is felt that Christian ethics are something that must be accepted in advance, standing quite firmly, not dependent on philosophy, and in no need of the fictitious props put to support them; and it is felt that Philosophy merely devises certain propositions in order that ethics may not contradict her, but may rather be bound to her and appear to flow from her. All such propositions, however, only appear to justify Christian ethics while they are considered in the abstract. As soon as they are applied to questions of practical life, the non-correspondence, and, more than that, the evident contradiction between the philosophic basis and what we consider morality, appears in full strength.

The unfortunate Nietzsche, who has latterly become so celebrated, rendered a valuable service by his exposure of this contradiction. He is incontrovertible when he says that all rules of morality, from the point of view of the current non-Christian philosophy, are mere lies and hypocrisy, and that it is much more profitable, pleasanter and more reasonable, for a man to devise his own Super-men (Uebermensch) and be one of them, than to be one of the mass which has to serve as the scaffold for these Super-men. No philosophical constructions founded on the pagan-religious view of life can prove to anyone that it is more profitable or wiser for him to live, not for a welfare he desires, comprehends, and sees to be possible for himself or for his family or his society, but for another's welfare—undesired, not understood, and unattainable by his puny human power. Philosophy founded on an understanding of life limited to the welfare of man, will never be able to prove to a rational man, who knows that he may die at any moment, that it is good for him, and that he ought, to forego his own desired, understood, and undoubted welfare—not even for any certain welfare to others (for he can never know what will result from his sacrifices), but—merely because it is right or good to do so : that it is a categorical imperative.

To prove this from the point of view of pagan philosophy is impossible. To prove that people are all equal—that it is better for a man to sacrifice his life in the service of others than to trample on the lives of others, making them serve him—one must redefine one's relation to the universe : one must prove that man's position is such that he has no option, since the meaning of his life lies only in the execution of the will of Him that sent him ; and the will of Him that sent him is, that he should give his life to the service of men. And such a change in man's relation to the universe comes only from religion.

Thus it is with the attempts to deduce Christian morality from, and to reconcile it with, the fundamental positions of pagan science. No sophistries or subtleties of thought can destroy this simple and clear position, that the law of evolution, which lies at the base of all the science of to-day, is founded on a general, eternal, and unalterable law—on the law of the struggle for existence, and the survival of the fittest ; and that, therefore, each man to attain his own and his group's welfare should try to be that 'fittest,' and to make his group such, in order that not he or his group should perish, but some other, less fit.

However much some naturalists, frightened by the logical consequences of this law and by their application to human life, may try to perplex the matter with words, and to exorcise this law—their efforts only make still more evident the irresistibility of that law, which rules the life of the whole organic world, and, therefore, that of man regarded as an animal.

Since I began writing this article, a Russian translation has appeared of an article by Mr. Huxley, composed of a speech on Evolution and Ethics* delivered by him to some English Society. In this article the learned Professor—like our well-known Professor Bekétof and many others who have written on the same subject, and with as little success as his predecessors—tries to prove that the struggle for existence does not infringe morality, and that side by side with the acknowledgement of the struggle for existence as a fundamental law of life, morality may not merely exist, but even progress. Mr. Huxley's article is full of all kinds of jokes, verses, and general views on ancient religion and philosophy, and is consequently so florid and complicated that it is only with great effort that one is able to reach its fundamental thought. That thought, however, is as follows : The law of evolution runs counter to the moral law ; this was known to the ancient Greeks and Hindus. The philosophy and religion of both those peoples brought them to the doctrine of self-renunciation. That doctrine, the author thinks, is not correct ; the correct one is this : A law exists, which the author calls the cosmic law, in

* Huxley's Romanes Lecture, delivered in 1894, and contained in *Evolution and Ethics*, issued by Macmillan and Co.

accord with which all beings struggle against one another, and only the fittest survive. Man also is subject to this law ; and thanks only to it has man become what he now is. But this law runs counter to morality. How, then, can it be reconciled with morality ? That can be accomplished in this way : A law of social progress exists, which seeks to check the cosmic process, and to replace it by another, an ethical, process, the object of which is the survival, not of the fittest, but of the best in an ethical sense. Where this ethical process sprang from, Mr. Huxley does not explain, but in his 20th foot-note he says that the basis of this process is, on the one hand, that people, like animals, prefer to be in company, and therefore suppress in themselves qualities harmful to societies ; and, on the other hand, that the members of a society forcibly suppress actions contrary to social welfare. It seems to Mr. Huxley that this process, obliging men to curb their passions for the sake of preserving the group of which they are members, and for fear of being punished if they disturbed the order of their group, supplies that ethical law the existence of which he wishes to demonstrate. It seems to Mr. Huxley, in the naïveté of his soul, that in English society, as it exists to-day—with its Irish problem, the poverty of its lowest classes, the insensate luxury of the rich, its trade in opium and spirits, its executions, its slaughter or extermination of tribes for the sake of trade and politics, its secret vice and its hypocrisy—the man who does not infringe the police regulations is a moral man, guided by the ethical law. He forgets that the qualities needful to maintain the society in which a man lives may be useful for that society—as the qualities of the members of a band of robbers may be useful to that band, and as in our own society we find a use for the qualities of executioners, gaolers, judges, soldiers, and hypocrite-priests, etc.— but that these qualities have nothing in common with morality.

Morality is something continually developing and growing, and, therefore, conformity to the existing rules of a certain society, and their preservation by means of the axe or the scaffold (to which Mr. Huxley alludes as to instruments of morality), will not only not be the maintenance, but will be the infringement of morality. And, on the contrary, every infringement of the existing order—such as were not only the infringements committed by Jesus and his disciples of the regulations of a Roman province, but the infringements of present-day regulations by one who should refuse to take part in legal proceedings, in military service, in the payment of taxes levied for warlike preparations—will not only not be an infringement of morality, but will be an inevitable condition of the manifestation of morality.

Every cannibal who perceives that he should not eat his fellow-men, and who acts accordingly, infringes the order of his society. And, therefore, though action infringing the order of any society *may* be immoral, every truly moral action which pushes forward the limits of morality will always be *sure* to be an infringement of the order of society. If, therefore, a law has appeared in society in accord with which people sacrifice their personal advantages for the preservation of the integrity of their group—that law is not the ethical law, but, on the contrary, will generally be a law contrary to all ethics—that same law of the struggle for existence, only in a hidden, latent form. It is the same struggle for existence, but carried over from the individual to a group of individuals. It is not the cessation of the fight, but only a backward swinging of the arm, to strike a harder blow.

If the law of the struggle for existence and the survival of the fittest is the eternal law of all life (and it cannot but be admitted to be so when we regard man as an animal)—then no tangled discussions about social progress and an ethical law supposed to flow from it, or to spring up from no one knows where, just when we happen to need it (like a *deus ex machina*), can disturb that law.

If social progress, as Mr. Huxley assures us, collects

people into groups, then the struggle and the survival will continue among those families, clans, and nations, and the struggle will not only not be more moral, but it will be even more cruel and more immoral than that between individuals, as we see in actual life. Even if we admit the impossible, and suppose that in another thousand years all humanity will, by social progress alone, be united into one whole, and will form a single nation and a single State—even then (not to mention that the struggle abolished between nations and States will continue between man and the animal world, and will always remain a struggle—that is, will remain an activity quite excluding the possibility of the Christian morality we confess)—even then the struggle between individuals forming this union, and between the groups of families, clans and nationalities, will not be diminished, but will continue in a new form, as we see in all aggregations of individuals, families, races and States. The members of a family quarrel and fight with one another as well as with outsiders, and often to a greater degree and with more venom. It is just the same thing in the State; among people living in one State, a struggle continues just as with people outside the State, only it is carried on under other forms. In the one case the slaughter is done with arrows and knives, in the other it is done by hunger. And if both in the family and in the State the weak are saved, that is not done by the social union, but occurs because among the people united in families and in States, love and self-sacrifice exist. If, outside the family, of two children only the fittest survives, while in a good mother's family both remain alive, this does not result from union into families, but from the fact that the mother possesses love and self-sacrifice. And neither self-sacrifice nor love can result from a social process.

To assert that a social process produces morality is like asserting that the construction of stoves produces heat.

Heat comes from the sun, and stoves produce heat only when fuel (the result of the sun's work) is put into them.    Just so morality comes from religion.    Special forms of social life produce morality only when the results of religious influence—which is morality—are put into them.

Stoves may be heated and give warmth, or may not be heated and may remain cold; just as social forms may contain morality, and may then have a moral influence on society, or may not contain morality, and will then remain without influence on society.

Christian morality cannot be based on a pagan or social conception of life, and cannot be deduced either from philosophy or from non-Christian science; and not only can it not be deduced from them, but it cannot even be reconciled with them.

That is how the matter has always been understood by every serious and strictly consistent philosophy and science, which said, quite reasonably: 'If our propositions do not tally with morality, so much the worse for morality,' and continued their investigations.

Ethical treatises not founded on religion, and even secular catechisms, are written and taught, and people may suppose that humanity is guided by them; but that only seems to be the case, because people are really guided not by those treatises and catechisms, but by the religions which they have always possessed and still possess; whereas these treatises and catechisms only counterfeit what flows naturally from religion.

The dictates of secular morality not based on a religious teaching are just like the action of a man who, though ignorant of music, should take the conductor's seat and begin to wave his arms before the experienced musicians who were performing.    The music would continue for awhile by its own momentum, and because of what the musicians had learned from former conductors; but evidently the waving of a stick by a man ignorant of music would not merely be useless, but it would in course of time certainly confuse the musicians and disorganize the orchestra.    A similar confusion begins to take place in people's minds at the present time, in consequence of attempts made by leading men to teach people a morality not founded on that highest religion which begins to be assimilated, and has already been partly assimilated, by Christian humanity.

It is indeed desirable to have moral teaching unmixed with superstition, but the fact is that moral teaching is a result of a certain relation man holds towards the universe or towards God. If that relation is expressed in forms which seem to us superstitious, we should, to right the matter, try to express that relation more reasonably, clearly, and exactly, or even to destroy the former relation (now become inadequate) of man to the universe, and to substitute for it one that is higher clearer, and more reasonable; but we should in no case devise a so-called secular, non-religious morality founded on sophistry, or simply founded on nothing at all.

The attempts to found a morality apart from religion, are like what children do when, wishing to transplant a flower that pleases them—they pluck it from the roots that do not please, and seem to them superfluous, and stick it rootless into the ground. Without religious roots there can be no real, sincere morality, just as without roots there can be no real flower.

So in answer to your two questions, I say: '*Religion is a certain relation established by man between his separate personality and the infinite universe or its Source. And morality is the ever-present guide to life which results from that relation.*'

[December 28, o.s., 1893.]

# VIII

# REASON AND RELIGION

### A LETTER TO AN INQUIRER

You ask me :

1. Should men of no special intellectual gifts seek to express in words truths they have reached relating to the inner life ?

2. Is it worth while to try to attain full and clear understanding of one's inner life ?

3. How in moments of struggle or doubt are we to know whether it is conscience that speaks to us, or whether it is intellect bribed by our infirmities ?  (This third question, for brevity's sake, I have restated in my own words without, I hope, altering your meaning.)

These three questions, it seems to me, are all summed up in one—the second ; for if we should not try to attain full and clear understanding of our inner life, then also we should not, and cannot, express in words the truths we have reached ; and in moments of doubt we shall have nothing to guide us in distinguishing between conscience and false reasoning.  But if it is right to seek the greatest clearness one's mental powers can reach (whether those powers be great or small), then we should also express in words the truths we have reached, and by those truths, elucidated to the utmost and expressed in words, we must be guided in moments of struggle or doubt.  And therefore I answer your root question in the affirmative ; namely, that every man, in order to accomplish the purpose for which he was sent here, and to attain true well-being (the two always accord), should exert the whole strength of his mind to elucidate for himself the religious foundations on which he rests; that is to say, he should clear up the purpose of his life.

Among uneducated navvies, whose work is paid for by the cubic fathom, I have often met with a prevalent conviction that mathematical calculations are deceptive and should not be trusted. Whether this is because they do not know mathematics, or because those who calculate the earth they have dug up often intentionally or unintentionally cheat them, the fact remains that disbelief in the sufficiency or applicability of mathematics to estimate quantities, has firmly established itself among these uneducated labourers, and for most of them has become an unquestioned verity, which they do not even consider it necessary to prove. A similar opinion has established itself among people whom I may safely call *irreligious*—an opinion to the effect that reason cannot solve religious questions; that the application of reason to these questions is the chief source of errors, and that to solve religious questions by reason is an act of wicked pride.

I mention this because the doubt expressed in your questions as to whether one should try to attain full and clear understanding, can only arise from the supposition that reason cannot be applied to the solution of religious questions. Yet that supposition is as strange and as obviously false as the supposition that calculation cannot solve mathematical questions.

Man has received direct from God only one instrument wherewith to know himself and to know his relation to the universe—he has no other—and that instrument is reason: but suddenly he is told that his reason may be used to elucidate his home, family, business, political, scientific or artistic problems, but may not be used to clear up the very thing for which it was chiefly granted him. It would seem that to clear up the most important truths, those on which his whole life depends, man must on no account use his reason, but must recognise such truths apart from his reason, though apart from his reason man can know nothing. People say : 'Recognise by inspiration, by faith': but the fact is, that man cannot even believe apart from his reason. If a man believes one thing and not another, he does this only because his reason tells him he should not believe this, but should believe that. To say a man should not be guided by reason, is the same as to say to a man carrying a lamp in a dark catacomb, that, to find the way out, he must extinguish his lamp and be guided, not by light, but by something else.

But perhaps it will be said (as you say in your letter) that not all men are gifted with great intellect, and especially not with capacity to express their thoughts ; and by an unskilful expression of their thoughts about religion they may, therefore, occasion error. To that I will reply in the words of the Gospel, that what is hidden from the wise is revealed to babes. And this saying is not an exaggeration or a paradox (as we are accustomed to consider sayings in the Gospels that do not please us), but is a statement of the simplest and most undoubted truth, namely, that to every being in the world a law is given which that being should follow, and that to enable him to perceive this law, every being has received suitable organs. And, therefore, every man is gifted with reason, and by that reason the law he should follow is revealed to each man. That law is hidden only from those who do not wish to follow it, and who, in order not to obey the law, reject reason, and, instead of using the reason given to them wherewith to discern truth, accept on faith the guidance of others who have also rejected reason.

The law man should follow is so simple that it is accessible to every child : especially as man need not rediscover this law of his life. Those who lived before us discovered and expressed it, and a man need only verify the propositions he finds expressed in tradition, by his own reason—accepting or rejecting them. But he must not do as people advise who prefer not to obey the law : he must not check his reason by tradition, but, contrariwise, must check tradition by reason.

Traditions may come from man and be false, but reason certainly comes from God and cannot be false. And, therefore, no specially great capacities are needed to know and express the truth, but we need only believe that reason not only is the highest, the divine quality in man, but that it is the only instrument he possesses for the attainment of truth.

Special talents and intellectual gifts are needed, not for the knowledge and statement of truth, but for the invention and statement of falsehood. Once they abandon the indications of reason, and, instead of believing them, credulously accept what is offered to them as truth, people pile up and credulously accept (usually in the guise of laws, revelations, and dogmas) such complex, unnatural and contradictory propositions, that to express them and connect them with any truth really needs great subtlety of mind and exceptional gifts. One need only imagine to one's self a man of our world, educated in the religious beliefs of any one of the Christian Churches—Catholic, Russo-Greek Orthodox, or Protestant—who should wish to elucidate the religious principles with which he has been inoculated in childhood, and to connect them with real life—what a complex intellectual labour he would have to perform in order to adjust all the contradictions contained in the faith with which his education had inoculated him : a God, who is the Creator and is good—creates evil, condemns people, and demands a ransom, etc. ; and we ourselves profess a law of love and forgiveness, yet we execute, make war, take their produce from the poor, etc.

For the disentanglement of these insoluble contradictions, or, rather, in order to hide them from one's self, great ability and special mental endowments are necessary ; but to know the law of one's life, or, as you express it, to attain full and clear understanding of one's belief, no special mental gifts are required —we only need be careful not to accept anything contrary to reason, not to deny our reason, religiously to guard our reason and believe in it alone. If the meaning of his life seems obscure to a man, this does not prove that his reason is incompetent to explain that meaning; it only indicates that he has credulously accepted too much that is irrational, and that what has not been verified by reason must be set aside.

And, therefore, my answer to your root question, as to whether we must strive to attain a clear understanding of our inner life, is, that that is the most necessary and important thing we can do in life.   It is necessary and important because the only reasonable meaning of our life consists in fulfilment of the will of God, who has sent us here.   But the will of God is known, not by some extraordinary miracle, the writing of the law by the finger of the Deity on stone tablets, the compilation by the aid of the Holy Ghost of an infallible book, or by the infallibility of any holy man or collection of men, but only by the use of reason by all men, transmitting both by deed and by word, one to another, the consciousness of truth that is ever more and more elucidating itself to them.   That knowledge never has been, nor ever will be, complete, but it ever increases as humanity advances : the longer we live the more clearly we know God's will, and, consequently, the more we know what we should do to fulfil it.   And so I think the clearing up by each man (however small he may seem to himself or to others—the least are the greatest) of all religious truth accessible to him, and its expression in words (for expression in words is one sure sign of complete clearness in thought), is one of the chief and most holy duties of man.

I shall be very glad if my reply, in any degree, satisfies you.

[1895.]

## IX

## SHAME !

THERE was a time, between 1820 and 1830, when the officers of the Seménof Regiment, the flower of the young generation of that time, men who were for the most part Freemasons, and subsequently Decembrists,* decided not to use corporal punishment in their regiment, and, notwithstanding the stringent discipline then required, without using corporal punishment, theirs continued to be a model regiment.

The officer in charge of one of the companies of this same Seménof Regiment, meeting Sergius Ivánovitch Mouravyóf—one of the best men of his, or indeed of any, time—spoke of a certain soldier, a thief and a drunkard, saying that such a man could only be tamed with rods. Sergius Mouravyóf did not agree with him, and proposed transferring the man into his own company.

The transfer was made, and almost the next day the soldier stole a comrade's boots, sold them for drink, and made a disturbance. Sergius Ivánovitch mustered the company, called the soldier out, and said to him : ' You know that in my regiment we neither strike men nor flog them, and I am not going to punish you. I shall pay, with my own money, for the boots you stole, but I ask you, not for my sake but for your own, to think over your way of life and to amend it.' And

* Members of the party which attempted, but failed, to secure by force a liberal constitution for Russia, in 1825, when Nicholas I. ascended the throne.

after giving the man some friendly counsel, Sergius Ivánovitch let him go.

The man again got drunk and fought, and again he was not punished but only exhorted : ' You are doing yourself great harm. If you will amend, you will yourself be the better for it. So I ask you not to do these things any more.'

The man was so struck by this new kind of treatment, that he completely altered, and became a model soldier.

This incident was told me by Sergius Ivánovitch's brother, Matthew Ivánovitch, who, like his brother and all the best men of his day, considered corporal punishment a shameful relic of barbarism, disgraceful to those who inflict it rather than to those who endure it. When telling this story he could never refrain from tears of emotion and pleasure. And indeed for those who heard him tell it, it was hard not to follow his example.

That is how, seventy-five years ago, educated Russians regarded corporal punishment. And in our day, seventy-five years later, the grandsons of these men take their places as magistrates at sessions, and calmly discuss whether such and such a full-grown man (often the father of a family, or sometimes even a grandfather) should, or should not, be flogged, and how many strokes of the rod he ought to receive.

The most advanced of these grandsons, meeting in committees and Local Government Councils, draw up declarations, addresses, and petitions, to the effect that, on certain hygienic or pedagogic grounds,* it would be better not to flog all the mouzhíks (people of the peasant

---

* By petitioning, openly, for the repeal of laws such as that empowering the local magistrates to have peasants flogged, the petitioners would risk being looked at askance by those in power. But members of local Health Committees, or Educational Committees sometimes find opportunities to utter veiled protests with a minimum amount of risk.

L

class), but only those who have not passed all the classes of the National Schools.

Evidently a great change has taken place in what we call the educated upper classes. The men of the 'twenties, who considered the infliction of corporal punishment disgraceful to themselves, were able to get rid of it even in the military service, where it was deemed indispensable; but the men of our day calmly apply it, not to soldiers only, but to any man of one special class of the Russian people, and cautiously, diplomatically, in their committees and assemblies, draw up addresses and petitions to the Government, with all sorts of reservations and circumlocutions, saying that there are hygienic objections to punishment by flogging, and therefore its use should be limited; or that it would be desirable only to flog those peasants who have not gone through a certain school course, or not to flog peasants referred to in the Manifesto issued on the occasion of the Tsar's marriage.

Evidently a terrible change has taken place among the so-called upper classes of Russian society. And what is most astonishing is that it has come about just while (during these same seventy-five years; and especially during the last thirty-five, since the emancipation of the serfs), in the very class which it is considered necessary to expose to this revolting, coarse, and stupid torture by flogging, an equally important change has taken place in the contrary direction.

While the upper, governing classes have sunk to a plane so coarse and morally degraded that they have legalized flogging and can calmly discuss it, the mental and moral plane of the peasant class has so risen that corporal punishment has become for them not only a physical, but also a moral, torture.

I have heard and read of cases of suicide committed by peasants sentenced to be flogged, and I cannot doubt that such cases occur, for I have myself seen a most ordinary young peasant turn white as a sheet and lose control of his voice at the mere mention, in the District Court, of the possibility of it being inflicted on him.

I have seen how another peasant of forty, who had been condemned to corporal punishment, wept when, in reply to my inquiry whether the sentence had been executed, he had to reply that it had been.

I know, too, the case of a respected, elderly peasant of my acquaintance, who was sentenced to be flogged because he had quarrelled with the Overseer, not noticing that the latter was wearing his badge of office. The man was brought to the District Court, and from there to the shed in which the punishment is usually inflicted. The watchman came with the rods, and the peasant was told to strip.

'Parmén Ermílitch, you know I have a son who is married,' said the peasant, addressing the Elder, and trembling all over. 'Can't this be avoided? You know it's a sin.'

'It's the authorities, Petróvitch. I should be glad enough myself, but there's no help for it,' replied the Elder abashed.

Petróvitch undressed and lay down.

'Christ suffered, and told us to,' said he.

The clerk, an eye-witness, told me the story, and said that every man's hand trembled and none of those present could look one another in the face—feeling that they were doing something dreadful. And these are the people whom it is considered necessary, and probably for some reason advantageous, to beat with rods, like animals, though it is forbidden to torture even animals.

For the benefit of our Christian and enlightened country, it is necessary to subject to this most stupid, most indecent, and most degrading punishment, not all members of this Christian and enlightened country, but only that class which is the most industrious, useful, moral, and numerous.

To prevent violations of the law, the highest authorities of an enormous Christian empire, nineteen centuries after Christ, can devise nothing wiser and more moral than to take the transgressors—grown-up and sometimes elderly people—undress them, lay them on the floor, and whip their bottoms with birches.*

And people who consider themselves most advanced, and who are grandsons of those who seventy-five years ago got rid of corporal punishment, now, in our day, most respectfully and quite seriously, petition his Excellency the Minister, or whoever it may be, not to allow so much flogging of grown-up Russians, because the doctors are of opinion that it is unhealthy; or beg that those who have a school diploma should not be whipped; or that those who were to be flogged at the time of the Emperor's marriage should be let off. And the wise Government meets such frivolous petitions with profound silence, or even prohibits them.

Can one seriously petition on this matter? Is there really any question? Surely there are some deeds which, whether perpetrated by private individuals or by Governments, one cannot calmly discuss, and condemn only under certain circumstances. And the flogging of adult members of one particular class of Russian people, in our time and among our mild and Christianly-enlightened folk, is such a deed. To hinder such crimes against all law, human and divine, one cannot diplomatically approach the Government under cover of hygienic or educational or loyalistic considerations. Of such deeds we must either not speak at all, or we must speak straight to the point and always with detestation and abhorrence. To ask that only those peasants who are literate should be exempt from being beaten on their bare buttocks, is as though in a land where the law decreed that unfaithful wives should be punished by being stripped and exposed in the streets, people were to petition that this punishment should only be inflicted on such as could not knit stockings, or do something of that kind.

* And why choose just this stupid and brutal method of causing pain and not some other? Why not stick needles into people's shoulders or other parts?—or squeeze their hands and feet in vices—or do something of that kind?— L. T.

About such deeds one cannot 'most humbly pray,' nor 'lay our petition at the foot of the throne,' etc.— such deeds must only, and can only, be denounced. And such deeds should be denounced, because when an appearance of legality is given to them they disgrace us all who live in the country in which they are committed. For if it is legal to flog a peasant, this has been enacted for my benefit also, to secure my tranquillity and well-being. And that is intolerable.

I will not and I cannot acknowledge a law which infringes all law human and divine ; and I cannot imagine myself confederate with those who enact and confirm such legalized crimes.

If such abominations must be discussed, there is but one thing to say—viz., that no such law can exist ; that no ukaze, nor insignia, nor seals, nor Imperial commands, can make a law out of a crime ; but that, on the contrary, the dressing-up in legal form of such crimes (as that the grown men of one—only one—class, may, at the will of another, a worse, class—the nobles and the officials—be subjected to an indecent, savage, and revolting punishment), shows, better than anything else, that where such sham legalization of crime is possible, no laws at all exist, but merely the savage licence of brute force.

If one has to speak of corporal punishment inflicted on the peasant class alone, the needful thing is—not to defend the rights of the Local Government, or appeal from a Governor (who has vetoed a petition to exempt literate peasants from flogging) to a Minister, and from the Minister to the Senate, and from the Senate to the Emperor (as was proposed by the Tambóf Local Assembly), but unceasingly to proclaim and cry aloud that such applications of a brutal punishment (already abandoned for children) to one—and that the best—class of Russians, is disgraceful to all who, directly or indirectly, participate in it.

Petróvitch, who lay down to be beaten after crossing himself and saying : 'Christ suffered and told us to,' forgave his tormentors, and remained after the flogging the man he was before. The only result of the torture inflicted upon him was to make him scorn the authority which decrees such punishments. But to many young people, not only the punishment itself but often even the knowledge that it is possible, acts debasingly on their moral feelings, brutalizing some and making others desperate. Yet even that is not the chief evil. The greatest evil is in the mental condition of those who arrange, sanction, and decree these abominations, of those who employ them as threats, and of all who live in the conviction that such violations of justice and humanity are needful conditions of a good and orderly life. What terrible moral perversion must exist in the minds and hearts of those—often young men—who, with an air of profound practical wisdom, say (as I have myself heard said) that it won't do not to flog peasants, and that it is better for the peasants themselves to be flogged.

These are the people most to be pitied for the debasement into which they have sunk, and in which they are stagnating.

Therefore, the emancipation of the Russian people from the degrading influence of a legalized crime is, from every aspect, a matter of enormous importance. And this emancipation will be accomplished, not when exemption from corporal punishment is obtained by those who have a school diploma, or by any other set of peasants, nor even when all the peasants but one are exempted, but it will only be accomplished when the governing classes confess their sin and humbly repent.

[December 14, o.s., 1895.]

# X

## LETTER TO PETER VERÍGIN, THE DOUKHOBÓR LEADER—I

Dear Brother,

I. M. Tregoúbof has sent on to me your letter to him, and I was much pleased to read it—pleased to get to know about you and, as it were, to hear your voice, and to know what you are thinking about, and how you think, and what is vital to you. I see by your letter that you live in a spiritual world and are occupied with spiritual questions. For a man's welfare, that is the chief thing : for only in spirit is man free, and only by the spirit is God's work done, and only in spirit does man feel himself at one with God, for 'God is a spirit.'

The thoughts expressed in your letter about the advantage of living intercourse over intercourse by means of dead books, pleased me much, and I share them. I write books, and therefore know all the evil they produce. I know how people who do not wish to receive the truth, can avoid reading books or understanding what goes against the grain and exposes them, and I know how they can misinterpret and pervert—as they have done with the Gospels. All this I know, but yet I consider books to be, in our time, inevitable. I say 'in our time' in contradistinction to the Gospel times, when there were no printing-presses and books were not used, and the means of communication were vocal. Then it was possible to do without books, for the enemies of truth had none. But now one cannot leave this powerful engine entirely for the enemies of truth to use for deception, but must also see that it is used on the side of truth.

To refuse to make use of a book or a letter to convey one's thoughts or get at the thoughts of others, would be like refusing to use one's strength of voice to convey to many people at once what one has to say; or to use one's ears to understand what some one is saying in a loud voice. It would be like refusing to acknowledge the possibility of conveying thought except *tête-à-tête*, or when conveyed in a whisper. Writing and printing have but multiplied a thousand, a hundred thousand, times the number of people by whom the thoughts expressed may be heard; but the relation between him who expresses and him who receives the thoughts remains as before: as in conversation the hearer may grasp and understand what is said, or may let it go in at one ear and out at the other, so it is with printed matter. As the reader of a book may twist it this way or that, so may he also do who hears spoken words. As in books (and we constantly see this) much may be written that is superfluous and empty, just so is it with speech. A difference exists, but it is a difference that is sometimes to the advantage of vocal, sometimes of printed communications. The advantage of vocal communication is that the hearer feels the spirit of the speaker, but the disadvantage is that very often empty talkers (for instance advocates) having a gift of words, sway men not by their reasonableness, but by their mastery of oratorical art, which is not the case with books. Another advantage of verbal communication is that a hearer who has not understood a matter can ask questions, but there is the accompanying disadvantage that those who have failed to understand (often purposely failed) can put questions which are not to the point, and can thus divert the stream of thought, which is not the case with books. The disadvantages of books are: First, that paper can endure all things, and people can have any nonsense printed, causing enormous labour to be wasted in papermaking and typesetting; which is not the case with vocal communication, for people can refuse to listen to nonsense. Secondly, that books are multiplying enormously, so that the good ones get lost in the sea of empty and harmful ones. But then again the advantages of the press are very great ; and consist chiefly in the fact that the circle of hearers is extended a hundredfold, or a thousandfold, as compared to the hearers of the spoken word. And this increase of the circle of readers is important not because there are many readers, but because among the millions of people of different nations and stations to whom a book becomes accessible, those who share similar thoughts discover one another, and while living thousands of miles apart, not knowing one another, are yet united and live by one spirit, having the spiritual joy and encouragement of feeling that they are not alone. Such communication I now have with you and with many, many men of other nations—men who have never seen me but who yet are nearer to me than sons or brothers of my own blood. The chief consideration in favour of books is, that since men reached a certain stage in development of the external conditions of life—books, and printing in general, have become a means of communication among men, and must, therefore, not be neglected. So many harmful books have been written and circulated, that the evil can only be met by other books. One wedge drives out another. Christ said : ' What I tell you in the ear, proclaim upon the housetops.' Printing is just that proclamation from the housetops. The printed word is a tongue—a tongue that reaches very far ; and for this reason all that is said of the tongue relates also to the printed word : ' Therewith bless we God, and therewith curse we men, made after the likeness of God.' Therefore one cannot be too careful what one says and listens to, nor what one prints and reads. I write all this not that I think you understand the matter differently (from your letter I conclude that you understand the matter as I do) but because these thoughts have come into my head, and I wish to share them with you. In your letter I was particularly pleased by your saying : 'If we observed all that has already been given us from above, we should be quite happy. What is necessary and right, must certainly exist in everyone, and comes directly from above, or is found in one's self.' That is quite true, and is just how I understand man's nature. Every man can undoubtedly know the truth of God— all he need know to fulfil what God demands of him in this life—if only this truth revealed to man be not darkened by false human interpretations. Therefore to know God's truth, man should first of all discard all false interpretations, and all the snares of the world tempting him to accept those interpretations, and then truth alone will remain, and will be accessible to little children, for it is native to the soul of man. The chief difficulty is, when discarding falsehood, not to throw away with it some part of the truth, and when explaining truth not to introduce new errors.

Thank you, dear brother, for the greetings you sent me. Write to me in Moscow, if there is no obstacle to your doing so. Cannot I be of any service to you ? You would please me very much if you would give me some commission to execute.

I embrace you as a brother.

LEO TOLSTOY.

[November 21, o.s., 1895.]

This letter and the one that follows were written to Peter Verígin while he was at Obdórsk, a small settlement near the mouth of the river Obi in Northern Siberia, undergoing his fifteen years' exile. He was released in 1902, and rejoined his sect in Canada.

## XI

## LETTER TO PETER VERÍGIN, THE DOUKHOBÓR LEADER—II

Dear Friend,

I received your letter yesterday, and hasten to reply. Letters from you and to you are long on the road, and I have not long to live.

In your arguments against books there is very much that is just and ingenious (for instance, the comparison to a medical assistant and a doctor) but the arguments themselves are invalid, chiefly because you contrast books with living intercourse, as though a book excluded living intercourse. In reality, the one does not exclude, but helps, the other.

To speak frankly, your stubborn contention against books seems to me a peculiarly sectarian method of defending a once accepted and expressed opinion. And such peculiarity does not accord with the conception I had formed of your intellect, and especially of your candour and sincerity. God leads men to Himself, and to the performance of His will, by all paths: they move consciously when they try to do His will, and unconsciously when, as they suppose, they are doing their own will.

To accomplish God's will—to establish His kingdom on earth—union among men is needed, that all may be one, as Jesus felt himself to be one with the Father. For this union, we need (1) an internal means: the recognition and clear expression of truth, such as Jesus achieved, and such as unites all men; and (2) an external means: the diffusion of this expression of truth — a diffusion accomplished by very diverse methods : by trade, and conquest, and travel, and books, and railroads, and telegraphs, and in many other ways, some of which, such as conquest, I have to repudiate, but others, such as books and means of rapid communication, I have no cause to repudiate, and cannot (unless I wish to deprive myself of a convenient means of serving God) refuse to utilize. As to your argument that to produce books and railroads people have to burrow underground for ore and to work at a furnace, why—all that has to be done before one can have even a ploughshare, or spade, or a scythe. And there is nothing bad in burrowing underground for ore, or working at a furnace ; and when I was young I would willingly have burrowed underground or worked at a furnace, to show my spirit, and so would any good young fellow to-day, provided the work were not compulsory, nor for life, and were surrounded by all the conveniences which will certainly be devised as soon as everyone is expected to work, and the labour is not put on wage-slaves only.

But let us not pursue this subject ; only believe me that if I write to you thus, I do it neither because I have written many books and still write them—I most heartily agree with you, that the very simplest good life is more precious than the most beautiful of books —nor because thanks to books I come into touch with other men—as happened this autumn with a Hindu who fully shares our Christian outlook (and who has sent me an English book by a lady, his compatriot, explaining the teachings of the Brahmans in conformity with the essentials of Christ's teaching), and again with some Japs who profess and teach a quite Christian morality, and two of whom visited me a few days ago. Not by these things am I withheld from agreeing with you, and from condemning book-printing, railroads, telephones, and other such things—but because when I see an ant-hill in the meadow I cannot admit that the ants have been mistaken in constructing that hill, and doing all they are doing in it. And in the same way, looking at all the material labours mankind has accomplished, I cannot admit that they have done it all by mistake. As a man and not an ant, I see defects in the human ant-hill, and cannot but wish to rectify them—in that lies my share of the common work—but I do not wish to destroy the whole hill of human labour, but only to arrange better what is ill-arranged in it. And in the human ant-hill there is very much that is ill-arranged, concerning which I have written and yet write, have suffered and yet suffer, and which as far as I have strength I try to alter.

What is wrong in our life is, first and foremost, the fact that the means are put in place of the aim, and what should be the aim (the welfare of our fellow-men) is sacrificed to the means. The welfare of man, even his life itself, is sacrificed to produce things of which only some are wanted by everyone, but some of which are only good to serve the caprice of a single man. So that human lives are sacrificed to produce articles wanted only by a few, or wanted by no one, or that are even simply harmful.

What is wrong is that people forget, have forgotten, or do not know, that (not to speak of the production of such things as looking-glasses) not even to produce the most important and necessary things—such as ploughshares or scythes—is it permissible or justifiable to sacrifice a single life, or to destroy the happiness of a single man—even the most apparently insignificant; for the meaning of human life lies solely in the welfare of all men. To infringe the life and welfare of any man for the welfare of mankind in general, is the same as if for an animal's welfare we were to cut off one of his limbs.

That is where the terrible mistake of our times is to be found; not in the fact that printing-offices, railroads, and other such things exist, but in the fact that men consider it allowable to sacrifice the welfare, were it only of a single man, for the accomplishment of any business however great. As soon as people lose sight of the meaning and aim of their activity (and there is only one aim—the welfare of one's neighbour), as soon as they decide that for business purposes it is permissible to sacrifice the life and welfare of a single old man, burdensome to everyone, or even of an idiot, then it becomes permissible to sacrifice those who are less old and less stupid, and no limit can any longer be found—all may be sacrificed for the sake of business. That is what is wrong, and against that we must fight.

It should be understood that, however useful and important book-printing, railroads, ploughs and scythes may seem to us, it were better to let them all perish and to do without them, until we can learn to get them without destroying the happiness and life of men. That is the whole question ; and it is here people generally get confused, trying to go round the point on one side or the other. Some say : ' You want to destroy all that humanity has achieved by its labour—you wish to return to barbarism, for the sake of some moral principle or other. Moral principles are wrong if they hinder the well-being humanity achieves in the course of its progress.' Others say (and I fear you hold this opinion, and it is an opinion people attribute to me) that since, in the process of attaining all the material ameliorations of life, moral principles have been violated, therefore all these ameliorations must, in themselves, be bad and should be abandoned.

To the upholders of the first view I reply, that what is needed is not to destroy anything, but only to remember that the aim of humanity is the welfare of *all*, and that consequently as soon as any amelioration deprives even a single man of welfare, that amelioration should be abandoned, and not introduced until means are found to produce it and to use it, without infringing the welfare of any single man. And I think that with such a view of life, very many empty and harmful productions would be abandoned, while we should very quickly find means to produce what is really useful without infringing the welfare of any man.

To the upholders of the second view I reply, that humanity in passing from the stone age to the bronze or iron age, and progressing to its present material condition, cannot have made a mistake, but has followed an unalterable law of progress, and to turn back is, I will not say undesirable, but is as impossible as it is for us again to become monkeys ; and that the problem for a man of to-day is not to dream about what people used to be like, and how to revert to what they were, but it is—to serve the welfare of men now living.  And what is necessary for the welfare of men now living is—that some men should not torment others or oppress them, should not deprive them of the products of their labour, nor compel them to work at things they do not need or may not have ; and chiefly that it should not be considered possible or right, for the sake of any practical advantage or material success, to sacrifice the life or welfare of one's neighbour, or, what is the same thing differently expressed, to infringe the law of love.

If people only knew that the aim of humanity is not material progress, but that that progress is an inevitable growth, and that the aim is simply the welfare of all men, and that this aim is superior to any material aim people can set themselves, then everything would fall into its proper place.  And it is to this, people of our time should devote all their strength.

But to weep because men cannot now live without implements, like wild beasts, feeding themselves on fruits, is as if I, an old man, were to weep for lack of teeth and black hair and the strength I had in my youth.  What I have to do is, not to insert false teeth, dye my hair, and do gymnastics, but to try to live in the way natural for an old man, putting first—not worldly affairs, but the affairs of God—union and love, and admitting worldly affairs only in so far as they do not infringe God's work.  The same should be done by humanity in its present stage of existence.

But to say that railroads, gas, electricity and book-printing are harmful, because for their sake human lives are sacrificed, is like saying that ploughing and sowing are harmful—merely because I ploughed a field at the wrong time, let it get overgrown with weeds, and then sowed seed without reploughing—that is to say, did things out of turn and at the wrong time.

I was very glad to see what you write about your own life ; and that even in the difficult circumstances in which you are placed you practise what you preach—earning your bread by your own work. In nothing else can a man's sincerity be so well seen. I have now become very faulty in that respect : surrounded as I am by all kinds of luxury, which I hate, but from which I have not the strength to escape. Your example encourages me, and I do not cease to make efforts.

Thanks for sending the extract from your diary. Concerning thoughts there expressed by you, I should like to share with you certain observations that tend in the same direction. I will do so another time.

Farewell meanwhile ; please do not let yourself feel any ill will towards me for my reply to the opinions expressed not only in your letter to me, but also in the letter to E. I. You are very dear to me, and I try to deal as straightforwardly as possible, like a brother, in relation to you.

Yours lovingly,
LEO TOLSTOY.

[October 14, o.s., 1896.]

# XII

## LETTER ON NON-RESISTANCE: TO ERNEST H. CROSBY, OF NEW YORK

DEAR MR. CROSBY,

I am very glad to have news of your activity, and to hear that your work begins to attract attention. Fifty years ago Lloyd Garrison's Declaration of Non-Resistance* only estranged people from him; and Ballou's† fifty years' labour in the same direction was constantly met by a conspiracy of silence. I now read with great pleasure in the *Voice* admirable thoughts by American writers on this question of Non-Resistance. I need only demur to the notion expressed by Mr. Bemis. It is an old but unfounded libel upon Christ to suppose that the expulsion of the cattle from the temple indicates that Jesus beat people with a whip and advised his disciples to behave in the same way.‡

The opinions expressed by these writers, especially by Heber Newton and G. D. Herron, are quite correct, but unfortunately they do not reply to the question Christ put to men, but to another question which has been substituted for it by those chief and most dangerous

---

* The Declaration of Non-Resistance drawn up by William Lloyd Garrison was adopted at a Peace Convention held in Boston, September 18-20, 1838.

† Adin Ballou (1803–1890), a Massachusetts Restorationist minister, founder of Hopedale Community (1842–1856), and author of *Christian Non-Resistance*.

‡ Christ's use of a scourge is mentioned only in St. John's Gospel. Our Revised Version, following the Greek, indicates that the scourge was for 'the sheep and the oxen.'

opponents of Christianity—the so-called 'orthodox' ecclesiastical authorities.

Mr. Higginson says, 'I do not believe Non-Resistance admissible as a universal rule.' Heber Newton says that 'People's opinion as to the practical results of the application of Christ's teaching will depend on the extent of people's belief in his authority.' Carlos Martyn considers 'The transition stage in which we live not suited for the application of the doctrine of Non-Resistance.' G. D. Herron holds 'That to obey the law of Non-Resistance we must learn how to apply it to life.' Mrs. Livermore, thinking that the law of Non-Resistance can be fully obeyed only in the future, says the same.

All these views refer to the question, 'What would happen if people were all obliged to obey the law of Non-Resistance?' But, in the first place, it is impossible to oblige everyone to accept this law. Secondly, if it were possible to do so, such compulsion would in itself be a direct negation of the very principle set up. Oblige all men to refrain from violence! Who then would enforce the decision? Thirdly, and this is the chief point, the question as put by Christ is not at all, Can Non-Resistance become a general law for humanity? but, How must each man act to fulfil his allotted task, to save his soul, and to do the will of God?—which are all really one and the same thing.

Christian teaching does not lay down laws for everybody, and does not say to people, 'You all, for fear of punishment, must obey such and such rules, and then you will all be happy'; but it explains to each individual his position in relation to the world, and lets him see what results, for him individually, inevitably flow from that relation. Christianity says to man (and to each man separately) that his personal life can have no rational meaning if he counts it as belonging to himself, or as having for its aim worldly happiness for himself or for other people. This is so because the happiness he seeks is unattainable : (1) because, as all beings strive after worldly advantages, the gain of one is the loss of others, and it is most probable that each individual will incur much superfluous suffering in the course of his vain efforts to seize unattainable blessings; (2) because, even if a man get worldly advantages, the more he obtains the less they satisfy him and the more he hankers after fresh ones; (3) and chiefly because the longer a man lives, the more inevitable becomes the approach of old age, sickness, and of death, destroying all possibility of worldly advantages.

So that if a man considers his life his own, to be spent in seeking worldly happiness for himself as well as for others, then that life can have no rational explanation for him.

Life has a rational meaning only when one understands that to consider our life our own, or to see its aim in worldly happiness for ourselves or for other people, is a delusion; that a man's life does not belong to him who has received it, but to Him who has given it; and its object should, therefore, be, not the attainment of worldly happiness either for one's self or for other individuals, but solely the fulfilment of the will of Him who created this life.

This conception alone gives life a rational meaning, and makes its aim (which is to fulfil the will of God) attainable. And, most important of all, only when enlightened by this conception does man see clearly the right direction for his own activity. Man is then no longer destined to suffer and to despair, as was inevitable under the former conception.

'The universe and I in it,' says to himself a man with this conception, 'exist by the will of God. I cannot know the whole of the universe (for in its immensity it transcends my comprehension), nor can I know my own position in it, but I do know with certainty what God, who has sent me into the world (infinite in time and space, and therefore incomprehensible to me), demands from me. This is revealed to me (1) by the collective wisdom of the best men who have gone before me, *i.e.*, by tradition, (2) by my own reason, and (3) by my heart, *i.e.*, by the highest aspiration of my nature.

Tradition (the collective wisdom of our greatest forerunners) tells me that I should do unto others as I would that they should do unto me.

My reason shows me that only by all men acting thus is the highest happiness for all men attainable.

Only when I yield myself to that intuition of love which demands obedience to this law, is my own heart happy and at rest. And not only can I then know how to act, but I can and do discern the work to co-operate in which my activity was designed and is required.

I cannot fathom God's whole design, for the sake of which the universe exists and lives; but the Divine work which is being accomplished in this world and in which I participate by living is comprehensible to me.

This work is the annihilation of discord and strife among men and among all creatures, and the establishment of the highest unity and concord and love.

It is the fulfilment of the promises of the Hebrew prophet who foretold a time when all men should be taught by truth, when spears should be turned into reaping-hooks, swords be beaten to ploughshares, and the lion lie down with the lamb.

So that a man of Christian intelligence not only knows what he has to do, but he also understands the work he is doing.

He has to act so as to co-operate towards the establishment of the kingdom of God on earth. For this a man must obey his intuition of God's will, *i.e.*, must act lovingly towards others, as he would that others should act towards him.

Thus the intuitive demands of man's soul coincide with the external aim of life which he sees before him.

According to Christian teaching, man in this world is God's labourer. A labourer does not know his master's whole design, but he does know the immediate object which he is set to work at. He receives definite instructions what to do, and especially what not to do, lest he hinder the attainment of the very aims towards which his labour should tend. For the rest he has full liberty given him. And, therefore, for a man who has grasped the Christian conception of life, the meaning of his life is perfectly plain and reasonable, nor can he have a moment's hesitation as to *how* he should act, or *what* he should do to fulfil the object for which he lives.

And yet in spite of such a twofold indication (clear and indubitable to a man of Christian understanding) of what is the real aim and meaning of human life, and of what men should do and should not do, we find people (and people calling themselves Christians) who decide that, in such and such circumstances, men ought to abandon God's law and reason's guidance and to act in opposition to them, because (according to their conception) the effects of actions performed in submission to God's law may be detrimental or inconvenient.

According to the law contained alike in tradition, in our reason, and in our hearts, man should always do unto others as he would that they should do unto him ; he should always co-operate in the development of love and union among created beings. But, in the judgment of these far-sighted people, on the contrary, as long as in their opinion it is premature to obey this law, man should do violence—imprison or kill people— and thereby evoke anger and venom instead of loving union in the hearts of men. It is as though a bricklayer, set to do a particular task and knowing that he was co-operating with others to build a house, after receiving clear and precise instructions from the master himself how to build a certain wall, accepted orders from some fellow-bricklayers (who like himself knew neither the plan of the house, nor what would fit in with it) to cease building his wall, and, instead, to pull down a wall that other workmen had erected.

Astonishing delusion ! A being who breathes to-day and has vanished to-morrow receives one definite indubitable law to guide him through the brief term of his life ; but, instead of obeying that law, he prefers to fancy that he knows what is necessary, advantageous, and well-timed for men and for all the world—this world which continually changes and evolves—and for the sake of some advantage (which each man pictures after his own fancy) he decides that he and other people should, temporarily, abandon the indubitable law given to him and to all men, and should act, not as he would that others should act towards him, nor to bring love into the world—but should do violence, imprison, kill, and bring into the world enmity whenever it seems to him advisable to do so. And he decides to act thus, though he knows that the most horrible cruelties, martyrdoms, and murders—from the Inquisition, and the murders and horrors of all the revolutions, down to the brutalities of contemporary Anarchists and their slaughter by the established authorities—have only occurred because people will imagine that they know what is necessary for mankind and for the world. But are there not always, at any given moment, two opposite parties, each of which declares that it is necessary to use force against the other ? The 'law-and-order' party against the Anarchist, the Anarchist against the 'law-and-order' men ; English against Americans, and Americans against English ; Germans against English, and English against Germans, and so forth in all possible combinations and rearrangements.

A man enlightened by Christianity sees that he has no reason to abandon the law of God, given to enable him to walk sure-footedly through life, in order to follow the chance, inconstant, and often contradictory demands of men. But besides this, if he has lived a Christian life for some time and has developed in himself a moral Christian sensibility, he literally cannot act as people demand of him. Not his reason alone but his feeling also makes it impossible.

To many people of our society it would be impossible to torture or kill a baby, even if they were told that by so doing they could save hundreds of other people. And in the same way, a man who has developed a

Christian sensibility of heart finds a whole series of actions become impossible for him. For instance, a Christian who is obliged to take part in judicial proceedings in which a man may be sentenced to death, or who is obliged to take part in evictions or in debating a proposal leading to war, or to participate in preparations for war (not to mention war itself), is in a position parallel to that of a kindly man called on to torture or to kill a baby. It is not reason alone that forbids him to do what is demanded of him ; he feels instinctively that he *cannot* do it. For certain actions are morally impossible, just as others are physically impossible. As a man cannot lift a mountain, and as a kindly man cannot kill an infant, so a man living a Christian life cannot take part in deeds of violence. Of what value to him, then, are arguments about the imaginary advantages of doing what it is morally impossible for him to do ?

But how is a man to act when he sees clearly the evil of following the law of love and its corollary law of Non-Resistance ? How (to use the stock example) is a man to act when he sees a robber killing or outraging a child, and he can only save the child by killing the robber ?

When such a case is put, it is generally assumed that the only possible reply is that one should kill the robber to save the child. But this answer is given so quickly and decidedly only because we are all so accustomed to the use of violence—not only to save a child, but even to prevent a neighbouring Government altering its frontier at the expense of ours, or someone from smuggling lace across that frontier, or even to defend our garden fruit from a passer-by.

It is assumed that to save the child the robber should be killed. But it is only necessary to consider the question, on what grounds a man (whether he be or be not a Christian) ought to act so, in order to come to the conclusion that such action has no reasonable foundation, and only seems to us necessary because up to two thousand years ago such conduct was considered right, and a habit of acting so was formed. Why should a non-Christian—not acknowledging God, nor regarding the fulfilment of His will as the aim of life—decide to kill the robber in order to defend the child? By killing the robber, he certainly kills; whereas he cannot know positively whether the robber would have killed the child or not. But letting that pass, who shall say whether the child's life was more needed, was better, than the robber's life?

Surely, if the non-Christian knows not God nor sees life's meaning in the performance of His will, the only rule for his actions must be a reckoning, a conception, of what is more profitable for him and for all men : a continuation of the robber's life or of the child's. To decide that, he needs to know what would become of the child whom he saves, and what—had he not killed him—would have been the future of the robber he kills. And as he cannot know this, the non-Christian has no sufficient rational ground for killing a robber to save a child.

If a man is a Christian, and consequently acknowledges God and sees the meaning of life in fulfilling His will, then, however ferocious the robber, however innocent and lovely the child, he has even less ground to abandon the God-given law and to do to the robber what the robber wishes to do to the child. He may plead with the robber, may interpose his own body between the robber and the victim, but there is one thing he cannot do : he cannot deliberately abandon the law he has received from God, the fulfilment of which alone gives meaning to his life. Very probably bad education, or his animal nature, may cause a man (Christian or non-Christian) to kill the robber, not only to save the child, but even to save himself or his purse, but it does not follow that he is right in acting thus, nor that he should accustom himself or others to think such conduct right.

What it does show is that, notwithstanding a coating of education and of Christianity, the habits of the Stone Age are yet so strong in man, that he still commits actions long since condemned by his reasonable conscience.

I see a robber killing a child, and I can save the child by killing the robber—therefore in certain cases violence must be used to resist evil. A man's life is in danger, and can be saved only by my telling a lie—therefore in certain cases one must lie. A man is starving, and one can save him only by stealing—therefore in certain cases one must steal.

I lately read a story by Coppée, in which an orderly kills his officer, whose life was insured, and thereby saves the honour and the family of the officer. Therefore in certain cases one must kill.

Such inventions, and the deductions from them, only prove that there are men who know that it is not well to steal, to lie, or to kill, but who are still so unwilling that people should cease to do these things, that they use all their mental powers to invent excuses for such conduct. There is no moral law concerning which we may not devise a case in which it is difficult to decide what is more moral : to disobey the law or to obey it? But all such inventions fail to prove that the laws, 'thou shalt not lie, steal, or kill,' are invalid.

It is the same with reference to the law of Non-Resistance. People know it is wrong to use violence, but they are so anxious to continue to live a life secured by the ' strong arm of the law,' that—instead of devoting their intellects to the elucidation of the evils which have flowed and are still flowing from admitting that man has a right to use violence to his fellow-men—they prefer to exert their mental powers in defence of that error.

'*Fais ce que dois, advienne que pourra*' ('Do what's right, come what may') is an expression of profound wisdom. We each can know indubitably what we ought to do, but what results will follow from our actions none of us either knows or can know. Therefore it follows that, besides feeling the call of duty, we are further driven to act as duty bids us, by the consideration that we have no other guidance, but are totally ignorant of what will result from our actions.

Christian teaching indicates what a man should do to perform the will of Him who sent him into life; but discussion as to what results we anticipate from such or such human actions have nothing to do with Christianity, but are just an example of the error Christianity eliminates.

None of us has ever yet met the imaginary robber with the imaginary child, but all the horrors which fill the annals of history and of our own times came and come from this one thing—that people will believe that they can foresee the results of hypothetical future actions.

The case is this: People once lived an animal life, and violated or killed whom they thought well to violate or to kill. They even ate each other; and public opinion approved of it. Thousands of years ago, as far back as the times of Moses, a day came when people realized that to violate or kill each other is bad. But there were people for whom the reign of force was advantageous, and these did not approve of the change, but assured themselves and others that to do deeds of violence and to kill people is not always bad, but that there are circumstances when it is necessary and even moral. And violence and even slaughter, though not so frequent or so cruel as before, continued—only with this difference, that those who committed or commended such acts excused themselves by pleading that they did it for the benefit of humanity.

It was just this sophistical justification of violence that Christ denounced. When two enemies fight, each may think his own conduct justified by the circumstances. Excuses can be made for every use of violence; and no infallible standard has ever been discovered by which to measure the worth of these excuses. Therefore Christ taught us to believe in no excuse for violence, and (contrary to what had been taught by them of old time) never to use violence.

One would have thought that those who professed

Christianity would have been indefatigable in exposing deception in this matter, for such an exposure forms one of the chief features of Christianity. What really happened was just the reverse. People who profited by violence, and who did not wish to give up their advantages, took on themselves a monopoly of Christian preaching, and declared that as cases can be found in which Non-Resistance causes more harm than the use of violence (the imaginary robber killing the imaginary child), therefore Christ's doctrine of Non-Resistance need not always be followed, and that one may deviate from his teaching to defend one's life or the life of others, to defend one's country, to save society from lunatics or criminals, and in many other cases. The decision of the question, In what cases should Christ's teaching be set aside? was left to the very people who employed violence. So that it ended by Christ's teaching, on the subject of not resisting evil, by violence being completely annulled. And, worst of all, the very people Christ denounced came to consider themselves the sole preachers and expositors of his doctrines. But the light shines through the darkness, and Christ's teaching is again exposing the pseudo-teachers of Christianity.

We may think about rearranging the world to suit our own taste—no one can prevent that—and we may try to do what seems to us pleasant or profitable, and with that object treat our fellow-creatures with violence on the pretext that we are doing good. But acting thus we cannot pretend to follow Christ's teaching, for Christ denounced just this deception. Truth sooner or later reappears, and the false teachers are unmasked, which is just what is happening to-day.

Only let the question of man's life be rightly put, as Christ put it, and not as it has been perversely put by the Churches, and the whole structure of falsehood which the Churches have built over Christ's teaching, will collapse of itself.

The real question is not whether it would be good or bad for a certain human society that people should follow the law of Love and the consequent law of Non-

Resistance, but it is this, Do you, who to-day live and to-morrow will die—who are indeed tending deathward every moment—do you wish now, immediately and entirely, to obey the law of Him who sent you into life, and who clearly showed you His will alike in tradition and in your mind and heart; or do you prefer to resist his will? And as soon as the question is put thus, only one reply is possible—I wish now, this moment, without delay or hesitation, to the very utmost of my strength, neither waiting for anyone nor counting the cost, to do that which alone is clearly demanded by Him who sent me into the world; and on no account, and under no conditions, do I wish to, or can I, act otherwise, for herein lies my only possibility of a rational and unharassed life.

[January 12, o.s., 1896.]

## XIII

## HOW TO READ THE GOSPELS, AND WHAT IS ESSENTIAL IN THEM

THERE is so much that is strange, improbable, unintelligible, and even contradictory, in what professes to be Christ's teaching, that people do not know how to understand it.

It is very differently understood by different people. Some say Redemption is the all-important matter; others say the all-important thing is grace, obtainable through the Sacraments; others, again, that submission to the Church is what is really essential. But the Churches themselves disagree, and interpret the teaching variously. The Roman Catholic Church holds that the Holy Ghost proceeds from the Father and the Son, that the Pope is infallible, and that salvation is obtainable chiefly through works. The Lutheran Church disagrees, and considers that faith is what is chiefly needed for salvation. The Orthodox Russo-Greek Church considers that the Holy Ghost proceeds from the Father only, and that both works and faith are necessary to salvation. And the Anglican and other Episcopalian Churches, the Presbyterian and the Methodist, not to mention hundreds of others, each interpret Christ's teaching in their own way.

Young men and men of the people, doubting the truth of the Church teaching in which they have been brought up, often come to me and ask what *my* teaching is, and how *I* understand Christ's teaching? Such questions always grieve and even shock me.

Christ, who the Churches say was God, came on

earth to reveal divine truth to men for their guidance in life. A man—even a plain, stupid man—if he wants to give people guidance of importance to them, will manage to impart it so that they can make out what he means. And is it possible that God, having come on earth specially to save people, was not able to say what he wanted to say clearly enough to prevent people from misinterpreting his words, and from disagreeing with each other about them?

This could not be so if Christ were God; nor even if Christ were not God, but were merely a great teacher, is it possible that he failed to express himself clearly. For a great teacher is great just because he is able to express the truth so that it can neither be hidden nor obscured, but is as plain as daylight.

In either case, therefore, the Gospels which transmit Christ's teaching must contain truth. And, indeed, the truth is there for all who will read the Gospels with a sincere wish to know the truth, without prejudice and, above all, without supposing that they contain some special sort of wisdom beyond human reason.

That is how I read the Gospels, and I found in them truth plain enough for little children to understand, as indeed is said in the Gospels. So that when I am asked what *my* teaching consists in, and how *I* understand Christ's teaching, I reply: 'I have no teaching, but I understand Christ's teaching as it is explained in the Gospels. If I have written books about Christ's teaching, I have done so only to show the falseness of interpretations given by commentators on the Gospels.'

To understand Christ's real teaching, the chief thing is not to interpret the Gospels, but to understand them as they are written. And therefore, to the question how Christ's teaching should be understood, I reply: 'If you wish to understand it, read the Gospels. Read them, putting aside all foregone conclusions; read them with the sole desire to understand what is there said. But just because the Gospels are holy books, read them considerately, reasonably, and with discernment, and not haphazard or mechanically, as though all the words were of equal weight.'

To understand any book one must choose out the parts that are quite clear, dividing them from what is obscure or confused. And from what is clear we must form our idea of the drift and spirit of the whole work. Then, on the basis of what we have understood, we may proceed to make out what is confused or not quite intelligible. That is how we read all kinds of books. And it is particularly necessary thus to read the Gospels, which have passed through a multiplicity of compilations, translations, and transcriptions, and were composed eighteen centuries ago, by men who were not highly educated, and who were superstitious.*

Therefore, in order to understand the Gospels, we must first of all separate what is quite simple and intelligible from what is confused and unintelligible, and must afterwards read this clear and intelligible part several times over, trying fully to assimilate it. Then, helped by the comprehension of the general meaning, we can try to explain to ourselves the drift of the parts which seemed involved and obscure. That was how I read the Gospels, and the meaning of Christ's teaching became so clear to me that it was impossible to have any doubts about it. And I advise everyone who wishes

---

* The Gospels, as is known to all who have studied their origin, far from being infallible expressions of divine truth, are the work of innumerable minds and hands, and are full of errors. Therefore the Gospels can in no case be taken as a production of the Holy Ghost, as Churchmen assert. Were that so, God would have revealed the Gospels as He is said to have revealed the Commandments on Mount Sinai ; or He would have transmitted the complete book to men, as the Mormons declare was the case with their Holy Scriptures. But we know how these works were written and collected, and how they were corrected and translated ; and therefore not only can we not accept them as infallible revelations, but we must, if we respect truth, correct errors that we find in them.—L. T.

to understand the true meaning of Christ's teaching to follow the same plan.

Let each man, in reading the Gospels, select all that seems to him quite plain, clear, and comprehensible, and let him score it down the margin—say with a blue pencil—and then, taking the marked passages first, let him separate Christ's words from those of the Evangelists by marking Christ's words a second time with, say, a red pencil. Then let him read over these doubly-scored passages several times. Only after he has thoroughly assimilated these, let him again read the words attributed to Christ which he did not understand when he first read them, and let him score, in red, those which have become plain to him. Let him leave unscored the words of Christ which remain quite unintelligible, and also unintelligible words by the writers of the Gospels. The passages marked in red will supply the reader with the essence of Christ's teaching. They will give what all men need, and what Christ therefore said in a way that all can understand. The places marked only in blue will give what the authors of the Gospels said that is intelligible.

Very likely in selecting what is, from what is not, fully comprehensible, people will not all choose the same passages. What is comprehensible to one may seem obscure to another. But all will certainly agree in what is most important, and these are things which will be found quite intelligible to everyone. It is just this—just what is fully comprehensible to all men—that constitutes the essence of Christ's teaching.

[July 22, o.s., 1896.]

# XIV

## A LETTER TO RUSSIAN LIBERALS*

I should be very glad to join you and your associates
—whose work I know and appreciate—in standing up
for the rights of the Literature Committee and opposing
the enemies of popular education. But in the sphere
in which you are working I see no way to resist them.

My only consolation is that I, too, am constantly
engaged in struggling against the same enemies of
enlightenment, though in another manner.

* Though published as *A Letter to Russian Liberals*, this
letter was, in the first instance, addressed to a Russian lady
who wrote to Tolstoy asking his advice or assistance when
the Literature Committee (Komitét Grámotnosti) was
closed. The circumstances were as follows : A 'Voluntary
Economic Society' (founded in the reign of Catherine the
Great) existed, and was allowed to debate economic problems
within certain limits. Its existence was sanctioned by, and
it was under the control of, the Ministry of the Interior. A
branch of this society was formed, called the 'Literature
Committee.' This branch aimed at spreading good and
wholesome literature among the people and in the schools,
by establishing libraries or in other ways. Their views as
to what books it is good for people to read did not, however, tally with those of the Government, and in 1896 it
was decreed that the 'Voluntary Economic Society' should
be transferred from the supervision of the Ministry of the
Interior to that of the Ministry of Education. This, translated into unofficial language, meant that the activity of
the Committee was to terminate, and the proceedings of the
society to be reduced to a formality.

Concerning the special question with which you are preoccupied, I think that in place of the Literature Committee which has been prohibited, a number of other Literature Associations to pursue the same objects should be formed without consulting the Government, and without asking permission from any censor. Let Government, if it likes, prosecute these Literature Associations, punish the members, banish them, etc. If the Government does that, it will merely cause people to attach special importance to good books and to libraries, and it will strengthen the trend towards enlightenment.

It seems to me that it is now specially important to do what is right quietly and persistently, not only without asking permission from Government, but consciously avoiding its participation. The strength of the Government lies in the people's ignorance, and the Government knows this, and will therefore always oppose true enlightenment. It is time we realized that fact. And it is most undesirable to let the Government, while it is spreading darkness, pretend to be busy with the enlightenment of the people. It is doing this now by means of all sorts of pseudo-educational establishments which it controls: schools, high-schools, universities, academies, and all kinds of committees and congresses. But good is good, and enlightenment is enlightenment, only when it is quite good and quite enlightened, and not when it is toned down to meet the requirements of Delyánof's* or Dournovó's circulars. And I am extremely sorry when I see valuable, disinterested, and self-sacrificing efforts spent unprofitably. It is strange to see good, wise people spending their strength in a struggle against the Government, but carrying on that struggle on the basis of whatever laws the Government itself likes to make.

This is how the matter appears to me:

There are people (we ourselves are such) who realize

* Delyánof was Minister of Education and Dournovó was Minister of the Interior when the Committee was suppressed.

that our Government is very bad, and who struggle against it. From before the days of Radístchef* and the Decembrists there have been two ways of carrying on the struggle. One way is that of Sténka Rázin,† Pougatchéf,‡ the Decembrists, the Revolutionary party of the 'sixties,§ the Terrorists of March 1,‖ and others. The other way is that which is preached and practised by you, the method of the 'Gradualists,' which consists in carrying on the struggle without violence and within the limits of the law, conquering constitutional rights bit by bit.

Within my memory both these methods have been employed unremittingly for more than half a century,

---

* Radístchef, the author of *A Journey from Petersburg to Moscow*, was a Liberal whose efforts towards the abolition of serfdom led to his being banished to Siberia. Recalled to Petersburg after five years, he recommenced his activity as a reformer, was reproved and threatened by the Government, became hypochondriac, and committed suicide in 1802.

As to the Decembrists, see footnote on p. 160.

† Sténka Rázin was a Cossack who raised a formidable insurrection in the seventeenth century. He was eventually defeated and captured, and was executed in Moscow in 1671.

‡ Pougatchéf headed the most formidable Russian insurrection of the eighteenth century. He was executed in Moscow in 1775.

§ The series of reforms, including the abolition of serfdom, which followed the Crimean War and the death of Nicholas I., were, from the first, adopted half-heartedly, and since the time of the Polish insurrection (1863) the control of the Government has been in reactionary hands. The more vehement members of the Liberal party, losing hope of constitutional reform, formed a Revolutionary party in the 'sixties, and later on the Terrorist party was started, which organized assassinations as a means towards liberty, equality, and fraternity.

‖ Alexander II. was killed by a bomb thrown at him in the streets of Petersburg on March 1, o.s. (March 13, n.s.), 1881. This assassination was organized by the Terrorist party.

and yet the state of things grows worse and worse. Even such signs of improvement as do show themselves have come, not from either of these kinds of activity, but from causes of which I will speak later on, and in spite of the harm done by these two kinds of activity. Meanwhile, the power against which we struggle grows ever greater, stronger, and more insolent. The last gleams of self-government—Local Government, public trial, your Literature Committee, etc., etc.—are all being done away with.

Now that both methods have been tried without effect for so long a time, we may, it seems to me, see clearly that neither the one nor the other will do, and see also why this is so. To me, at least, who have always disliked our Government, but have never adopted either of the above methods of resisting it, the defects of both methods are apparent.

The first method is unsatisfactory, because even could an attempt to alter the existing régime by violent means succeed, there would be no guarantee that the new organization would be durable, and that the enemies of that new order would not, at some convenient opportunity, triumph by using violence such as had been used against them, as has happened over and over again in France and wherever else there have been revolutions. And so the new order of things, established by violence, would have continually to be supported by violence—*i.e.*, by wrong-doing. And, consequently, it would inevitably, and very quickly, be vitiated, like the order it replaced. And in case of failure the violence of the Revolutionists only strengthens the order of things they strive against (as has always been the case, in our Russian experience, from Pougatchéf's rebellion to the attempt of March 1), for it drives the whole crowd of undecided people—who stand wavering between the two parties—into the camp of the conservative and retrograde party. So I think that, guided both by reason and experience, we may boldly say that this means, besides being immoral, is irrational and ineffectual.

The other method is, in my opinion, even less effectual or rational. It is ineffectual and irrational because Government—holding in its grasp the whole power (the army, the administration, the Church, the schools, and the police), and framing what are called the laws on the basis of which the Liberals wish to resist it—this Government knows very well what is really dangerous to it, and will never let people who submit to it and act under its guidance do anything that will undermine its authority. For instance, take the case before us : a Government such as ours, or any other which rests on the ignorance of the people, will never consent to their being really enlightened. It will sanction all kinds of pseudo-educational organizations controlled by itself—schools, high schools, universities, academies, and all kinds of committees and congresses and publications sanctioned by the censor—so long as these organizations and publications serve its purpose—that is, stupefy the people, or at least do not hinder their stupefaction. But as soon as those organizations or publications attempt to cure that on which the power of Government rests (namely, the blindness of the people), the Government will simply, and without rendering any account to anyone, or saying why it acts so and not otherwise, pronounce its veto, and will rearrange or close the establishments and organizations, and forbid the publications. And therefore, as both reason and experience clearly show, such an illusory, gradual conquest of rights is a self-deception which suits the Government admirably, and which it, therefore, is even ready to encourage.

But not only is this activity irrational and ineffectual, it is also harmful. It is harmful because enlightened, good, and honest people by entering the ranks of the Government give it a moral authority which but for them it would not possess. If the Government were made up entirely of that coarse element—the men of violence, self-seekers, and flatterers—who form its core, it could not continue to exist. The fact that honest and enlightened people are found participating in the affairs of the Government gives Government whatever moral prestige it possesses.

That is one evil resulting from the activity of Liberals who participate in the affairs of Government, or who come to terms with it. Another evil of such activity is that to secure opportunities to carry on their work, these highly-enlightened and honest people have to begin to compromise, and so, little by little, come to consider that for a good end one may swerve somewhat from truth in word and deed. For instance, that one may, though not believing in the established Church, take part in its ceremonies; may take oaths; may, when necessary for the success of some affair, present petitions couched in language which is untruthful and derogatory to man's natural dignity; may enter the army; may take part in a Local Government which has been stripped of all its powers; may serve as a master or a professor, teaching not what one considers necessary one's self, but what one is told to teach by the Government; that one may even become a *Zémsky Natchálnik*\* submitting to Governmental demands and instructions which violate one's conscience; may edit newspapers and periodicals, remaining silent about what ought to be mentioned, and printing what one is ordered to print: and entering into these compromises—the limits of which cannot be foreseen—enlightened and honest people, who alone could form some barrier to the infringements of human liberty by the Government,

---

\* During the Reform period, in the reign of Alexander II., many iniquities of the old judicial system were abolished. Among other innovations 'Judges of the Peace' were appointed to act as magistrates. They were elected (indirectly); if possessed of a certain property qualification, men of any class were eligible, and the regulations under which they acted were drawn up in a comparatively liberal spirit. Under Alexander III. the office of 'Judge of the Peace' was abolished, and was replaced by *Zémsky Natchálniks*. Only members of the aristocracy were eligible; they were not elected, but appointed by Government, and they were armed with authority to have peasants flogged.

retreating, little by little, further and further from the demands of conscience, fall at last into a position of complete dependency on the Government. They receive rewards and salaries from it, and, continuing to imagine that they are forwarding Liberal ideas, become the humble servants and supporters of the very order against which they set out to fight.

It is true that there are also better, sincere people in the Liberal camp, whom the Government cannot bribe, and who remain unbought and free from salaries and position. But even these people, having been ensnared in the nets spread by Government, beat their wings in their cages (as you are now doing in your Committee), unable to advance from the spot they are on. Or else, becoming enraged, they go over to the revolutionary camp; or they shoot themselves; or take to drink; or they abandon the whole struggle in despair, and, oftenest of all, retire into literary activity, in which, yielding to the demands of the censor, they say only what they are allowed to say, and by that very silence about what is most important convey to the public distorted views, which just suit the Government. But they continue to imagine that they are serving society by the writings which give them means of subsistence.

Thus, reflection and experience alike show me that both the means of combating Government used heretofore, are not only ineffectual, but actually tend to strengthen the power and irresponsibility of the Government.

What is to be done? Evidently not what for seventy years past has proved fruitless, and has only produced reverse results. What is to be done? Just what those have done, to whose activity we owe the progress towards light and good that has been achieved since the world began, and that is still being achieved to-day. That is what must be done! And what is it?

Merely the simple, quiet, truthful carrying on of what you consider good and needful, quite independently of the Government, or of whether it likes it or not.   In other words : standing up for one's rights, not as a member of the 'Literature Committee,' nor as a deputy, nor as a land-owner, nor as a merchant, nor even as a Member of Parliament ; but standing up for one's rights as a rational and free man, and defending them—not as the rights of Local Boards or Committees are defended, with concessions and compromises, but without any concessions or compromises—in the only way in which moral and human dignity can be defended.

Successfully to defend a fortress, one has to burn all the houses in the suburbs and leave only what is strong, and what you intend not to surrender on any account. Only from the basis of this firm stronghold can we conquer all we require.   True, the rights of a Member of Parliament, or even of a member of a Local Board, are greater than the rights of an ordinary man ; and it seems as though we could do much by using those rights.   But the hitch is that to obtain the rights of a Member of Parliament, or of a committee-man, one has to abandon part of one's rights as a man.   And having abandoned part of one's rights as a man, there is no longer any fixed point of leverage, and one can no longer either conquer or maintain any real right. In order to lift others out of a quagmire one must one's self stand on firm ground ; and if, hoping the better to assist others, you go into the quagmire, you will not pull others out, but will yourself sink in.

It may be very desirable and useful to get an eight-hours' day legalized by Parliament, or to get a Liberal programme for school libraries sanctioned through your Committee ; but if as a means to this end a Member of Parliament must publicly lift up his hand and lie, lie when taking an oath, by expressing in words respect for what he does not respect; or (in our own case) if, in order to pass programmes however Liberal, it is necessary to take part in public worship, to be sworn, to wear a uniform, to write mendacious and flattering petitions, and to make speeches of a similar character, etc., etc.—then, by doing these things and foregoing our dignity as men, we lose much more than we gain, and by trying to reach one definite aim (which very often is not reached) we deprive ourselves of the possibility of reaching other aims which are of supreme importance. Only people who have something which they will on no account and under no circumstances yield can resist a Government and curb it. To have power to resist, you must stand on firm ground.

And the Government knows this very well, and is, above all else, concerned to worm out of men that which will not yield—namely, their dignity as men. When that is wormed out of them, the Government calmly proceeds to do what it likes, knowing that it will no longer meet any real resistance. A man who consents publicly to swear, pronouncing the degrading and mendacious words of the oath ; or submissively to wait several hours, dressed up in a uniform, at a Minister's reception ; or to inscribe himself as a Special Constable for the Coronation ; or to fast and receive Communion for respectability's sake ; or to ask the Head-Censor whether he may, or may not, express such and such thoughts, etc.—such a man is no longer feared by Government.

Alexander II. said he did not fear the Liberals, because he knew they could all be bought—if not with money, then with honours.

People who take part in Government, or work under its direction, may deceive themselves or their sympathizers by making a show of struggling ; but those against whom they struggle (the Government) know quite well, by the strength of the resistance experienced, that these people are not really pulling, but are only pretending to. Our Government knows this with respect to the Liberals, and constantly tests the quality of the opposition, and finding that genuine resistance is practically non-existent, it continues its course in full assurance that it can do what it likes with such opponents.

The Government of Alexander III. knew this very

well, and, knowing it, deliberately destroyed all that the Liberals thought they had achieved, and were so proud of. It altered and limited Trial by Jury; it abolished the office of Judge of the Peace; it cancelled the rights of the Universities; it perverted the whole system of instruction in the High Schools; it re-established the Cadet Corps, and even the State-sale of intoxicants; it established the *Zémsky Natchálniks*; it legalized flogging; it almost abolished the Local Government; it gave uncontrolled power to the Governors of Provinces; it encouraged the quartering of troops on the peasants in punishment; it increased the practice of 'administrative'* banishment and imprisonment, and the capital punishment of political offenders; it renewed religious persecutions; it brought to a climax the use of barbarous superstitions; it legalized murder in duels; under the name of a 'State of Siege'† it established lawlessness with capital punishment as a normal condition of things—and in all this it met with no protest except from one honourable woman,‡ who boldly told the Government the truth as she saw it.

The Liberals whispered among themselves that these things displeased them, but they continued to take part

---

* Sentenced by *Administrative Order* means sentenced by the arbitrary will of the Government, or by the Chief of the Gendarmes of a Province. Administrative sentences are often inflicted without the victim being heard in his own defence, or even knowing what he is punished for.

† The 'Statute of Increased Protection,' usually translated 'State of Siege,' was first applied to Petersburg and Moscow only, but was subsequently extended to Odessa, Kief, Khárkof, and Warsaw. Under this law, practically absolute power, including that of capital punishment, was entrusted to the Governors-General of the Provinces in question.

‡ Madame Tsébrikof, a well-known writer and literary critic, wrote a polite but honest letter to Alexander III., pointing out what was being done by the Government. She was banished to a distant province.

in legal proceedings, and in the Local Governments, and in the Universities, and in Government service, and on the Press. In the Press they hinted at what they were allowed to hint at, and kept silence on matters they had to be silent about, but they printed whatever they were told to print. So that every reader (not privy to the whisperings of the editorial rooms), on receiving a Liberal paper or magazine, read the announcement of the most cruel and irrational measures unaccompanied by comment or sign of disapproval, together with sycophantic and flattering addresses to those guilty of enacting these measures, and frequently even praise of the measures themselves. Thus all the dismal activity of the Government of Alexander III.—destroying whatever good had begun to take root in the days of Alexander II., and striving to turn Russia back to the barbarity of the commencement of this century—all this dismal activity of gallows, rods, persecutions, and stupefaction of the people, has become (even in the Liberal papers and magazines) the basis of an insane laudation of Alexander III. and of his acclamation as a great man and a model of human dignity.

This same thing is being continued in the new reign. The young man who succeeded the late Tsar, having no understanding of life, was assured by the men in power, to whom it was profitable to say so, that the best way to rule a hundred million people is to do as his father did—that is, not to ask advice from anyone, but to do just what comes into his head, or what the first flatterer about him advises. And, fancying that unlimited autocracy is a sacred life-principle of the Russian people, the young man begins to reign ; and instead of asking the representatives of the Russian people to help him with their advice in the task of ruling (about which he, educated in a cavalry regiment, knows nothing and can know nothing), he rudely and insolently shouts at those representatives of the Russian people who visit him with congratulations, and he calls the desire, timidly expressed by some of them,* to be allowed to inform the authorities of their needs, 'insensate dreams.'

And what followed? Was Russian society shocked? Did enlightened and honest people—the Liberals—express their indignation and repulsion? Did they at least refrain from laudation of this Government, and from participating in it and encouraging it? Not at all. From that time a specially intense competition in adulation commenced, both of the father and of the son who imitated him. And not a protesting voice was heard, except in one anonymous letter, cautiously expressing disapproval of the young Tsar's conduct. From all sides fulsome and flattering addresses were brought to the Tsar, as well as (for some reason or other) icóns† which nobody wanted and which serve merely as objects of idolatry to benighted people. An insane expenditure of money: a Coronation amazing in its absurdity, was arranged; the arrogance of the rulers and their contempt of the people caused thousands to perish in a fearful calamity—which was regarded as a slight eclipse of the festivities, which did not terminate on that account.‡ An exhibition§ was organized, which no one wanted except those who organized it, and which cost millions of roubles. In the Chancellery of the Holy Synod, with unparalleled effrontery, a new

* By the representatives of the Local Government of Tver and others, at a reception in the Winter Palace on the accession of Nicholas II.

† Icóns are conventional paintings of God, Jesus, angels, saints, the 'Mother of God,' etc., usually done on bits of wood, with much gilding. They are hung up in the corners of the rooms, as well as in churches, etc., to be prayed to.

‡ As part of the Coronation festivities, a 'People's Fête' was arranged to take place on the Hodínskoe Field, near Moscow. Owing to bad arrangements, some 3,000 people were killed when trying to enter the grounds, and many others were injured. This occurred on Saturday, May 18, o.s., 1896. That same evening the Emperor danced at the grand ball given by the French Ambassador in Moscow.

§ The unsuccessful Exhibition at Nízhni Nóvgorod in 1896.

and supremely stupid means of mystifying people was devised—namely, the enshrinement of the incorruptible body of a Saint whom nobody knew anything about.* The stringency of the Censor was increased. Religious persecution was made more severe. The State of Siege (*i.e.*, the legalization of lawlessness) was continued, and the state of things is still becoming worse and worse.

And I think that all this would not have happened if those enlightened, honest people who are now occupied in Liberal activity on the basis of legality, in Local Governments, in the Committees, in Censor-ruled literature, etc., had not devoted their energies to the task of circumventing the Government and—without abandoning the forms it has itself arranged—of finding ways to make it act so as to harm and injure itself :† but, abstaining from taking any part in Government or in any business bound up with Government, had merely claimed their rights as men.

'You wish, instead of Judges of the Peace, to institute *Zémsky Natchálniks* with birch-rods : that is your business, but we will not go to law before your *Zémsky Natchálniks*, and will not ourselves accept appointment to such an office. You wish to make trial by jury a mere formality : that is your business, but we will not serve as judges, or as advocates, or as jurymen. You wish, under the name of a "State of Siege," to establish despotism : that is your business, but we will not participate in it, and will plainly call the "State of Siege"

* The 'incorruptible' body of St. Theodosius was exhibited to the people and to the pilgrims who assembled from all parts of Russia, and was then enshrined with great pomp in the Cathedral of Tchernígof in 1896. These relics performed miracles, which were fully reported in the official papers, and no papers ventured to express any doubts as to the genuine nature of these occurrences.

† Sometimes it seems to me simply laughable that people can occupy themselves with such an evidently hopeless business ; it is like undertaking to cut off an animal's leg without letting it notice it.—L. T.

despotism, and capital punishment inflicted without trial—murder. You wish to organize Cadet Corps, or Classical High Schools in which military exercises and the Orthodox Faith are taught : that is your affair, but we will not teach in such schools, nor send our children to them, but will educate our children as seems to us right. You decide to reduce the Local Governments to impotence : we will not take part in them. You prohibit the publication of literature that displeases you : you may seize books and punish the printers, but you cannot prevent our speaking and writing, and we shall continue to do so. You demand an oath of allegiance to the Tsar : we will not accede to what is so stupid, false, and degrading. You order us to serve in the army : we will not do so, because wholesale murder is as opposed to our conscience as individual murder, and, above all, because to promise to murder whomsoever a commander may tell us to murder is the meanest act a man can commit. You profess a religion which is a thousand years behind the times, with an "Iberian Mother of God"* relics, and coronations: that is your affair, but we do not acknowledge idolatry and superstition to be religion, but call them idolatry and superstition, and we try to free people from them.'

And what can the Government do against such activity? It can banish or imprison a man for preparing a bomb, or even for printing a proclamation to working men ; it can transfer your Literature Committee from one Ministry to another, or close a Parliament ; but what can a Government do with a man who is not willing publicly to lie with uplifted hand, or who is not willing to send his children to an establishment which he considers bad, or who is not willing to learn to kill people, or is not willing to take part in idolatry, or is not willing to take part in coronations, deputa-

---

* ' The Iberian Mother of God ' in Moscow is a wonder-working icón of the Virgin Mary, which draws a large revenue. It is frequently taken to visit the sick, and travels about with six horses ; the attendant priest sits in the carriage bareheaded.

tions and addresses, or who says and writes what he thinks and feels? By prosecuting such a man the Government secures for him general sympathy, making him a martyr, and it undermines the foundations on which it is itself built, for, in so acting, instead of protecting human rights it itself infringes them.

And it is only necessary for all those good, enlightened, and honest people whose strength is now wasted in Revolutionary, Socialistic, or Liberal activity (harmful to themselves and to their cause) to begin to act thus, and a nucleus of honest, enlightened, and moral people would form around them, united in the same thoughts and the same feelings. And to this nucleus the ever-wavering crowd of average people would at once gravitate, and public opinion—the only power which subdues Governments—would become evident, demanding freedom of speech, freedom of conscience, justice and humanity. And as soon as public opinion was formulated, not only would it be impossible to suppress the Literature Committee, but all those inhuman organizations—the 'State of Siege,' the Secret Police, the Censor, Schlüsselburg,* the Holy Synod, and the rest—against which the Revolutionists and the Liberals are now struggling, would disappear of themselves.

So that two methods of opposing the Government have been tried, both unsuccessfully, and it now remains to try a third and last method, one not yet tried, but one which, I think, cannot but be successful. Briefly, it is this: That all enlightened and honest people should try to be as good as they can; and not even good in all respects but only in one, namely, in observing one of the most elementary virtues—to be honest and not to lie, but so to act and speak that your motives should be intelligible to an affectionate seven-year-old boy; to act so that your boy should not say: 'But why, papa, did you say so-and-so, and now you do and say something quite different?' This method

* The most terrible of the places of imprisonment in Petersburg.

seems very weak, and yet I am convinced that it is this method, and this method alone, that has moved humanity since the race began. Only because there were straight men—truthful and courageous, who made no concessions that infringed their dignity as men— have all those beneficent revolutions been accomplished of which mankind now has the advantage—from the abolition of torture and slavery up to liberty of speech and of conscience. Nor can this be otherwise, for what is demanded by conscience (the highest fore-feeling man possesses of the truth to which he can attain) is always and in all respects the thing most fruitful and most necessary for humanity at the given time. Only a man who lives according to his conscience can exert influence on people, and only activity that accords with one's conscience can be useful.

But I must make my meaning quite plain. To say that the most effectual means of achieving the ends towards which Revolutionists and Liberals are striving is by activity in accord with their consciences, does not mean that people can begin to live conscientiously in order to achieve those ends. To begin to live conscientiously on purpose to achieve external ends is impossible.

To live according to one's conscience is possible only as a result of firm and clear religious convictions; the beneficent result of these on our external life will inevitably follow. Therefore the gist of what I wished to say to you is this : That it is unprofitable for good, sincere people to spend their powers of mind and soul on gaining small practical ends—for instance, in the various struggles of nationalities, or parties, or in Liberal wire-pulling—while they have not reached a clear and firm religious perception, that is, a conscious-ness of the meaning and purpose of life. I think that all the powers of soul and mind of good men, who wish to be of service to humanity, should be directed to that end. When that is accomplished all else will also be accomplished.

Forgive me for sending you so long a letter, which

perhaps you did not at all need, but I have long wished to express my views on this question. I even began a long article about it, but I shall hardly have time to finish it before death comes, and therefore I wished to get at least part of it said. Forgive me if I am in error about anything.

[August 31, o.s., 1896.]

## XV

## TIMOTHY BÓNDAREF

How strange and odd it would have seemed to the educated Romans of the middle of the first century, had anyone told them that the obscure, confused, and often unintelligible letters addressed by a wandering Jew to his friends and pupils would have a hundred, a thousand, a hundred thousand times more readers, more circulation, and more influence over people, than all the poems, odes, elegies, and elegant epistles of the authors of that age! And yet that is what has happened.

Equally strange and odd must my assertion seem to people to-day, that Bóndaref's work—at the naïveté of which we condescendingly smile from the height of our mental grandeur—will survive all the other works described in this Dictionary, and have more effect on people than all the other books mentioned in it put together. And yet I am convinced that such will be the case. And the reason of my conviction is, that just as there are an innumerable quantity of false paths that lead nowhere and are therefore unnecessary, but only one true path that leads us to our aim and is therefore necessary, so also there are an innumerable quantity of false, unnecessary thoughts, but only one true and needful thought, or, rather, direction of thought ; and that true and needful direction of thought in our time has been expressed by Bóndaref in his book, with a force, clearness and conviction with which no one else has expressed it. Therefore, the many works that now seem so important and necessary may vanish completely and be forgotten; but what Bóndaref has said, and that to which he has called men, will not be forgotten —for life itself will bring men more and more to see the force of his statements.

All discoveries of truth, whether in science (abstract or applied), in philosophy, in morals, or in economics, are reached by people going round the new truths in ever-narrowing circles, drawing nearer and nearer to them, and sometimes slightly touching them, until some bold, free, and gifted man seizes the very centre of the new truth, and places it on a height where it is visible to all. This is just what Bóndaref has done for the moral-economic truth which was awaiting discovery and elucidation in our time. Many have said, and are saying, the same thing. Some consider physical labour necessary for health; others consider it essential for a just economic order; a third group show its necessity for the normal, all-round development of man's capacities; while a fourth group considers it essential for man's moral progress. Thus, for instance, Ruskin— one of the greatest English writers, and one of the greatest authors of our age (almost as little esteemed as our own Bóndaref by the cultured crowd of to-day) —notwithstanding the fact that he is a most highly educated and refined man (*i.e.*, notwithstanding the fact that he stands at the opposite pole of society from Bóndaref), in Letter 67 of his *Fors Clavigera*, says:— '*It is physically impossible that true religious knowledge, or pure morality, should exist among any classes of a nation who do not work with their hands for their bread.*'

Many go round this truth and express it (as Ruskin does) with various reservations, but no one else has done what Bóndaref does in acknowledging bread-labour to be the fundamental religious law of life. And he has not done this, as it pleases people to suppose, because he is an ignorant and foolish man who does not know all that we know; but he has done it because he is a man of genius, who knows that truth is only *then* the truth, when it is expressed, not with limitations, reservations and retrenchments, but when it is expressed fully. As the truth that the sum of the angles in a right-angled triangle is equal to two right angles, loses all meaning and importance if it is expressed thus : that the sum of the angles in the triangle will be approximately equal to two right angles—so also the truth that a man ought to work with his hands, if expressed in the form of advice, or of an expression of its desirability, or of an assertion that perhaps it may be useful from certain points of view, etc., loses all its meaning and importance. This truth has meaning and importance only when it is expressed as an absolute law, the infringement of which involves inevitable ills and sufferings, and the observance of which is demanded of us by God, or by reason—as Bóndaref expresses it. Bóndaref does not demand that every man should absolutely put on peasant's shoes and follow the plough, though he says that that would be desirable and would liberate people sunk in luxury from the delusions that torment them (really, nothing but good would come from exact obedience even to that demand) ; but Bóndaref says that every man should consider the duty of physical labour—of direct participation in those labours of which he enjoys the fruits— as his first, chief, and indubitably sacred obligation, and that people should be brought up to recognise that duty. And I cannot conceive how any honest and thoughtful person can disagree with that opinion.

[1897.]

The above article was contributed to Vengérof's *Biographical Dictionary of Russian Writers*. Concerning Bóndaref, see foot-note, p. 1, of this volume.

# LETTERS ON HENRY GEORGE

I.

*To T. M. Bóndaref, who had written from Siberia asking for information about the Single-Tax.*

This is Henry George's plan:

The advantage and convenience of using land is not everywhere the same; there will always be many applicants for land that is fertile, well situated, or near a populous place; and the better and more profitable the land, the more people will wish to have it. All such land should, therefore, be valued according to its advantages: the more profitable—dearer; the less profitable—cheaper. Land for which there are few applicants should not be valued at all, but allotted gratuitously to those who wish to work it themselves.

With such a valuation of the land—here in the Toúla Government, for instance,—good arable land might be estimated at about 5 or 6 roubles* the desyatína;† kitchen-gardens in the villages, at about 10 roubles the desyatína; meadows that are fertilized by spring floods at about 15 roubles, and so on. In towns the valuation would be 100 to 500 roubles the desyatína, and in crowded parts of Moscow or Petersburg, or at the landing-places of navigable rivers, it would amount to several thousands or even tens of thousands of roubles the desyatína.

* The rouble is a little more than 25 pence.
† The desyatína is nearly 2¾ acres.

When all the land in the country has been valued in this way, Henry George proposes that a law should be made by which, after a certain date in a certain year, the land should no longer belong to any one individual, but to the whole nation—the whole people ; and that everyone holding land should, therefore, pay to the nation (that is, to the whole people) the yearly value at which it has been assessed. This payment should be used to meet all public or national expenses, and should replace all other rates, taxes, or customs dues.

The result of this would be that a landed proprietor who now holds, say, 2,000 desyatína, might continue to hold them if he liked, but he would have to pay to the treasury—here in the Toúla Government, for instance (as his holding would include both meadow-land and homestead)—12,000 or 15,000 roubles a year ; and, as no large land-owners could stand such a payment, they would all abandon their land. But it would mean that a Toúla peasant, in the same district, would pay a couple of roubles per desyatína less than he pays now, and could have plenty of available land near by, which he would take up at 5 or 6 roubles per desyatína. Besides, he would have no other rates or taxes to pay, and would be able to buy all the things he requires, foreign or Russian, free of duty. In towns, the owners of houses and manufactories might continue to own them, but would have to pay to the public treasury the amount of the assessment on their land.

The advantages of such an arrangement would be :

1. That no one will be unable to get land for use.

2. That there will be no idle people owning land and making others work for them in return for permission to use that land.

3. That the land will be in the possession of those who use it, and not of those who do not use it.

4. That as the land will be available for people who wish to work on it, they will cease to enslave themselves as hands in factories and works, or as servants in towns, and will settle in the country districts.

5. That there will be no more inspectors and collectors of taxes in mills, factories, refineries and workshops, but there will only be collectors of the tax on land which cannot be stolen, and from which a tax can be most easily collected.

6 (and chiefly). That the non-workers will be saved from the sin of exploiting other people's labour (in doing which they are often not the guilty parties, for they have from childhood been educated in idleness, and do not know how to work), and from the yet greater sin of all kinds of shuffling and lying to justify themselves in commiting that sin ; and the workers will be saved from the temptation and sin of envying, condemning and being exasperated with the non-workers, so that one cause of separation among men will be destroyed.

II.

*To a German Propagandist of Henry George's Views.*

It is with particular pleasure that I hasten to answer your letter, and say that I have known of Henry George since the appearance of his *Social Problems*. I read that book and was struck by the justice of his main thought—by the exceptional manner (unparalleled in scientific literature), clear, popular and forcible, in which he stated his cause—and especially by (what is also exceptional in scientific literature) the Christian spirit that permeates the whole work. After reading it I went back to his earlier *Progress and Poverty*, and still more deeply appreciated the importance of its author's activity.

You ask what I think of Henry George's activity, and of his Single-Tax system. My opinion is the following :

Humanity constantly advances: on the one hand clearing its consciousness and conscience, and on the other hand rearranging its modes of life to suit this changing consciousness. Thus, at each period of the life of humanity, the double process goes on : the clearing up of conscience, and the incorporation into life of what has been made clear to conscience.

At the end of the eighteenth century and the commencement of the nineteenth, a clearing up of conscience took place in Christendom with reference to the labouring classes—who lived under various forms of slavery—and this was followed by a corresponding readjustment of the forms of social life, to suit this clearer consciousness : namely, the abolition of slavery, and the organization of free wage-labour in its place. At the present time an enlightenment of men's consciences is going on in relation to the way land is used ; and soon, it seems to me, a practical application of this new consciousness must follow.

And in this process (the enlightenment of conscience as to the utilization of land, and the practical application of that new consciousness), which is one of the chief problems of our time, the leader and organizer of the movement was and is Henry George. In this lies his immense, his pre-eminent, importance. He has helped by his excellent books, both to clear men's minds and consciences on this question, and to place it on a practical footing.

But in relation to the abolition of the shameful right to own landed estates, something is occurring similar to what happened (within our own recollection) with reference to the abolition of serfdom. The Government and the governing classes—knowing that their position and privileges are bound up with the land question—pretend that they are preoccupied with the welfare of the people, organizing savings banks for workmen, factory inspection, income taxes, even eight-hours working days—and carefully ignore the land question, or even, aided by compliant science, which will demonstrate anything they like, declare that the expropriation of the land is useless, harmful, and impossible.

Just the same thing occurs, as occurred in connection with slavery. At the end of the eighteenth and the beginning of the nineteenth centuries, men had long felt that slavery was a terrible anachronism, revolting to the human soul; but pseudo-religion and pseudo-science demonstrated that slavery was not wrong, that it was necessary, or at least that it was premature to abolish it. The same thing is now being repeated with reference to landed property. As before, pseudo-religion and pseudo-science demonstrate that there is nothing wrong in the private ownership of landed estates, and that there is no need to abolish the present system.

One would think it would be plain to every educated man of our time that an exclusive control of land by people who do not work on it, but who prevent hundreds and thousands of poor families from using it, is a thing as plainly bad and shameful as it was to own slaves; yet we see educated, refined aristocrats—English, Austrian, Prussian, and Russian—making use of this cruel and shameful right, and not only not feeling ashamed, but feeling proud of it.

Religion blesses such possessions, and the science of political economy demonstrates that the present state of things is the one that should exist for the greatest benefit of mankind.

The service rendered by Henry George is, that he has not only mastered the sophistries with which religion and science try to justify private ownership of land, and simplified the question to the uttermost, so that it is impossible not to admit the wrongfulness of land-ownership—unless one simply stops one's ears—but he was also the first to show how the question can be practically solved. He first gave a clear and direct reply to the excuses, used by the enemies of every reform, to the effect that the demands of progress are unpractical and inapplicable dreams.

Henry George's plan destroys that excuse, by putting the question in such a form that a committee might be assembled to-morrow to discuss the project and to convert it into law. In Russia, for instance, the discussion of land purchase, or of nationalizing the land without compensation, could begin to-morrow; and the project might—after undergoing various vicissitudes—

be carried into operation, as occurred thirty-three years ago* with the project for the emancipation of the serfs.

The need of altering the present system has been explained, and the possibility of the change has been shown (there may be alterations and amendments of the Single-Tax system, but its fundamental idea is practicable); and, therefore, it will be impossible for people not to do what their reason demands. It is only necessary that this thought should become public opinion; and in order that it may become public opinion it must be spread abroad and explained— which is just what you are doing, and is a work with which I sympathize with my whole soul, and in which I wish you success.

[1897.]

* The Emancipation of the Serfs in Russia was decreed in 1861, and was accomplished during the following few years.

# XVII

## MODERN SCIENCE*

*παντὶ λόγῳ λόγος ἴσος ἀντικεῖται.†*

I THINK this article of Carpenter's on Modern Science should be particularly useful in Russian society, in which, more than in any other in Europe, a superstition is prevalent and deeply rooted which considers that humanity for its welfare does not need the diffusion of true religious and moral knowledge, but only the study of experimental science, and that such science will satisfy all the spiritual demands of mankind.

It is evident how harmful an influence (quite like that of religious superstition) so gross a superstition must have on men's moral life. And, therefore, the publication of the thoughts of writers who treat experimental science and its method critically is specially desirable in our society.

Carpenter shows that neither Astronomy, nor Physics, nor Chemistry, nor Biology, nor Sociology, supplies us with true knowledge of actual facts; that all the laws discovered by those sciences are merely generalizations, having but an approximate value as laws, and *that* only as long as we do not know, or leave

---

* Written as preface to a Russian translation, by Count Sergius Tolstoy, of Edward Carpenter's essay, *Modern Science: a Criticism*, which forms part of the volume *Civilization: its Cause and Cure*, published by Swan Sonnenschein and Co., London.

† To every argument an equal argument is matched.

out of account, certain other factors ; and that even these laws seem laws to us only because we discover them in a region so far away from us in time and space that we cannot detect their non-correspondence with actual fact.

Moreover, Carpenter points out that the method of science, which consists in explaining things near and important to us by things more remote and indifferent, is a false method which can never bring us to the desired result.

He says that every science tries to explain the facts it is investigating by means of conceptions of a lower order. 'Each science has been (as far as possible) reduced to its lowest terms. Ethics has been made a question of utility and inherited experience. Political Economy has been exhausted of all conceptions of justice between man and man, of charity, affection, and the instinct of solidarity, and has been founded on its lowest discoverable factor, namely, self-interest. Biology has been denuded of the force of personality in plants, animals, and men ; the 'self' here has been set aside, and the attempt made to reduce the science to a question of chemical and cellular affinities, protoplasm, and the laws of osmose. Chemical affinities, again, and all the wonderful phenomena of Physics are emptied down into a flight of atoms ; and the flight of atoms (and of astronomic orbs as well) is reduced to the laws of dynamics.'

It is supposed that the reduction of questions of a higher order to questions of a lower order will explain the former. But an explanation is never obtained in this way, and what happens is merely that, descending in one's investigations ever lower and lower, from the most important questions to less important ones, science reaches at last a sphere quite foreign to man, with which he is barely in touch, and confines its attention to that sphere, leaving all unsolved the questions most important to him.

What takes place is as if a man, wishing to understand the use of an object lying before him—instead of coming close to it, examining it from all sides and handling it—were to retire further and further from it, until he was at such a distance from the object that all its peculiarities of colour and inequalities of surface had disappeared, and only its outline was still visible against the horizon ; and as if, from there, he were to begin writing a minute description of the object, imagining that now, at last, he clearly understood it, and that this understanding, formed at such a distance, would assist a complete comprehension of it. And it is this self-deception that is partly exposed by Carpenter's criticism, which shows, first, that the knowledge afforded us by the natural sciences amounts merely to convenient generalizations, which certainly do not express actual facts ; and, secondly, that the method of science by which facts of a higher order are reduced to facts of a lower order, will never furnish us with an explanation of the former.

But without predetermining the question whether experimental science will, or will not, by its methods, ever bring us to the solution of the most serious problems of human life, the activity of experimental science itself, in its relation to the eternal and most reasonable demands of man, is so anomalous as to amaze one.

People must live. But in order to live they must know how to live. And all men always obtained this knowledge—well or ill—and in conformity with it have lived, and progressed ; and this knowledge of how men should live has from the days of Moses, Solon, and Confucius been always considered a science—the very essence of science. And only in our time has it come to be considered that the science telling us how to live, is not a science at all, but that only experimental science—commencing with Mathematics and ending in Sociology—is real science.

And a strange misunderstanding results.

A plain, reasonable working man supposes, in the old way which is also the common-sense way, that if there are people who spend their lives in study, whom he feeds and keeps while they think for him—then no doubt these men are engaged in studying things men need to know; and he expects of science that it will solve for him the questions on which his welfare, and that of all men, depends. He expects science to tell him how he ought to live: how to treat his family, his neighbours and the men of other tribes, how to restrain his passions, what to believe in and what not to believe in, and much else. And what does our science say to him on these matters?

It triumphantly tells him: how many million miles it is from the earth to the sun; at what rate light travels through space; how many million vibrations of ether per second are caused by light, and how many vibrations of air by sound; it tells of the chemical components of the Milky Way, of a new element—helium—of micro-organisms and their excrements, of the points on the hand at which electricity collects, of X rays, and similar things.

'But I don't want any of those things,' says a plain and reasonable man—'I want to know how to live.'

'What does it matter what you want?' replies science. 'What you are asking about relates to Sociology. Before replying to sociological questions, we have yet to solve questions of Zoology, Botany, Physiology, and, in general, of Biology; but to solve those questions we have first to solve questions of Physics, and then of Chemistry, and have also to agree as to the shape of the infinitesimal atoms, and how it is that imponderable and incompressible ether transmits energy.'

And people—chiefly those who sit on the backs of others, and to whom it is therefore convenient to wait —are content with such replies, and sit blinking, awaiting the fulfilment of these promises; but a plain and reasonable working man—such as those on whose backs these others sit while occupying themselves with science —the whole great mass of men, the whole of humanity, cannot be satisfied by such answers, but naturally ask in perplexity : ' But when will this be done ?   We cannot wait.   You say yourselves that you will discover these things after some generations.   But we are alive now—alive to-day and dead to-morrow—and we want to know how to live our life while we have it.   So teach us !'

' What a stupid and uneducated man !' replies science. ' He does not understand that science exists not for use, but for *science*.   Science studies whatever presents itself for study, and cannot select the subjects to be studied. Science studies *everything*.   That is the characteristic of science.'

And scientists are really convinced that to be occupied with trifles, while neglecting what is more essential and important, is a characteristic not of themselves, but of science.   The plain, reasonable man, however, begins to suspect that this characteristic pertains not to science, but to men who are inclined to occupy themselves with trifles and to attach great importance to those trifles.

' Science studies *everything*,' say the scientists.   But, really, *everything* is too much.   Everything is an infinite quantity of objects ;  it is impossible at one and the same time to study *all*.   As a lantern cannot light up everything, but only lights up the place on which it is turned or the direction in which the man carrying it is walking, so also science cannot study everything, but inevitably only studies that to which its attention is directed.   And as a lantern lights up most strongly the place nearest to it, and less and less strongly objects that are more and more remote from it, and does not at all light up those things its light does not reach, so also human science, of whatever kind, has always studied and still studies most carefully what seems most important to the investigators, less carefully what seems to them less important, and quite neglects the whole remaining infinite quantity of objects.   And what for men has defined and still defines the subjects they are to consider most important, less important, and unimportant, is the general understanding of the meaning and purpose of life (that is to say, the religion) possessed by those who occupy themselves with science. But men of science to-day—not acknowledging any religion, and having therefore no standard by which to choose the subjects most important for study, or to discriminate them from less important subjects and, ultimately, from that infinite quantity of objects which the limitations of the human mind, and the infinity of the number of those objects, will always cause to remain uninvestigated—have formed for themselves a theory of 'science for science's sake,' according to which science is to study not what mankind needs, but *everything*.

And, indeed, experimental science studies every-thing, not in the sense of the totality of objects, but in the sense of disorder—chaos in the arrangement of the objects studied.   That is to say, science does not devote most attention to what people most need, less to what they need less, and none at all to what is quite useless, but it studies anything that happens to come to hand. Though Comte's and other classifications of the sciences exist, these classifications do not govern the selection of subjects for study, but that selection is dependent on the human weaknesses common to men of science as well as to the rest of mankind.   So that, in reality, scientists study not *everything*, as they imagine and de-clare, but they study what is more profitable and easier to study.   And it is more profitable to study things that conduce to the well-being of the upper classes, with whom the men of science are connected ; and it is easier to study things that lack life.   Accordingly, many men of science study books, monuments, and inanimate bodies.

Such study is considered the most real 'science.' So that in our day what is considered to be the most real 'science,' the only one (as the Bible was considered the only book worthy of the name), is, not the con-templation and investigation of how to make the life of

man more kindly and more happy, but the compilation
and copying from many books into one of all that our
predecessors wrote on a certain subject, the pouring of
liquids out of one glass bottle into another, the skilful
slicing of microscopic preparations, the cultivation of
bacteria, the cutting up of frogs and dogs, the investigation of X rays, the theory of numbers, the chemical
composition of the stars, etc.

Meanwhile all those sciences which aim at making
human life kindlier and happier—religious, moral, and
social science—are considered by the dominant science
to be unscientific, and are abandoned to the theologians,
philosophers, jurists, historians, and political economists ; who, under the guise of scientific investigation,
are chiefly occupied in demonstrating that the existing
order of society (the advantages of which they enjoy)
is the very one which ought to exist, and that, therefore, it must not only not be changed, but must be
maintained by all means.

Not to mention Theology and Jurisprudence,
Political Economy, the most advanced of the sciences
of this group, is remarkable in this respect. The most
prevalent Political Economy (that of Karl Marx),*
accepting the existing order of life as though it were
what it ought to be, not only does not call on men to
alter that order—that is to say, does not point out to
them how they ought to live that their condition may
improve—but, on the contrary, it demands an increase
in the cruelty of the existing order of things, that its
more-than-questionable predictions may be fulfilled,
concerning what will happen if people continue to live
as badly as they are now living.

And, as always occurs, the lower a human activity
descends—the more widely it diverges from what it
should be—the more its self-confidence increases. That

---

* In Russia the rigid theories of Karl Marx, and the
German type of Social Democracy, have had, and still have,
more vogue than in England.

P

is just what has happened with the science of to-day. True science is never appreciated by its contemporaries, but on the contrary is usually persecuted. Nor can this be otherwise. True science shows men their mistakes, and points to new, unaccustomed ways of life. And both these services are unpleasant to the ruling section of society. But present-day science not only does not run counter to the tastes and demands of the ruling section of society, but it quite complies with them: it satisfies idle curiosity, excites people's wonder, and promises them increase of pleasure. And so, whereas all that is truly great is calm, modest and unnoticed, the science of to-day knows no limits to its self-laudation.

'All former methods were erroneous, and all that used to be considered science was an imposture, a blunder, and of no account. Only our method is true, and the only true science is ours. The success of our science is such that thousands of years have not done what we have accomplished in the last century. In the future, travelling the same path, our science will solve all questions, and make all mankind happy. Our science is the most important activity in the world, and we, men of science, are the most important and necessary people in the world.'

So think and say the scientists of to-day, and the cultured crowd echo it, but really at no previous time and among no people has science—the whole of science with all its knowledge—stood on so low a level as at present. One part of it, which should study the things that make human life kind and happy, is occupied in justifying the existing evil order of society; another part is engaged in solving questions of idle curiosity.

'What?—Idle curiosity?' I hear voices ask in indignation at such blasphemy. 'What about steam, and electricity, and telephones, and all our technical improvements? Not to speak of their scientific importance, see what practical results they have produced! Man has conquered Nature and subjugated its forces' . . . with more to the same effect.

'But all the practical results of the victories over Nature have till now—for a considerable time past—gone to factories that injure the workmen's health; have produced weapons to kill men with, and increased luxury and corruption'—replies a plain, reasonable man—'and, therefore, the victory of man over Nature has not only failed to increase the welfare of human beings, but has, on the contrary, made their condition worse.'

If the arrangement of society is bad (as ours is), and a small number of people have power over the majority and oppress it, every victory over Nature will inevitably only serve to increase that power and that oppression. That is what is actually happening.

With a science which aims not at studying how people ought to live, but at studying whatever exists—and which is therefore occupied chiefly in investigating inanimate things while allowing the order of human society to remain as it is—no improvements, no victories over Nature, can better the state of humanity.

'But medical science? You are forgetting the beneficent progress made by medicine. And bacteriological inoculations? And recent surgical operations?' exclaim the defenders of science,—adducing as a last resource the success of medical science to prove the utility of all science. 'By inoculations we can prevent illness, or can cure it; we can perform painless operations: cut open a man's inside and clean it out, and can straighten hunched-backs,' is what is usually said by the defenders of present-day science, who seem to think that the curing of one child from diphtheria, among those Russian children of whom 50 per cent. (and even 80 per cent. in the Foundling Hospitals) die as a regular thing apart from diphtheria—must convince anyone of the beneficence of science in general.

Our life is so arranged that from bad food, excessive and harmful work, bad dwellings and clothes, or from want, not children only, but a majority of people, die before they have lived half the years that should be

P 2

theirs. The order of things is such that children's ill-nesses, consumption, syphilis and alcoholism seize an ever-increasing number of victims, while a great part of men's labour is taken from them to prepare for wars, and every ten or twenty years millions of men are slaughtered in wars; and all this because science, instead of supplying correct religious, moral and social ideas, which would cause these ills to disappear of themselves, is occupied on the one hand in justifying the existing order, and on the other hand—with toys. And, in proof of the fruitfulness of science, we are told that it cures one in a thousand of the sick, who are sick only because science has neglected its proper business.

Yes, if science would devote but a small part of those efforts, and of that attention and labour which it now spends on trifles, to supplying men with correct re-ligious, moral, social, or even hygienic ideas, there would not be a one-hundredth part of the diphtheria, the diseases of the womb, or the deformities, the occa-sional cure of which now makes science so proud, though they are effected in clinical hospitals, the cost of whose luxurious appointments is too great for them to be at the service of all who need them.

It is as though men who had ploughed badly, and sown badly with poor seeds, were to go over the ground tending some broken ears of corn and trampling on others that grew alongside, and should then exhibit their skill in healing the injured ears, as a proof of their knowledge of agriculture.

Our science, in order to become science and to be really useful and not harmful to humanity, must first of all renounce its experimental method, which causes it to consider as its duty the study merely of what exists, and must return to the only reasonable and fruitful conception of science, which is, that the object of science is to show how people ought to live. Therein lies the aim and importance of science; and the study of things as they exist can only be a subject for science in so far as that study co-operates towards the know-ledge of how men should live.

It is just to the admission of its bankruptcy by experimental science, and to the need of adopting another method, that Carpenter draws attention in this article.

[1898.]

Chapter xx. of *What is Art?* forms a companion article to the above essay. They were both written at the same period and deal with the same topic.

# XVIII

## LETTER TO A NON-COMMISSIONED OFFICER

You are surprised that soldiers are taught that it is right to kill people in certain cases and in war, while in the books admitted to be holy by those who so teach, there is nothing like such a permission, but, on the contrary, not only is all murder forbidden but all insulting of others is forbidden also, and we are told not to do to others what we do not wish done to us. And you ask, Is there not some fraud in all this? And if so, then for whose sake is it committed?

Yes, there is a fraud, committed for the sake of those accustomed to live on the sweat and blood of other men, and who therefore have perverted, and still pervert, Christ's teaching, given to man for his good, but which has now, in its perverted form, become a chief source of human misery.

The thing has come about in this way:

The Government and all those of the upper classes near the Government who live by other people's work, need some means of dominating the workers, and find this means in the control of the army. Defence against foreign enemies is only an excuse. The German Government frightens its subjects about the Russians and the French; the French Government frightens its people about the Germans; the Russian Government frightens its people about the French and the Germans; and that is the way with all Governments. But neither Germans nor Russians nor Frenchmen desire to fight their neighbours or other people; but, living in peace, they dread war more than anything else in the world. The Government and the upper, governing classes, to excuse their domination of the labourers, behave like a gipsy who whips his horse before he turns a corner and then pretends he cannot hold it in. They stir up their own people and some foreign Government, and then pretend that for the well-being, or the defence, of their people they must declare war: which again brings profit only to generals, officers, officials, merchants, and, in general, to the rich. In reality war is an inevitable result of the existence of armies; and armies are only needed by Governments to dominate their own working classes.

The thing is a crime, but the worst of it is that the Government, in order to have a plausible basis for its domination of the people, has to pretend that it holds the highest religious teaching known to man (the Christian), and that it brings up its subjects in this teaching. That teaching, however, is in its very nature opposed not only to murder but to all violence, and therefore the Governments, in order to dominate the people and to be considered Christian, had to pervert Christianity and to hide its true meaning from the people, and thus deprive men of the well-being Christ offered them.

This perversion was accomplished long ago, in the time of that scoundrel the Emperor Constantine, who for doing it was enrolled among the saints.* All subsequent Governments, especially our Russian Government, do their utmost to preserve this perverted understanding, and to prevent people from seeing the real meaning of Christianity; because having once seen the real meaning of Christianity, the people would perceive that the Governments, with their taxes, soldiers, prisons, gallows, and false priests, are not only not the pillars of Christianity they profess to be, but are its greatest enemies.

In consequence of this perversion, those frauds which

* Constantine the Great was decreed to be a god by the Roman Senate, and was made a Christian saint by the Eastern Church.

have surprised you are possible, and all those terrible misfortunes occur from which men suffer.

The people are oppressed and robbed, and are poor, ignorant, dying of hunger. Why? Because the land is in the hands of the rich; and the people are enslaved in mills and in factories, obliged to earn money because taxes are demanded from them, and the price of their labour is diminished while the price of things they need is increased.

How are they to escape? By taking the land from the rich? But if this is done, soldiers will come, and will kill the rebels or put them in prison. Seize the mills and factories? The same will happen. Organize and maintain a strike? It is sure to fail. The rich will hold out longer than the workers, and the armies are always on the side of the capitalists. The people will never extricate themselves from the want in which they are kept as long as the army is in the hands of the governing classes.

But who compose these armies that keep the people in this state of slavery? Who are these soldiers that will fire at peasants who take the land, or at strikers who will not disperse, or at smugglers who bring in goods without paying taxes? Who put in prison and guard there those who refuse to pay taxes? The soldiers are these same peasants who are deprived of land, these same strikers who want better wages, these same taxpayers who want to be rid of these taxes.

And why do these people shoot at their brothers? Because it has been instilled into them that the oath they were obliged to take on entering the service is binding, and that though it is generally wrong to kill people, it is right to do so at the command of one's superiors. That is to say, the same fraud is played off upon them which has struck you. But here we meet the question, How is it that sensible people— often people who can read, and even educated people— believe such an evident lie? However little education a man may have, he cannot but know that Christ did not sanction murder, but taught kindness, meekness, forgiveness of injuries, love of one's enemies; and therefore he cannot help seeing that on the basis of Christian teaching he cannot pledge himself in advance to kill all whom he may be ordered to kill.

The question is, How can sensible people believe—as all now serving in the army have believed and still believe—such an evident falsehood? The answer is that it is not this one fraud by itself that takes people in, but they have from childhood been deprived of the proper use of their reason by a whole series of deceptions, a whole system of frauds, called the Orthodox Faith, which is nothing but the grossest idolatry. In this faith people are taught: that God is triple, that besides this triple God there is a Queen of Heaven,* and besides this Queen there are various saints whose corpses have not decayed,† and besides these saints there are icóns‡ of the Gods and of the Queen of Heaven, to which one should offer candles and pray with one's hands; and that the most important and holy thing on earth is the pap§ which the priest makes of wine and white bread on Sundays, behind a partition; and that after the priest has whispered over it,

* The Holy Virgin, the 'Mother of God' and 'Queen of Heaven,' plays a prominent part in the Orthodox Eastern Church.

† One proof of holiness adduced as justifying admission to the rank of sainthood is the non-decomposition of the holy person's corpse. These miraculously preserved bodies are enshrined in chapels, monasteries and cathedrals, and are there visited by pilgrims, who offer up prayers at the shrine, place candles before it, and usually leave some contribution for the benefit of the establishment.

‡ The icóns of the Eastern Church are not 'graven images,' but are pictures painted in a conventional cadaverous manner on wood; these are often covered with an embossed metal cover allowing only the hands and face to be seen, and making the icón as much like an image as a picture.

§ The mixture of bread and wine administered by the priests of the Orthodox Eastern Church at the celebration of the Eucharist.

the wine is no longer wine, and the white bread is not bread, but they are the blood and flesh of one of the triple Gods, etc. All this is so stupid and senseless that it is quite impossible to understand what it all means. And the very people who teach this faith do not ask you to understand it, but only tell you to believe it ; and people trained to believe these things from childhood can believe any kind of nonsense that is told them. And when men have been so befooled that they believe that God hangs in the corner,* or sits in a morsel of pap which the priest gives out in a spoon ; that to kiss a board or some relic and put candles in front of them, is useful for life here and hereafter—they are next called on to enter the military service, where they are humbugged to any extent ; being first made to swear on the Gospel (in which swearing is prohibited) that they will do just what is forbidden in those Gospels, and then taught that to kill people at the word of those in command is not a sin, but that to refuse to obey those in command is a sin. So that the fraud played off on soldiers when it is instilled into them that they may, without sin, kill people at the wish of those in command, is not an isolated fraud, but is bound up with a whole system of deception without which this one fraud would not deceive them.

Only a man quite befooled by the false faith called Orthodoxy, palmed off upon him for true Christian faith, can believe that it is no sin for a Christian to enter the army, promising blindly to obey any man who ranks above him in the service, and, at the will of others, learning to kill, and committing that most terrible crime forbidden by all moral law.

A man free from the pseudo-Christian faith that is called Orthodoxy, will not believe that.

And that is why the so-called Sectarians—Christians

* This refers to the common practice of hanging an icón in the corner of each dwelling-room. These icóns are called ' gods,' and are prayed to in a way that often amounts to idolatry.

who have repudiated the Orthodox teaching, and acknowledge Christ's teaching as explained in the Gospels, and especially in the Sermon on the Mount—are not tricked by this deception, but have frequently refused, and still do refuse, to be soldiers, considering such an occupation incompatible with Christianity, and preferring to bear all kinds of persecution, as hundreds and thousands of people are doing : in Russia many of the Doukhobórs and Molokáns; in Austria the Nazarenes, and in Sweden, Switzerland, and Germany some members of the Evangelical sects. The Government knows this, and is therefore exceedingly anxious that the general Church deception, without which its power could not be maintained, should be commenced with every child from early infancy and be continually maintained in such a way that none may escape it. The Government tolerates anything else : drunkenness and vice (and not only tolerates but even organizes drunkenness and vice—they help to stupefy people), but by all means in its power it hinders those who have escaped out of its trap from assisting others to escape.

The Russian Government perpetrates this fraud with special craft and cruelty. It orders all its subjects to baptize their children during infancy into the false faith called Orthodoxy, and it threatens to punish them if they disobey. And when the children are baptized—that is, are reckoned as Orthodox—then, under threats of criminal penalties, they are forbidden to discuss the faith into which, without their wish, they were baptized; and for such discussion of that faith, as well as for renouncing it and changing to another, they are actually punished. So that it cannot be said of Russians in general that they believe the Orthodox Faith—they do not know whether they believe it or not. They were converted to it during infancy, and kept in it by violence —that is, by the fear of punishment. All Russians were entrapped into Orthodoxy by cunning fraud, and are kept in it by cruel force.

Using the power it wields, the Government perpetrates and maintains this fraud, and by means of it retains power.

And, therefore, the sole way to free people from their many miseries lies in freeing them from the false faith instilled into them by Government, and in their imbibing the true Christian teaching, which this false teaching hides. The true Christian teaching is very simple, clear, and obvious to all, as Christ said. But it is simple and accessible only when man is freed from that falsehood in which we were all educated, and which is passed off upon us as God's Truth.

Nothing useful can be poured into a vessel that is already full of what is useless. We must first empty out what is useless. So it is with the acquirement of true Christian teaching. We have first to understand that all the stories telling how God made the world 6,000 years ago; how Adam sinned and the human race fell, and how the Son of God (a God born of a virgin) came on earth and redeemed man; and all the fables in the Old Testament and in the Gospels, and all the lives of the saints with their stories of miracles and relics—are all nothing but a gross hash of Jewish super-stitions and priestly frauds. Only to a man quite free from this deception can the clear and simple teaching of Christ, which needs no explanation, be accessible and comprehensible. That teaching tells us nothing of the beginning, or of the end, of the world, nor about God and His purpose, nor, in general, about things which we cannot and need not know; but it speaks only of what man must do to save himself—that is, how best to live the life he has come into, in this world, from birth to death. For that purpose it is only necessary to act towards others as we wish them to act towards us. In *that* is all the law and the prophets, as Christ said. And to act in this way we need neither icóns, nor relics, nor church services, nor priests, nor catechisms, nor Governments, but, on the contrary, we need perfect freedom from all that; for to do to others as we wish them to do to us is only possible when a man is free from the fables which the priests give out as the only truth, and when he is not bound by promises to act as other people may order.  Only such a man will be capable of fulfilling—not his own will nor that of other men, but—the will of God.

And the will of God is not that we should fight and oppress the weak, but that we should acknowledge all men to be our brothers and should serve one another.

These are the thoughts your letter has aroused in me. I shall be very glad if they help to clear up the questions you are thinking about.

[1899.]

## XIX

## PATRIOTISM AND GOVERNMENT

The time is fast approaching when to call a man a
patriot will be the deepest insult you can offer him.
Patriotism now means advocating plunder in the interests
of the privileged classes of the particular State system into
which we have happened to be born.'—E. BELFORT BAX.

### I.

I HAVE already several times expressed the thought
that in our day the feeling of patriotism is an unnatural,
irrational, and harmful feeling, and a cause of a great
part of the ills from which mankind is suffering ; and
that, consequently, this feeling should not be cultivated,
as is now being done, but should, on the contrary, be
suppressed and eradicated by all means available to
rational men. Yet, strange to say—though it is undeniable that the universal armaments and destructive wars
which are ruining the peoples result from that one
feeling—all my arguments showing the backwardness,
anachronism, and harmfulness of patriotism have been
met, and are still met, either by silence, by intentional
misinterpretation, or by a strange unvarying reply to
the effect that only bad patriotism (Jingoism, or Chau-
vinism) is evil, but that real good patriotism is a very
elevated moral feeling, to condemn which is not only
irrational but wicked.

What this real, good patriotism consists in, we are
never told ; or, if anything is said about it, instead
of explanation we get declamatory, inflated phrases,
or, finally, some other conception is substituted for

patriotism—something which has nothing in common with the patriotism we all know, and from the results of which we all suffer so severely.

It is generally said that the real, good patriotism consists in desiring for one's own people or State such real benefits as do not infringe the well-being of other nations.

Talking recently to an Englishman about the present war,* I said to him that the real cause of the war was not avarice, as people generally say, but patriotism, as is evident from the temper of the whole of English society.  The Englishman did not agree with me, and said that even were the case so, it resulted from the fact that the patriotism at present inspiring Englishmen is a bad patriotism ; but that good patriotism, such as he was imbued with, would cause Englishmen, his compatriots, to act well.

'Then do you wish only Englishmen to act well?' I asked.

'I wish all men to do so,' said he ; indicating clearly by that reply the characteristic of true benefits— whether moral, scientific, or even material and practical —which is that they spread out to all men.  But, evidently, to wish such benefits to everyone, not only is not patriotic, but is the reverse of patriotic.

Neither do the peculiarities of each people constitute patriotism, though these things are purposely substituted for the conception of patriotism by its defenders. They say that the peculiarities of each people are an essential condition of human progress, and that patriotism, which seeks to maintain those peculiarities, is, therefore, a good and useful feeling.  But is it not quite evident that if, once upon a time, these peculiarities of each people—these customs, creeds, languages— were conditions necessary for the life of humanity, in our time these same peculiarities form the chief obstacle to what is already recognised as an ideal—the brotherly union of the peoples?  And therefore the maintenance and defence of any nationality—Russian, German,

* That is, the South African War of 1899-1902.

French, or Anglo-Saxon, provoking the corresponding maintenance and defence not only of Hungarian, Polish, and Irish nationalities, but also of Basque, Provençal, Mordvá,* Tchouvásh, and many other nationalities—serves not to harmonize and unite men, but to estrange and divide them more and more from one another.

So that not the imaginary but the real patriotism, which we all know, by which most people to-day are swayed and from which humanity suffers so severely, is not the wish for spiritual benefits for one's own people (it is impossible to desire spiritual benefits for one's own people only), but is a very definite feeling of preference for one's own people or State above all other peoples and States, and a consequent wish to get for that people or State the greatest advantages and power that can be got—things which are obtainable only at the expense of the advantages and power of other peoples or States.

It would, therefore, seem obvious that patriotism as a feeling is bad and harmful, and as a doctrine is stupid. For it is clear that if each people and each State considers itself the best of peoples and States, they all live in a gross and harmful delusion.

II.

One would expect the harmfulness and irrationality of patriotism to be evident to everybody. But the surprising fact is that cultured and learned men not only do not themselves notice the harm and stupidity of patriotism, but they resist every exposure of it with the greatest obstinacy and ardour (though without any rational grounds), and continue to belaud it as beneficent and elevating.

What does this mean?

* The Mordvá (or Mordvinian) and Tchouvásh tribes are of Finnish origin, and inhabit chiefly the governments of the Middle Volga.

Only one explanation of this amazing fact presents itself to me.

All human history, from the earliest times to our own day, may be considered as a movement of the consciousness, both of individuals and of homogeneous groups, from lower ideas to higher ones.

The whole path travelled both by individuals and by homogeneous groups may be represented as a consecutive flight of steps from the lowest, on the level of animal life, to the highest attained by the consciousness of man at a given moment of history.

Each man, like each separate homogeneous group, nation, or State, always moved and moves up this ladder of ideas. Some portions of humanity are in front, others lag far behind, others, again — the majority—move somewhere between the most advanced and the most backward. But all, whatever stage they may have reached, are inevitably and irresistibly moving from lower to higher ideas. And always, at any given moment, both the individuals and the separate groups of people—advanced, middle, or backward—stand in three different relations to the three stages of ideas amid which they move.

Always, both for the individual and for the separate groups of people, there are the ideas of the past, which are worn out and have become strange to them, and to which they cannot revert: as, for instance, in our Christian world, the ideas of cannibalism, universal plunder, the rape of wives, and other customs of which only a record remains.

And there are the ideas of the present, instilled into men's minds by education, by example, and by the general activity of all around them ; ideas under the power of which they live at a given time : for instance, in our own day, the ideas of property, State organization, trade, utilization of domestic animals, etc.

And there are the ideas of the future, of which some are already approaching realization and are obliging people to change their way of life and to struggle against the former ways : such ideas in our world as those of freeing the labourers, of giving equality to women, of disusing flesh food, etc. ; while others, though already recognised, have not yet come into practical conflict with the old forms of life : such in our times are the ideas (which we call ideals) of the extermination of violence, the arrangement of a communal system of property, of a universal religion, and of a general brotherhood of men.

And, therefore, every man and every homogeneous group of men, on whatever level they may stand, having behind them the worn-out remembrances of the past, and before them the ideals of the future, are always in a state of struggle between the moribund ideas of the present and the ideas of the future that are coming to life. It usually happens that when an idea which has been useful and even necessary in the past becomes superfluous, that idea, after a more or less prolonged struggle, yields its place to a new idea which was till then an ideal, but which thus becomes a present idea.

But it does occur that an antiquated idea, already replaced in people's consciousness by a higher one, is of such a kind that its maintenance is profitable to those people who have the greatest influence in their society. And then it happens that this antiquated idea, though it is in sharp contradiction to the whole surrounding form of life, which has been altering in other respects, continues to influence people and to sway their actions. Such retention of antiquated ideas always has occurred, and still does occur, in the region of religion. The cause is, that the priests, whose profitable positions are bound up with the antiquated religious idea, purposely use their power to hold people to this antiquated idea.

The same thing occurs, and for similar reasons, in the political sphere, with reference to the patriotic idea, on which all arbitrary power is based. People to whom it is profitable to do so, maintain that idea by artificial means, though it now lacks both sense and utility. And as these people possess the most powerful means of influencing others, they are able to achieve their object.

In this, it seems to me, lies the explanation of the strange contrast between the antiquated patriotic idea, and that whole drift of ideas making in a contrary direction, which have already entered into the consciousness of the Christian world.

### III.

Patriotism, as a feeling of exclusive love for one's own people, and as a doctrine of the virtue of sacrificing one's tranquillity, one's property, and even one's life, in defence of one's own people from slaughter and outrage by their enemies, was the highest idea of the period when each nation considered it feasible and just, for its own advantage, to subject to slaughter and outrage the people of other nations.

But, already some 2,000 years ago, humanity, in the person of the highest representatives of its wisdom, began to recognise the higher idea of a brotherhood of man ; and that idea, penetrating man's consciousness more and more, has in our time attained most varied forms of realization.  Thanks to improved means of communication, and to the unity of industry, of trade, of the arts, and of science, men are to-day so bound one to another that the danger of conquest, massacre, or outrage by a neighbouring people, has quite disappeared, and all peoples (the peoples, but not the Governments) live together in peaceful, mutually advantageous, and friendly commercial, industrial, artistic, and scientific relations, which they have no need and no desire to disturb.  One would think, therefore, that the antiquated feeling of patriotism— being superfluous and incompatible with the consciousness we have reached of the existence of brotherhood among men of different nationalities—should dwindle more and more until it completely disappears.  Yet the very opposite of this occurs : this harmful and antiquated feeling not only continues to exist, but burns more and more fiercely.

The peoples, without any reasonable ground, and contrary alike to their conception of right and to their own advantage, not only sympathize with Governments in their attacks on other nations, in their seizures of foreign possessions, and in defending by force what they have already stolen, but even themselves demand such attacks, seizures, and defences : are glad of them, and take pride in them. The small oppressed nationalities which have fallen under the power of the great States—the Poles, Irish, Bohemians, Finns, or Armenians—resenting the patriotism of their conquerors, which is the cause of their oppression, catch from them the infection of this feeling of patriotism—which has ceased to be necessary, and is now obsolete, unmeaning, and harmful—and catch it to such a degree that all their activity is concentrated upon it, and they, themselves suffering from the patriotism of the stronger nations, are ready, for the sake of patriotism, to perpetrate on other peoples the very same deeds that their oppressors have perpetrated and are perpetrating on them.

This occurs because the ruling classes (including not only the actual rulers with their officials, but all the classes who enjoy an exceptionally advantageous position : the capitalists, journalists, and most of the artists and scientists) can retain their position—exceptionally advantageous in comparison with that of the labouring masses—thanks only to the Government organization, which rests on patriotism. They have in their hands all the most powerful means of influencing the people, and always sedulously support patriotic feelings in themselves and in others, more especially as those feelings which uphold the Government's power are those that are always best rewarded by that power.

Every official prospers the more in his career, the more patriotic he is ; so also the army man gets promotion in time of war—the war is produced by patriotism.

Patriotism and its result—wars—give an enormous revenue to the newspaper trade, and profits to many other trades. Every writer, teacher, and professor is more secure in his place the more he preaches patriotism. Every Emperor and King obtains the more fame the more he is addicted to patriotism.

The ruling classes have in their hands the army, money, the schools, the churches, and the press. In the schools they kindle patriotism in the children by means of histories describing their own people as the best of all peoples and always in the right. Among adults they kindle it by spectacles, jubilees, monuments, and by a lying patriotic press. Above all, they inflame patriotism in this way : perpetrating every kind of injustice and harshness against other nations, they provoke in them enmity towards their own people, and then in turn exploit that enmity to embitter their people against the foreigner.

The intensification of this terrible feeling of patriotism has gone on among the European peoples in a rapidly increasing progression, and in our time has reached the utmost limits, beyond which there is no room for it to extend.

IV.

Within the memory of people not yet old, an occurrence took place showing most obviously the amazing intoxication caused by patriotism among the people of Christendom.

The ruling classes of Germany excited the patriotism of the masses of their people to such a degree that, in the second half of the nineteenth century, a law was proposed in accordance with which all the men had to become soldiers : all the sons, husbands, fathers, learned men, and godly men, had to learn to murder, to become submissive slaves of those above them in military rank, and be absolutely ready to kill whomsoever they were ordered to kill ; to kill men of oppressed nationalities, and their own working-men standing up for their rights, and even their own fathers and brothers—as was publicly proclaimed by that most impudent of potentates, William II.

That horrible measure, outraging all man's best feelings in the grossest manner, was, under the influence of patriotism, acquiesced in without murmur by the people of Germany. It resulted in their victory over the French. That victory yet further excited the patriotism of Germany, and, by reaction, that of France, Russia, and the other Powers; and the men of the European countries unresistingly submitted to the introduction of general military service—*i.e.*, to a state of slavery involving a degree of humiliation and submission incomparably worse than any slavery of the ancient world. After this servile submission of the masses to the calls of patriotism, the audacity, cruelty, and insanity of the Governments knew no bounds. A competition in the usurpation of other peoples' lands in Asia, Africa, and America began—evoked partly by whim, partly by vanity, and partly by covetousness— and was accompanied by ever greater and greater distrust and enmity between the Governments.

The destruction of the inhabitants on the lands seized was accepted as a quite natural proceeding. The only question was, who should be first in seizing other peoples' land and destroying the inhabitants? All the Governments not only most evidently infringed, and are infringing, the elementary demands of justice in relation to the conquered peoples, and in relation to one another, but they were guilty, and continue to be guilty, of every kind of cheating, swindling, bribing, fraud, spying, robbery, and murder; and the peoples not only sympathized, and still sympathize, with them in all this, but they rejoice when it is their own Government and not another Government that commits such crimes.

The mutual enmity between the different peoples and States has reached latterly such amazing dimensions that, notwithstanding the fact that there is no reason why one State should attack another, everyone knows that all the Governments stand with their claws out and showing their teeth, and only waiting for someone to be in trouble, or become weak, in order to tear him to pieces with as little risk as possible.

All the peoples of the so-called Christian world have been reduced by patriotism to such a state of brutality, that not only those who are obliged to kill or be killed desire slaughter and rejoice in murder, but all the people of Europe and America, living peaceably in their homes exposed to no danger, are, at each war— thanks to easy means of communication and to the press—in the position of the spectators in a Roman circus, and, like them, delight in the slaughter, and raise the bloodthirsty cry, ' *Pollice verso.*'*

Not adults only, but also children, pure, wise children, rejoice, according to their nationality, when they hear that the number killed and lacerated by lyddite or other shells on some particular day was not 700 but 1,000 Englishmen or Boers.

And parents (I know such cases) encourage their children in such brutality.

But that is not all.   Every increase in the army of one nation (and each nation, being in danger, seeks to increase its army for patriotic reasons) obliges its neighbours to increase their armies, also from patriotism, and this evokes a fresh increase by the first nation.

And the same thing occurs with fortifications and navies : one State has built ten ironclads, a neighbour builds eleven ; then the first builds twelve, and so on to infinity.

' I'll pinch you.'   ' And I'll punch your head.'   ' And I'll stab you with a dagger.'   ' And I'll bludgeon you.' ' And I'll shoot you.'  . . .   Only bad children, drunken men, or animals, quarrel or fight so, but yet it is just what is going on among the highest representatives of the most enlightened Governments, the very men who undertake to direct the education and the morality of their subjects.

* *Pollice verso* (' thumb down ') was the sign given in the Roman amphitheatres by the spectators who wished a defeated gladiator to be slain.

v.

The position is becoming worse and worse, and there is no stopping this descent towards evident perdition.

The one way of escape believed in by credulous people has now been closed by recent events. I refer to the Hague Conference, and to the war between England and the Transvaal which immediately followed it.

If people who think little, or but superficially, were able to comfort themselves with the idea that international courts of arbitration would supersede wars and ever-increasing armaments, the Hague Conference and the war that followed it demonstrated in the most palpable manner the impossibility of finding a solution of the difficulty in that way. After the Hague Conference, it became obvious that as long as Governments with armies exist, the termination of armaments and of wars is impossible. That an agreement should become possible, it is necessary that the parties to it should *trust* each other. And in order that the Powers should trust each other, they must lay down their arms, as is done by the bearers of a flag of truce when they meet for a conference.

So long as Governments, distrusting one another, not only do not disband or decrease their armies, but always increase them in correspondence with augmentations made by their neighbours, and by means of spies watch every movement of troops, knowing that each of the Powers will attack its neighbour as soon as it sees its way to do so, no agreement is possible, and every conference is either a stupidity, or a pastime, or a fraud, or an impertinence, or all of these together.

It was particularly becoming for the Russian rather than any other Government to be the *enfant terrible* of the Hague Conference. No one at home being allowed to reply to all its evidently mendacious manifestations and rescripts, the Russian Government is so spoilt, that —having without the least scruple ruined its own people with armaments, strangled Poland, plundered Turkestan and China, and being specially engaged in suffocating Finland—it proposed disarmament to the Governments, in full assurance that it would be trusted!

But strange, unexpected, and indecent as such a proposal was—especially at the very time when orders were being given to increase its army—the words publicly uttered in the hearing of the people were such, that for the sake of appearances the Governments of the other Powers could not decline the comical and evidently insincere consultation; and so the delegates met—knowing in advance that nothing would come of it—and for several weeks (during which they drew good salaries) though they were laughing in their sleeves, they all conscientiously pretended to be much occupied in arranging peace among the nations.

The Hague Conference, followed up as it was by the terrible bloodshed of the Transvaal War, which no one attempted, or is now attempting, to stop, was, nevertheless, of some use, though not at all in the way expected of it—it was useful because it showed in the most obvious manner that the evils from which the peoples are suffering cannot be cured by Governments. That Governments, even if they wished to, can terminate neither armaments nor wars.

Governments, to have a reason for existing, must defend their people from other people's attack. But not one people wishes to attack, or does attack, another. And therefore Governments, far from wishing for peace, carefully excite the anger of other nations against themselves. And having excited other people's anger against themselves, and stirred up the patriotism of their own people, each Government then assures its people that it is in danger and must be defended.

And having the power in their hands, the Governments can both irritate other nations and excite patriotism at home, and they carefully do both the one and the other; nor can they act otherwise, for their existence depends on thus acting.

If, in former times, Governments were necessary to defend their people from other people's attacks, now, on the contrary, Governments artificially disturb the peace that exists between the nations, and provoke enmity among them.

When it was necessary to plough in order to sow, ploughing was wise; but evidently it is absurd and harmful to go on ploughing after the seed has been sown. But this is just what the Governments are obliging their people to do: to infringe the unity which exists, and which nothing would infringe if it were not for the Governments.

### VI.

In reality what are these Governments, without which people think they could not exist?

There may have been a time when such Governments were necessary, and when the evil of supporting a Government was less than that of being defenceless against organized neighbours; but now such Governments have become unnecessary, and are a far greater evil than all the dangers with which they frighten their subjects.

Not only military Governments, but Governments in general, could be, I will not say useful, but at least harmless, only if they consisted of immaculate, holy people, as is theoretically the case among the Chinese. But then Governments, by the nature of their activity, which consists in committing acts of violence,* are always composed of elements the most contrary to holiness—of the most audacious, unscrupulous, and perverted people.

A Government, therefore, and especially a Government entrusted with military power, is the most dangerous organization possible.

---

* The word *government* is frequently used in an indefinite sense as almost equivalent to management or direction; but in the sense in which the word is used in the present article, the characteristic feature of a Government is that it claims a moral right to inflict physical penalties, and by its decree to make murder a good action.

The Government, in the widest sense, including capitalists and the Press, is nothing else than an organization which places the greater part of the people in the power of a smaller part, who dominate them ; that smaller part is subject to a yet smaller part, and that again to a yet smaller, and so on, reaching at last a few people, or one single man, who by means of military force has power over all the rest.   So that all this organization resembles a cone, of which all the parts are completely in the power of those people, or of that one person, who happen to be at the apex.

The apex of the cone is seized by those who are more cunning, audacious, and unscrupulous than the rest, or by someone who happens to be the heir of those who were audacious and unscrupulous.

To-day it may be Borís Godunóf,* and to-morrow Gregory Otrépyef.†  To-day the licentious Catherine, who with her paramours has murdered her husband ; to-morrow Pougatchéf ;‡  then Paul the madman, Nicholas I., or Alexander III.

To-day it may be Napoleon, to-morrow a Bourbon or an Orléans, a Boulanger or a Panama Company ; to-day it may be Gladstone, to-morrow Salisbury, Chamberlain, or Rhodes.

And to such Governments is allowed full power, not only over property and lives, but even over the spiritual and moral development, the education, and the religious guidance of everybody.

People construct such a terrible machine of power, they allow any one to seize it who can (and the chances always are that it will be seized by the most morally worthless)—they slavishly submit to him, and are then

* Borís Godunóf, brother-in-law of the weak Tsar Fyódor Ivánovitch, succeeded in becoming Tsar, and reigned in Moscow from 1598 to 1605.

† Gregory Otrépyef was a pretender who, passing himself off as Dimítry, son of Iván the Terrible, reigned in Moscow in 1605 and 1606.

‡ Pougatchéf was the leader of a most formidable insurrection in 1773-1775, and was executed in Moscow in 1775.

surprised that evil comes of it. They are afraid of Anarchists' bombs, and are not afraid of this terrible organization which is always threatening them with the greatest calamities.

People found it useful to tie themselves together in order to resist their enemies, as the Circassians* did when resisting attacks. But the danger is quite past, and yet people go on tying themselves together.

They carefully tie themselves up so that one man can have them all at his mercy ; then they throw away the end of the rope that ties them, and leave it trailing for some rascal or fool to seize and to do them whatever harm he likes.

Really, what are people doing but just that—when they set up, submit to, and maintain an organized and military Government?

## VII.

To deliver men from the terrible and ever-increasing evils of armaments and wars, we want neither congresses nor conferences, nor treaties, nor courts of arbitration, but the destruction of those instruments of violence which are called Governments, and from which humanity's greatest evils flow.

To destroy Governmental *violence*, only one thing is needed : it is that people should understand that the feeling of patriotism, which alone supports that instrument of violence, is a rude, harmful, disgraceful, and bad feeling, and, above all, is immoral. It is a rude feeling, because it is one natural only to people standing on the lowest level of morality, and expecting from other nations such outrages as they themselves are ready to inflict ; it is a harmful feeling, because it disturbs advantageous and joyous, peaceful relations with other peoples, and above all produces that Governmental organization under which power may fall, and

* The Circassians, when surrounded, used to tie themselves together leg to leg, that none might escape, but all die fighting. Instances of this kind occurred when their country was being annexed by Russia.

does fall, into the hands of the worst men ; it is a disgraceful feeling, because it turns man not merely into a slave, but into a fighting cock, a bull, or a gladiator, who wastes his strength and his life for objects which are not his own but his Governments' ; and it is an immoral feeling, because, instead of confessing one's self a son of God (as Christianity teaches us) or even a free man guided by his own reason, each man under the influence of patriotism confesses himself the son of his fatherland and the slave of his Government, and commits actions contrary to his reason and his conscience.

It is only necessary that people should understand this, and the terrible bond, called Government, by which we are chained together, will fall to pieces of itself without struggle ; and with it will cease the terrible and useless evils it produces.

And people are already beginning to understand this. This, for instance, is what a citizen of the United States writes :

'We are farmers, mechanics, merchants, manufacturers, teachers, and all we ask is the privilege of attending to our own business. We own our homes, love our friends, are devoted to our families, and do not interfere with our neighbours—we have work to do, and wish to work.

'Leave us alone !

'But they will not—these politicians. They insist on governing us and living off our labour. They tax us, eat our substance, conscript us, draft our boys into their wars. All the myriads of men who live off the Government depend upon the Government to tax us, and, in order to tax us successfully, standing armies are maintained. The plea that the army is needed for the protection of the country is pure fraud and pretence. The French Government affrights the people by telling them that the Germans are ready and anxious to fall upon them ; the Russians fear the British ; the British fear everybody ; and now in America we are told we must increase our navy and add to our army because Europe may at any moment combine against us.

'This is fraud and untruth. The plain people in France, Germany, England, and America are opposed to war. We only wish to be let alone. Men with wives, children, sweethearts, homes, aged parents, do not want to go off and fight someone. We are peaceable and we fear war ; we hate it.

'We would like to obey the Golden Rule.

'War is the sure result of the existence of armed men. That country which maintains a large standing army will sooner or later have a war on hand. The man who prides himself on fisticuffs is going some day to meet a man who considers himself the better man, and they will fight. Germany and France have no issue save a desire to see which is the better man. They have fought many times—and they will fight again. Not that the people want to fight, but the Superior Class fan fright into fury, and make men think they must fight to protect their homes.

'So the people who wish to follow the teachings of Christ are not allowed to do so, but are taxed, outraged, deceived by Governments.

'Christ taught humility, meekness, the forgiveness of one's enemies, and that to kill was wrong. The Bible teaches men not to swear ; but the Superior Class swear us on the Bible in which they do not believe.

'The question is, How are we to relieve ourselves of these cormorants who toil not, but who are clothed in broadcloth and blue, with brass buttons and many costly accoutrements ; who feed upon our substance, and for whom we delve and dig?

'Shall we fight them?

'No, we do not believe in bloodshed ; and besides that, they have the guns and the money, and they can hold out longer than we.

'But who composes this army that they would order to fire upon us?

'Why, our neighbours and brothers—deceived into the idea that they are doing God's service by protecting their country from its enemies. When the fact is, our country has no enemies save the Superior Class, that pretends to look out for our interests if we will only obey and consent to be taxed.

'Thus do they siphon our resources and turn our true brothers upon us to subdue and humiliate us. You cannot send a telegram to your wife, nor an express package to your friend, nor draw a cheque for your grocer, until you first pay the tax to maintain armed men, who can quickly be used to kill you; and who surely will imprison you if you do not pay.

'The only relief lies in education. Educate men that it is wrong to kill. Teach them the Golden Rule, and yet again teach them the Golden Rule. Silently defy this Superior Class by refusing to bow down to their fetich of bullets. Cease supporting the preachers who cry for war and spout patriotism for a consideration. Let them go to work as we do. We believe in Christ—they do not. Christ spoke what he thought; they speak what they think will please the men in power—the Superior Class.

'We will not enlist. We will not shoot on their order. We will not "charge bayonet" upon a mild and gentle people. We will not fire upon shepherds and farmers, fighting for their firesides, upon a suggestion of Cecil Rhodes. Your false cry of "Wolf! wolf!" shall not alarm us. We pay your taxes only because we have to, and we will pay no longer than we have to. We will pay no pew-rents, no tithes to your sham charities, and we will speak our minds upon occasion.

'We will educate men.

'And all the time our silent influence will be going out, and even the men who are conscripted will be half-hearted and refuse to fight. We will educate men into the thought that the Christ Life of Peace and Good-will is better than the Life of Strife, Bloodshed, and War.

'"Peace on earth!"—it can only come when men do away with armies, and are willing to do unto other men as they would be done by.'

So writes a citizen of the United States; and from

various sides, in various forms, such voices are sounding.

This is what a German soldier writes:

'I went through two campaigns with the Prussian Guards (in 1866 and 1870), and I hate war from the bottom of my soul, for it has made me inexpressibly unfortunate. We wounded soldiers generally receive such a miserable recompense that we have indeed to be ashamed of having once been patriots. I, for instance, get ninepence a day for my right arm, which was shot through at the attack on St. Privat, August 18, 1870. Some hunting dogs have more allowed for their keep. And I have suffered for years from my twice wounded arm. Already in 1866 I took part in the war against Austria, and fought at Trautenau and Königgrätz, and saw horrors enough. In 1870, being in the reserve I was called out again; and, as I have already said, I was wounded in the attack at St. Privat: my right arm was twice shot through lengthwise. I had to leave a good place in a brewery, and was unable afterwards to regain it. Since then I have never been able to get on my feet again. The intoxication soon passed, and there was nothing left for the wounded invalid but to keep himself alive on a beggarly pittance eked out by charity. . . .

'In a world in which people run round like trained animals, and are not capable of any other idea than that of overreaching one another for the sake of mammon—in such a world let people think me a crank; but, for all that, I feel in myself the divine idea of peace, which is so beautifully expressed in the Sermon on the Mount. My deepest conviction is that war is only trade on a larger scale—the ambitious and powerful trade with the happiness of the peoples.

'And what horrors do we not suffer from it! Never shall I forget the pitiful groans that pierced one to the marrow!

'People who never did each other any harm begin to slaughter one another like wild animals, and petty, slavish souls—implicate the good God, making Him their confederate in such deeds.

'My neighbour in the ranks had his jaw broken by a
bullet. The poor wretch went wild with pain. He ran
like a madman, and in the scorching summer heat could
not even get water to cool his horrible wound. Our
commander, the Crown Prince (who was afterwards the
noble Emperor Frederick), wrote in his diary : "War
—is an irony on the Gospels." . . .'

People are beginning to understand the fraud of
patriotism, in which all the Governments take such
pains to keep them involved.

## VIII.

'But,' it is usually asked, 'what will there be instead
of Governments ?'

There will be nothing. Something that has long
been useless, and therefore superfluous and bad, will be
abolished. An organ that, being unnecessary, has
become harmful, will be abolished.

'But,' people generally say, 'if there is no Government, people will violate and kill each other.'

Why ? Why should the abolition of the organization
which arose in consequence of violence, and which has
been handed down from generation to generation to do
violence—why should the abolition of such an organization, now devoid of use, cause people to outrage and
kill one another ? On the contrary, the presumption
is that the abolition of the organ of violence would
result in people ceasing to violate and kill one another.

Now, some men are specially educated and trained to
kill and to do violence to other people—there are men
who are supposed to have a right to use violence, and
who make use of an organization which exists for that
purpose. Such deeds of violence and such killing are
considered good and worthy deeds.

But then, people will not be so brought up, and no
one will have a right to use violence to others, and
there will be no organization to do violence, and—as is
natural to people of our time—violence and murder will
always be considered bad actions, no matter who commits them.

R

But should acts of violence continue to be committed even after the abolition of the Governments, such acts will certainly be fewer than are committed now, when an organization exists specially devised to commit acts of violence, and a state of things exists in which acts of violence and murders are considered good and useful deeds.

The abolition of Governments will merely rid us of an unnecessary organization which we have inherited from the past, an organization for the commission of violence and for its justification.

'But there will then be no laws, no property, no courts of justice, no police, no popular education,' say people who intentionally confuse the use of violence by Governments with various social activities.

The abolition of the organization of Government formed to do violence, does not at all involve the abolition of what is reasonable and good, and therefore not based on violence, in laws or law courts, or in property, or in police regulations, or in financial arrangements, or in popular education. On the contrary, the absence of the brutal power of Government, which is needed only for its own support, will facilitate a juster and more reasonable social organization, needing no violence. Courts of justice, and public affairs, and popular education, will all exist to the extent to which they are really needed by the people, but in a shape which will not involve the evils contained in the present form of Government. Only that will be destroyed which was evil and hindered the free expression of the people's will.

But even if we assume that with the absence of Governments there would be disturbances and civil strife, even then the position of the people would be better than it is at present. The position now is such that it is difficult to imagine anything worse. The people are ruined, and their ruin is becoming more and more complete. The men are all converted into war-slaves, and have from day to day to expect orders to go to kill and to be killed. What more? Are the ruined

peoples to die of hunger?  Even that is already beginning in Russia, in Italy, and in India.  Or are the
women as well as the men to go to be soldiers?  In the
Transvaal even that has begun.

So that even if the absence of Government really
meant Anarchy in the negative, disorderly sense of that
word—which is far from being the case—even then no
anarchical disorder could be worse than the position to
which Governments have already led their peoples, and
to which they are leading them.

And therefore emancipation from patriotism, and the
destruction of the despotism of Government that rests
upon it, cannot but be beneficial to mankind.


IX.

Men, recollect yourselves!  For the sake of your
well-being, physical and spiritual, for the sake of your
brothers and sisters, pause, consider, and think of what
you are doing!

Reflect, and you will understand that your foes are
not the Boers, or the English, or the French, or the
Germans, or the Finns, or the Russians, but that your
foes—your only foes—are you yourselves, who by your
patriotism maintain the Governments that oppress you
and make you unhappy.

They have undertaken to protect you from danger,
and they have brought that pseudo-protection to such
a point that you have all become soldiers—slaves, and
are all ruined, or are being ruined more and more, and
at any moment may and should expect that the tight-
stretched cord will snap, and a horrible slaughter of
you and your children will commence.

And however great that slaughter may be, and however that conflict may end, the same state of things will
continue.  In the same way, and with yet greater
intensity, the Governments will arm, and ruin, and
pervert you and your children, and no one will help
you to stop it or to prevent it, if you do not help yourselves.

And there is only one kind of help possible—it lies in the abolition of that terrible linking up into a cone of violence, which enables the person or persons who succeed in seizing the apex to have power over all the rest, and to hold that power the more firmly the more cruel and inhuman they are, as we see by the cases of the Napoleons, Nicholas I., Bismarck, Chamberlain, Rhodes, and our Russian Dictators who rule the people in the Tsar's name.

And there is only one way to destroy this binding together—it is by shaking off the hypnotism of patriotism.

Understand that all the evils from which you suffer, you yourselves cause by yielding to the suggestions by which Emperors, Kings, Members of Parliament, Governors, officers, capitalists, priests, authors, artists, and all who need this fraud of patriotism in order to live upon your labour, deceive you !

Whoever you may be—Frenchman, Russian, Pole, Englishman, Irishman, or Bohemian—understand that all your real human interests, whatever they may be—agricultural, industrial, commercial, artistic, or scientific—as well as your pleasures and joys, in no way run counter to the interests of other peoples or States ; and that you are united, by mutual co-operation, by interchange of services, by the joy of wide brotherly intercourse, and by the interchange not merely of goods but also of thoughts and feelings, with the folk of other lands.

Understand that the question as to who manages to seize Wei-hai-wei, Port Arthur, or Cuba—your Government or another—does not affect you, or, rather, that every such seizure made by your Government injures you, by inevitably bringing in its train all sorts of pressure on you by your Government to force you to take part in the robbery and violence by which alone such seizures are made, or can be retained when made. Understand that your life can in no way be bettered by Alsace becoming German or French, and Ireland or Poland being free or enslaved—whoever holds them.

you are free to live where you will, if even you be an Alsatian, an Irishman, or a Pole.  Understand, too, that by stirring up patriotism you will only make the case worse, for the subjection in which your people are kept has resulted simply from the struggle between patriotisms, and every manifestation of patriotism in one nation provokes a corresponding reaction in another. Understand that salvation from your woes is only possible when you free yourself from the obsolete idea of patriotism and from the obedience to Governments that is based upon it, and when you boldly enter into the region of that higher idea, the brotherly union of the peoples, which has long since come to life, and from all sides is calling you to itself.

If people would but understand that they are not the sons of some fatherland or other, nor of Governments, but are sons of God, and can therefore neither be slaves nor enemies one to another—those insane, unnecessary, worn-out, pernicious organizations called Governments, and all the sufferings, violations, humiliations, and crimes which they occasion, would cease.

[May 10, o.s., 1900.]

# XX

## 'THOU SHALT NOT KILL'

'Thou shalt not kill.'—Exod. xx. 13.

'The disciple is not above his master: but every one when he is perfected shall be as his master.'—Luke vi. 40.

'For all they that take the sword shall perish with the sword.'—Matt. xxvi. 52.

'Therefore all things whatsoever ye would that men should do to you, do ye even so to them.'—Matt. vii. 12.

When Kings are executed after trial, as in the case of Charles I., Louis XVI., and Maximilian of Mexico; or when they are killed in Court conspiracies, like Peter III., Paul, and various Sultans, Shahs, and Khans—little is said about it; but when they are killed without a trial and without a Court conspiracy—as in the case of Henry IV. of France, Alexander II., the Empress of Austria, the late Shah of Persia, and, recently, Humbert—such murders excite the greatest surprise and indignation among Kings and Emperors and their adherents, just as if they themselves never took part in murders, nor profited by them, nor instigated them. But, in fact, the mildest of the murdered Kings (Alexander II. or Humbert, for instance), not to speak of executions in their own countries, were instigators of, and accomplices and partakers in, the murder of tens of thousands of men who perished on the field of battle; while more cruel Kings and Emperors have been guilty of hundreds of thousands, and even millions, of murders.

The teaching of Christ repeals the law, 'An eye for an eye, and a tooth for a tooth'; but those who have always clung to that law, and still cling to it, and who apply it to a terrible degree—not only claiming 'an eye for an eye,' but without provocation decreeing the slaughter of thousands, as they do when they declare war—have no right to be indignant at the application of that same law to themselves in so small and insignificant a degree that hardly one King or Emperor is killed for each hundred thousand, or perhaps even for each million, who are killed by the order and with the consent of Kings and Emperors. Kings and Emperors not only should not be indignant at such murders as those of Alexander II. and Humbert, but they should be surprised that such murders are so rare, considering the continual and universal example of murder that they give to mankind.

The crowd are so hypnotized that they see what is going on before their eyes, but do not understand its meaning. They see what constant care Kings, Emperors, and Presidents devote to their disciplined armies ; they see the reviews, parades, and manœuvres the rulers hold, about which they boast to one another ; and the people crowd to see their own brothers, brightly dressed up in fools' clothes, turned into machines to the sound of drum and trumpet, all, at the shout of one man, making one and the same movement at one and the same moment—but they do not understand what it all means. Yet the meaning of this drilling is very clear and simple : it is nothing but a preparation for killing.

It is stupefying men in order to make them fit instruments for murder. And those who do this, who chiefly direct this and are proud of it, are the Kings, Emperors and Presidents. And it is just these men—who are specially occupied in organizing murder and who have made murder their profession, who wear military uniforms and carry murderous weapons (swords) at their sides—that are horrified and indignant when one of themselves is murdered.

The murder of Kings—the murder of Humbert—is terrible, but not on account of its cruelty. The things done by command of Kings and Emperors—not only past events such as the massacre of St. Bartholomew, religious butcheries, the terrible repressions of peasant rebellions, and Paris *coups d'état*, but the present-day Government executions, the doing-to-death of prisoners in solitary confinement, the Disciplinary Battalions, the hangings, the beheadings, the shootings and slaughter in wars—are incomparably more cruel than the murders committed by Anarchists. Nor are these murders terrible because undeserved. If Alexander II. and Humbert did not deserve death, still less did the thousands of Russians who perished at Plevna, or of Italians who perished in Abyssinia. Such murders are terrible, not because they are cruel or unmerited, but because of the unreasonableness of those who commit them.

If the regicides act under the influence of personal feelings of indignation evoked by the sufferings of an oppressed people, for which they hold Alexander or Carnot or Humbert responsible ; or if they act from personal feelings of revenge, then—however immoral their conduct may be—it is at least intelligible ; but how is it that a body of men (Anarchists, we are told) such as those by whom Bresci was sent, and who are now threatening another Emperor—how is that they cannot devise any better means of improving the condition of humanity than by killing people whose destruction can no more be of use than the decapitation of that mythical monster on whose neck a new head appeared as soon as one was cut off ? Kings and Emperors have long ago arranged for themselves a system like that of a magazine-rifle : as soon as one bullet has been discharged another takes its place. *Le roi est mort, vive le roi !* So what is the use of killing them ?

Only on a most superficial view, can the killing of these men seem a means of saving the nations from oppression and from wars destructive of human life.

One only need remember that similar oppression and similar war went on, no matter who was at the head of the Government—Nicholas or Alexander, Frederick or Wilhelm, Napoleon or Louis, Palmerston or Gladstone, McKinley or anyone else—in order to understand that it is not any particular person who causes these oppressions and these wars from which the nations suffer. The misery of nations is caused not by particular persons, but by the particular order of Society under which the people are so tied up together that they find themselves all in the power of a few men, or more often in the power of one single man : a man so perverted by his unnatural position as arbiter of the fate and lives of millions, that he is always in an unhealthy state, and always suffers more or less from a mania of self-aggrandizement, which only his exceptional position conceals from general notice.

Apart from the fact that such men are surrounded from earliest childhood to the grave by the most insensate luxury and an atmosphere of falsehood and flattery which always accompanies them, their whole education and all their occupations are centred on one object : learning about former murders, the best present-day ways of murdering, and the best preparations for future murder. From childhood they learn about killing in all its possible forms. They always carry about with them murderous weapons—swords or sabres ; they dress themselves in various uniforms ; they attend parades, reviews and manœuvres ; they visit one another, presenting one another with Orders and nominating one another to the command of regiments—and not only does no one tell them plainly what they are doing, or say that to busy one's self with preparations for killing is revolting and criminal, but from all sides they hear nothing but approval and enthusiasm for all this activity of theirs. Every time they go out, and at each parade and review, crowds of people flock to greet them with enthusiasm, and it seems to them as if the whole nation approves of their conduct. The only part of the Press that reaches them, and that seems to them the expression of the feelings of the whole people, or at least of its best representatives, most slavishly extols their every word and action, however silly or wicked they may be. Those around them, men and women, clergy and laity —all people who do not prize human dignity—vying with one another in refined flattery, agree with them about anything and deceive them about everything, making it impossible for them to see life as it is. Such rulers might live a hundred years without ever seeing one single really independent man or ever hearing the truth spoken. One is sometimes appalled to hear of the words and deeds of these men ; but one need only consider their position in order to understand that any-one in their place would act as they do. If a reasonable man found himself in their place, there is only one reasonable action he could perform, and that would be to get away from such a position. Any one remaining in it would behave as they do.

What, indeed, must go on in the head of some Wilhelm of Germany—a narrow-minded, ill-educated, vain man, with the ideals of a German Junker—when there is nothing he can say so stupid or so horrid that it will not be met by an enthusiastic ' *Hoch !*' and be commented on by the Press of the entire world as though it were something highly important. When he says that, at his word, soldiers should be ready to kill their own fathers, people shout ' Hurrah !' When he says that the Gospel must be introduced with an iron fist—' Hurrah !' When he says the army is to take no prisoners in China, but to slaughter everybody, he is not put into a lunatic asylum, but people shout ' Hurrah !' and set sail for China to execute his com-mands. Or Nicholas II. (a man naturally modest) begins his reign by announcing to venerable old men who had expressed a wish to be allowed to discuss their own affairs, that such ideas of self-government were ' insensate dreams,'—and the organs of the Press he sees, and the people he meets, praise him for it. He proposes a childish, silly, and hypocritical project of universal peace, while at the same time ordering an increase in the army—and there are no limits to the laudations of his wisdom and virtue. Without any need, he foolishly and mercilessly insults and oppresses a whole nation, the Finns, and again he hears nothing but praise. Finally, he arranges the Chinese slaughter —terrible in its injustice, cruelty and incompatibility with his peace projects—and, from all sides, people applaud him, both as a victor and as a continuer of his father's peace policy.

What, indeed, must be going on in the heads and hearts of these men?

So it is not the Alexanders and Humberts, nor the Wilhelms, Nicholases, and Chamberlains—though they decree these oppressions of the nations and these wars —who are really the most guilty of these sins, but it is rather those who place and support them in the position of arbiters over the lives of their fellow-men. And, therefore, the thing to do is not to kill Alexanders, Nicholases, Wilhelms, and Humberts, but to cease to support the arrangement of society of which they are a result. And what supports the present order of society is the selfishness and stupefaction of the people, who sell their freedom and honour for insignificant material advantages.

People who stand on the lowest rung of the ladder— partly as a result of being stupefied by a patriotic and pseudo-religious education, and partly for the sake of personal advantages—cede their freedom and sense of human dignity at the bidding of these who stand above them and offer them material advantages. In the same way—in consequence of stupefaction, and chiefly for the sake of advantages—those who are a little higher up the ladder cede their freedom and manly dignity, and the same thing repeats itself with those standing yet higher, and so on to the topmost rung—to those who, or to him who, standing at the apex of the social cone have nothing more to obtain: for whom the only motives of action are love of power and vanity, and who are generally so perverted and stupefied by the power of life and death which they hold over their fellow-men, and by the consequent servility and flattery of those who surround them, that, without ceasing to do evil, they feel quite assured that they are benefactors to the human race.

It is the people who sacrifice their dignity as men for material profit that produce these men who cannot act otherwise than as they do act, and with whom it is useless to be angry for their stupid and wicked actions. To kill such men is like whipping children whom one has first spoilt.

That nations should not be oppressed, and that there should be none of these useless wars, and that men may not be indignant with those who seem to cause these evils, and may not kill them—it seems that only a very small thing is necessary. It is necessary that men should understand things as they are, should call them by their right names, and should know that an army is an instrument for killing, and that the enrolment and management of an army—the very things which Kings, Emperors, and Presidents occupy themselves with so self-confidently—is a preparation for murder.

If only each King, Emperor, and President understood that his work of directing armies is not an honourable and important duty, as his flatterers persuade him it is, but a bad and shameful act of preparation for murder—and if each private individual understood that the payment of taxes wherewith to hire and equip soldiers, and, above all, army-service itself, are not matters of indifference, but are bad and shameful actions by which he not only permits but participates in murder—then this power of Emperors, Kings, and Presidents, which now arouses our indignation, and which causes them to be murdered, would disappear of itself.

So that the Alexanders, Carnots, Humberts, and others should not be murdered, but it should be explained to them that they are themselves murderers, and, chiefly, they should not be allowed to kill people : men should refuse to murder at their command.

If people do not yet act in this way, it is only because Governments, to maintain themselves, diligently exercise a hypnotic influence upon the people.

And, therefore, we may help to prevent people killing either Kings or one another, not by killing—murder only increases the hypnotism—but by arousing people from their hypnotic condition.

And it is this I have tried to do by these remarks.

[August 8, o.s., 1900.]

Prohibited in Russia, an attempt was made to print this article in the Russian language in Germany; but the edition was seized in July, 1903, and after a trial in the Provincial Court of Leipzig (August, 1903) it was pronounced to be insulting to the German Kaiser, and all copies were ordered to be destroyed.

# XXI

## TO THE TSAR AND HIS ASSISTANTS

AGAIN there are murders, again disturbances and slaughter in the streets, again we shall have executions, terror, false accusations, threats and anger on the one side ; and hatred, thirst for vengeance, and readiness for self-sacrifice, on the other. Again all Russians are divided into two hostile camps, and are committing and preparing to commit the greatest crimes.

Very possibly the disturbances that have now broken out may be suppressed, though it is also possible that the troops of soldiers and of police, on whom the Government place such reliance, may realize that they are being called on to commit the terrible crime of fratricide—and may refuse to obey. But even if the present disturbance is suppressed, it will not be extinguished, but will burn in secret more and more fiercely, and will inevitably burst out sooner or later with increased strength, and produce yet greater sufferings and crimes.

Why is this ? Why should these things occur, when they might so easily be avoided ?

We address all you who are in power, from the Tsar, the members of the Council of State, and Ministers, to the relations—uncles, brothers, and entourage of the Tsar, and all who can influence him by persuasion. We appeal to you not as to enemies, but as to brothers, who, whether willingly or not, are inseparably bound up with us, so that all the sufferings we undergo react on you also—and react much more painfully if you feel that you could remove these sufferings but have failed to do so—we appeal to you to act so that the existing state of things may cease.

It seems to you, or to most of you, that it has all happened because, amid the regular current of life, some troublesome, dissatisfied men have arisen, who disturb the people and interrupt this regular current ; and that what is wrong is all the fault of these people. So that these troublesome, dissatisfied people should be subdued and repressed, and then everything will again go all right, and nothing will need to be altered.

But if, really, it were all due to troublesome and wicked men, it would be only necessary to catch them and shut them up in prison and execute them, and all disturbances would be at end. But, in fact, during more than thirty years, these people have been caught, imprisoned and executed, or banished by thousands— yet their number is ever increasing, and discontent with the present conditions of life not only grows, but spreads so that it has now reached millions of the working classes—the great majority of the whole nation. Evidently this dissatisfaction is not caused by troublesome and wicked men, but by something else. And you of the Government need only turn your attention for a moment from the acute strife in which you are now absorbed, and cease to credit naïvely the statement made by the Minister of the Interior in a recent circular, namely, that 'it is only necessary for the police to disperse the crowd promptly, and to fire at it if it does not disperse, for all to be tranquil and quiet,' and you will clearly see the cause that produces discontent among the people, and finds expression in disturbances which are assuming ever greater and wider and deeper dimensions.

Those causes are, that because, unfortunately, a Tsar who had freed the serfs happened to be murdered by a small group of people who mistakenly imagined that they would thereby serve the nation, the Government has not only decided not to advance in the direction of gradually discarding despotic methods (at variance with

all the present conditions of life), but, on the contrary,
imagining safety to lie in those coarse and obsolete
methods of despotism—instead of advancing in agreement with the general development and increasing complexity of modern life—has, for twenty years, not even
stood still, but has receded, and by this retrograde
movement has separated itself more and more from
the people and their demands.

So that it is not some wicked and troublesome people,
but it is you yourselves—the rulers, who do not wish to
consider anything but your own tranquillity for the
passing moment.  The thing needed is not that you
should defend yourselves from enemies who wish to
injure you—no one wishes to injure you—but the thing
needed is, that having recognised the cause of the social
discontent you should remove it.  Men, as a whole,
cannot desire discord and enmity, but always prefer to
live in agreement and amity with their fellows.  And
if they now are disquiet and seem to wish you ill, it is
only because you appear to them as an obstacle depriving
not only them, but millions of their brothers, of the
best human blessings—freedom and enlightenment.

That they may cease to be perturbed and to attack
you, very little is required, and that little is so necessary for you yourselves, and would so evidently give
you peace, that it will be strange indeed if you do not
grant it.

What needs to be done at once is very little.  Only
the following :

*First :* To grant the peasants equal rights with all
other citizens, and therefore to—

(*a*) Abolish the stupid, arbitrary institution of the
*Zémsky Natchálniks.**

(*b*) Repeal the special rules, framed to regulate the
relations between workmen and their employers.

(*c*) Free the peasants from the constraint of needing
passports to move from place to place, and also from
the compulsion laid only on them, to furnish lodging
and horses for officials, and men for police service.

* See footnote, p. 198.

(*d*) Free them from the unjust law which makes them jointly responsible for other peasants' debts, and from the land-redemption payments which have already, long ago, exceeded the value of the land received by them at the time of their emancipation.

(*e*) And, chiefly, abolish the senseless, utterly unnecessary and shameful system of corporal punishment, which has been retained only for the most industrious, moral, and numerous class of the population.

To equalize the rights of the peasantry (who form the immense majority of the people) with the rights of the other classes is particularly important, for no social system can be durable or stable, under which the majority does not enjoy equal rights but is kept in a servile position, and is bound by exceptional laws. Only when the labouring majority have the same rights as all other citizens, and are freed from shameful disabilities, is a firm order of society possible.

*Secondly :* The Statute of Increased Protection*— which abolishes all existing laws and hands over the population into the power of officials, who are often immoral, stupid, and cruel—must cease to be applied. Its disuse is specially important because, by stopping the action of the common law, it develops the practice of secret denunciations and the spy system, it encourages and evokes gross violence, often employed against working men who have differences with their employers or with the land-owners (nowhere are such cruelties practised as in the districts where this statute is in force). But above all is its disuse important, because to this terrible measure, and to it alone, do we owe the introduction and more and more frequent infliction of capital punishment—which most surely depraves men, is contrary to the Christian spirit of the Russian people, was formerly unknown in our code of laws, and is itself the greatest of crimes, and one forbidden by God and by conscience.

*Thirdly :* All barriers to education, instruction, and

* See footnote, p. 202.

S

to imparting knowledge, should be destroyed.  It is
necessary—

(*a*) To make no distinctions debarring people of any
class from education, and therefore to abolish all
restrictions aimed specially at the peasant class (forbidding popular readings, classes, and books, for some
reason supposed to be bad for the common people).

(*b*) To allow people of any race or religion (not
excepting the Jews, who for some reason are now
deprived of that right) to have access to all schools.

(*c*) To cease to hinder teachers from using in school
the language spoken by the children who attend the
school.

(*d*) And, above all, to allow the establishment and
continuance of all sorts of private schools (elementary
and higher) by all who wish to devote themselves to
education.

To set education and instruction free from the restraints now imposed upon them is important, because
these restraints alone hinder the working people from
freeing themselves from that very ignorance which now
serves the Government as a chief excuse for imposing
restraints on the peasants.  The liberation of the working classes from Governmental interference in matters
of education would be the easiest and quickest way to
enable the people to gain all the knowledge they
need, in place of such knowledge as is now being
forced upon them.  Liberty for private schools to be
opened and maintained by private people would end
the disturbances now continually arising among students
dissatisfied with the management of the establishments
in which they find themselves.  Were there no obstacles
to opening private schools and colleges, both elementary and advanced, young people dissatisfied with the
management of the Government educational institutions would enter private establishments which suited
their requirements.

Lastly, *fourthly*, and most important of all, all
limitation of religious liberty should be abolished.  It
is necessary—

(*a*) To repeal all the laws under which any secession from the established Church is punished as a crime.

(*b*) To allow Old-Believers,* Baptists, Molokáns,† Stundists,‡ and others, to open and maintain churches, chapels, and houses of prayer.

(*c*) To allow religious meetings and the preaching of all faiths.

(*d*) Not to hinder people of different faiths from educating their children in those faiths.

It is necessary to do this because, apart from the fact shown by history and science, and generally admitted, that religious persecutions fail to effect their object, and even produce a reverse effect by strengthening what people wish to destroy—and apart from the fact that the intervention of Government in matters of faith produces that most harmful and therefore worst of vices, hypocrisy, which Christ so strongly denounced, —not to speak of all that, the interference of Government in matters of faith hinders each individual and the whole people from attaining that highest blessing— union with one another. For union is attained, not by the forcible and impossible retention of all men in the bonds of one and the same external, once-accepted, confession of a religious teaching to which infallibility is attributed, but only by the free advance of the whole of humanity towards truth, which alone, therefore, can truly unite men.

Such are the modest and easily realizable desires, we believe, of the immense majority of the Russian people.

* The Old-Believers is a general name for the sects that separated from the Russo-Greek Church in the seventeenth and early in the eighteenth centuries.

† The Molokáns are a more modern sect. They reject the Sacraments and the ceremonial of the Russo-Greek Church, and pay much attention to the Bible.

‡ Stundist is a general name for the Protestant and rationalistic sects of many shades that have rapidly sprung up and increased, chiefly in South Russia, during the last quarter of a century.

The adoption of these measures would undoubtedly pacify the people, and free them from those terrible sufferings and (what is worse than sufferings) crimes, which will inevitably be committed on both sides, if the Government busies itself only with the suppression of these disturbances, leaving their cause untouched.

We appeal to you all—to the Tsar, to the Ministers, to the Members of the Council of State, to the Privy Councillors, and to those who surround the Tsar—to all, in general, who have power : to help to give peace to the nation, and free it from suffering and crime. We appeal to you, not as to men of a hostile camp, but as to men who must of necessity agree with us, as to fellow-workers and brothers.

It cannot be that, in a society of men mutually bound together, one section should feel at ease while it is ill with another. And especially is this so if it is the majority that suffers. It can be well for all, only when it is well for the strongest and most industrious majority, which supports the whole society.

Help, then, to improve the position of that majority, and help it in that which is most important : in what regards its freedom and enlightenment. Only then can your position also be safe and really strong.

This is written by Leo Tolstoy, who in writing it has tried to express not his own thoughts only, but the opinion of many of the best, kindest, most disinterested, most reasonable people—who all desire these things.

[March 15, o.s., 1901.]

# XXII

## A REPLY TO THE SYNOD'S EDICT OF EXCOMMUNICATION, AND TO LETTERS RECEIVED BY ME CONCERNING IT

'He who begins by loving Christianity better than truth, will proceed by loving his own sect or church better than Christianity, and end in loving himself better than all.'— COLERIDGE.

AT first I did not wish to reply to the Synod's Edict about me but it has called forth very many letters in which correspondents unknown to me write—some of them scolding me for rejecting things I never rejected; others exhorting me to believe in things I have always believed in; others, again, expressing an agreement with me which probably does not really exist, and a sympathy to which I am hardly entitled. So I have decided to reply both to the Edict itself—indicating what is unjust in it—and to the communications of my unknown correspondents.

The Edict of the Synod has, in general, many defects. It is either illegal, or else intentionally equivocal; it is arbitrary, unfounded, untruthful, and is also libellous, and incites to evil feelings and deeds.

It is illegal or intentionally equivocal; for if it is intended as an Excommunication from the Church, it fails to conform to the Church regulations subject to which Excommunications can be pronounced; while if it is merely an announcement of the fact that one who does not believe in the Church and its dogmas does not belong to the Church—that is self-evident, and the announcement can have no purpose other than to pass for an Excommunication without really being one ; as happened, in fact, for that is how the Edict has been understood.

It is arbitrary, for it accuses only me of disbelief in all the points enumerated in the Edict ; whereas many, in fact almost all educated people, share that disbelief and have constantly expressed and still express it both in conversations, in lectures, in pamphlets and in books.

It is unfounded because it gives as a chief cause of its publication the great circulation of the false teaching wherewith I pervert the people—whereas I am well assured that hardly a hundred people can be found who share my views, and the circulation of my writings on religion, thanks to the Censor, is so insignificant that the majority of those who have read the Synod's Edict have not the least notion of what I may have written about religion—as is shown by the letters I have received.

It contains an obvious falsehood, for it says that efforts have been made by the Church to show me my errors, but that these efforts have been unsuccessful. Nothing of the kind ever took place.

It constitutes what in legal terminology is called a libel, for it contains assertions known to be false and tending to my hurt.

It is, finally, an incentive to evil feelings and deeds, for, as was to be expected, it evoked, in unenlightened and unreasoning people, anger and hatred against me, culminating in threats of murder expressed in letters I received. One writes : ' Now thou hast been anathematized, and after death wilt go to everlasting torments, and wilt perish like a dog . . . anathema upon thee, old devil . . . be damned.' Another blames the Government for not having, as yet, shut me up in a monastery, and fills his letter with abuse. A third writes : ' If the Government does not get rid of you, we will ourselves make you shut your mouth,' and the letter ends with curses. ' May you be destroyed—you blackguard !' writes a fourth ; ' I shall find means to do it . . . and then follows indecent abuse. After the publication of the Synod's Edict I also noticed indications of anger of this kind in some of the people I met. On the very day (February 25) when the Edict was made public, while crossing a public square I heard the words: 'See! there goes the devil in human form,' and had the crowd been composed of other elements I should very likely have been beaten to death, as happened some years ago to a man at the Panteléymon Chapel.

So that, altogether, the Synod's Edict is very bad; and the statement, at the end, that those who sign it pray that I may become such as they are, does not make it any better.

That relates to the Edict as a whole; as to details, it is wrong in the following particulars. It is said in the Edict: 'A writer well known to the world, Russian by birth, Orthodox by baptism and education—Count Tolstoy—under the seduction of his intellectual pride has insolently risen against the Lord and against his Christ and against his holy heritage, and has publicly, in the sight of all men, renounced the Orthodox Mother Church which has reared him and educated him.'

That I have renounced the Church which calls itself Orthodox is perfectly correct.

But I renounced it not because I had risen against the Lord, but, on the contrary, only because with all the strength of my soul I wished to serve him. Before renouncing the Church, and fellowship with the people which was inexpressibly dear to me, I—having seen some reasons to doubt the Church's integrity—devoted several years to the investigation of its theoretic and practical teachings. For the theory, I read all I could about Church doctrine, and studied and critically analyzed dogmatic theology; while as to practice, for more than a year I followed strictly all the injunctions of the Church, observing all the fasts and all the services. And I became convinced that Church doctrine is theoretically a crafty and harmful lie, and practically a collection of the grossest superstitions and sorcery, which completely conceals the whole meaning of Christ's teaching.*

And I really repudiated the Church, ceased to observe its ceremonies, and wrote a will instructing those near me, that when I die they should not allow any servants of the Church to have access to me, but should put away my dead body as quickly as possible—without having any incantations or prayers over it—just as one puts away any objectionable and useless object, that it may not be an inconvenience to the living.

As to the statements made about me, that I devote the 'literary activity and the talent given to him by God, to disseminating among the people teachings contrary to Christ and to the Church,' and that, 'in his works and in letters issued by him and by his disciples in great quantities, over the whole world, but particularly within the limits of our dear fatherland, he preaches with the zeal of a fanatic the overthrow of all the dogmas of the Orthodox Church and the very essence of the Christian faith'—this is not true. I never troubled myself about the propagation of my teaching. It is true that for myself I have expressed in writings my understanding of Christ's teaching, and have not hidden these works from those who wished to become acquainted with them, but I never published them

* One need only read the Prayer-Book, and follow the ritual which is continually performed by the Orthodox priests, and which is considered a Christian worship of God, to see that all these ceremonies are nothing but different kinds of sorcery, adapted to all the incidents of life. That a child in case of death should go to Paradise, one has to know how to oil him and how to immerse him while pronouncing certain words; in order that after child-birth a mother may cease to be unclean, certain incantations have to be pronounced; to be successful in one's affairs, to live comfortably in a new house, that corn may grow well, that a drought may cease, to recover from sickness, to ease the condition in the next world of one who is dying,—for all these and a thousand other incidents there are certain incantations which, at a certain place, for a certain consideration, are pronounced by the priest.—L. T.

myself. Only when they have asked me about it, have I told people how I understand Christ's teaching. To those that asked, I said what I thought, and (when I had them) gave them my books.

Then it is said that ' he denies God worshipped in the Holy Trinity, the Creator and Protector of the universe; denies our Lord Jesus Christ, God-man, Redeemer and Saviour of the world, who suffered for us men and for our salvation, and was raised from the dead; denies the immaculate conception of the Lord Christ as man, and the virginity before his birth and after his birth of the Most Pure Mother of God.' That I deny the incomprehensible Trinity; the fable, which is altogether meaningless in our time, of the fall of the first man; the blasphemous story of a God born of a virgin to redeem the human race—is perfectly true. But God, a Spirit; God, love; the only God— the Source of all,—I not only do not deny, but I attribute real existence to God alone, and I see the whole meaning of life only in fulfilling his will, which is expressed in the Christian teaching.

It is also said: ' He does not acknowledge a life and retribution beyond the grave.' If one is to understand, by life beyond the grave, the Second Advent, a hell with eternal torments, devils, and a Paradise of perpetual happiness—it is perfectly true that I do not acknowledge such a life beyond the grave; but eternal life and retribution here and everywhere, now and for ever, I acknowledge to such an extent that, standing now, at my age, on the verge of my grave, I often have to make an effort to restrain myself from desiring the death of this body—that is, birth to a new life; and I believe every good action increases the true welfare of my eternal life, and every evil action decreases it.

It is also stated that I reject all the Sacraments. That is quite true. I consider all the Sacraments to be coarse, degrading sorcery, incompatible with the idea of God or with the Christian teaching, and also as infringements of very plain injunctions in the Gospels. In the Baptism of Infants I see a palpable perversion of the whole meaning which might be attached to the baptism of adults who consciously accepted Christianity; in the performance of the Sacrament of Marriage over those who are known to have had other sexual unions, in the permission of divorce, and in the consecration of the marriages of divorced people, I see a direct infringement both of the meaning and of the words of the Gospel teaching.

In the periodical absolution of sins at Confession I see a harmful deception, which only encourages immorality and causes men not to fear to sin.

Both in Extreme Unction and in Anointing I see methods of gross sorcery—as in the worship of icóns and relics, and as in all the rites, prayers and exorcisms which fill the Prayer-Book. In the Sacrament I see a deification of the flesh, and a perversion of Christian teaching. In Ordination I see (beside an obvious preparation for deception) a direct infringement of the words of Jesus, which plainly forbid anyone to be called teacher, father, or master.*

It is stated, finally, as the last and greatest of my sins, that, ' reviling the most sacred objects of the faith of the Orthodox people, he has not shrunk from subjecting to derision the greatest of Sacraments, the Holy Eucharist.'† That I did not shrink from describing simply and objectively what the priest does when preparing this so-called Sacrament is perfectly true; but that this so-called Sacrament is anything holy, and that to describe it simply, just as it is performed, is blasphemy, is quite untrue. Blasphemy does not consist in calling a partition a partition, and not an icono-

---

* Matt. xxiii. 8-10: 'But be not ye called Rabbi: for one is your teacher, and all ye are brethren. And call no man your father on the earth: for one is your Father, which is in heaven. Neither be ye called masters: for one is your Master, even the Christ.'

† See chapter xxxix., book i., of *Resurrection;* but see also, as a probable provocative of Tolstoy's Excommunication, the description of the Head of the Holy Synod in chapter xxvii., book ii., of that work.

stasis,* and a cup a cup, and not a chalice, etc.; but it is a most terrible, continual, and revolting blasphemy that men (using all possible means of deception and hypnotization) assure children and simple-minded folk that if bits of bread are cut up in a particular manner while certain words are pronounced over them, and if they are put into wine,† God will enter into those bits of bread, and any living person named by the priest when he takes out one of these sops will be healthy, and any dead person named by the priest when he takes out one of these sops will be better off in the other world on that account; and that into the man who eats such a sop—God himself will enter.

Surely that is terrible!

They undertake to teach us to understand the personality of Christ, but his teaching, which destroys evil in the world, and blesses men so simply, easily, and undoubtedly, if only they do not pervert it, is all hidden, is all transformed into a gross sorcery of washings, smearing with oil, gestures, exorcisms, eating of bits of bread, etc., so that of the true teaching nothing remains. And if, at any time, some one tries to remind men that Christ's teaching consists not in this sorcery, not in public prayer, liturgies, candles, and icóns, but in loving one another, in not returning evil for evil, in not judging or killing one another—the anger of those to whom deception is profitable is aroused, and with incomprehensible audacity they publicly declare in churches, and print in books, newspapers, and catechisms, that Jesus never forbade oaths (swearing allegiance, or swearing in courts of law), never forbade

---

* The iconostasis in Russo-Greek churches corresponds, somewhat, both to the Western altar-rails and to a rood-screen.

† In the Greek Church the priest mixes the sacramental bread with the wine before administering it to the communicant. The reader will note in this article allusions to several practices (baptism by immersion, unction, etc.) which do not exist, or are differently carried out, in the Church of England.

murder (executions and wars), and that the teaching of non-resistance to evil has with Satanic ingenuity been invented by the enemies of Christ.*

What is most terrible is that people to whom it is profitable, not only deceive adults, but (having power to do so) deceive children also—those very children concerning whom Jesus pronounced woe on him who deceives them. It is terrible that these people for such petty advantages do such fearful harm, by hiding from men the truth that was revealed by Jesus, and that gives blessings such as are not counterbalanced even to the extent of a one-thousandth part by the advantages these men secure for themselves. They behave like a robber who killed a whole family of five or six people to carry off an old coat and tenpence in money. They would willingly have given him all their clothes and all their money not to be killed; but he could not act otherwise.

So it is with the religious deceivers. It would be worth while keeping them ten times better, and letting them live in the greatest luxury, if only they would refrain from ruining men with their deceptions. But they cannot act differently. That is what is awful. And, therefore, we not only may, but should, unmask their deceptions. If there be a sacred thing, it is surely not what they call Sacraments, but just this very duty of unmasking their religious deceptions when one detects them.

When a Tchouvásh smears his idol with sour cream, or beats it, I can refrain from insulting his faith, and can pass by with equanimity, for he does these things in the name of a superstition of his own, foreign to me, and he does not interfere with what to me is holy. But when, with their barbarous superstitions, men (however numerous, however ancient their superstitions, and however powerful they may be) in the name of the God by whom I live, and of that teaching of Christ's which has given life to me and is capable of giving life to all men, preach gross sorcery, I cannot endure it pas-

* Speech by Ambrosius, Bishop of Khárkof.—L. T.

sively. And if I call what they are doing by its name, I only do my duty and what I cannot refrain from doing because I believe in God and in the Christian teaching. If they call the exposure of their imposture 'blasphemy,' that only shows the strength of their deception, and should increase the efforts to destroy this deception, made by those who believe in God and in Christ's teaching, and who see that this deception hides the true God from men's sight.

They should say of Christ—who drove bulls and sheep and dealers from the temple—that he blasphemed. Were he to come now, and see what is done in his name in church, he would surely, with yet greater and most just anger, throw out all these horrible altar-cloths,* lances, crosses, and cups and candles and icóns and all the things wherewith the priests—carrying on their sorcery—hide God and his truth from mankind.

So that is what is true and what is untrue in the Synod's Edict about me. I certainly do not believe in what they say they believe in. But I believe in much they wish to persuade people that I dis-believe in.

I believe in this : I believe in God, whom I understand as Spirit, as Love, as the Source of all. I believe that he is in me and I in him. I believe that the will of God is most clearly and intelligibly expressed in the teaching of the man Jesus, whom to consider as God, and pray to, I esteem the greatest blasphemy. I believe that man's true welfare lies in fulfilling God's will, and his will is that men should love one another, and should consequently do to others as they wish others to do to them—of which it is said in the Gospels that in this is the law and the prophets. I believe, therefore, that the meaning of the life of every man is to be found only in increasing the love that is in him ;

---

* The altar-cloths referred to are those containing frag-ments of holy relics, on which alone mass can be celebrated. The 'lances' are diminutive ones with which the priest cuts bits out of the holy bread, in remembrance of the lance that pierced Christ's side.

that this increase of love leads man, even in this life, to ever greater and greater blessedness, and after death gives him the more blessedness the more love he has, and helps more than anything else towards the establishment of the Kingdom of God on earth : that is, to the establishment of an order of life in which the discord, deception and violence that now rule will be replaced by free accord, by truth, and by the brotherly love of one for another. I believe that to obtain progress in love there is only one means : prayer—not public prayer in churches, plainly forbidden by Jesus,* but private prayer, like the sample given them by Jesus, consisting of the renewing and strengthening, in their consciousness, of the meaning of life and of their dependence solely on the will of God.

Whether these beliefs of mine offend, grieve, or prove a stumbling-block to anyone, or hinder anything, or give displeasure to anybody, or not, I can as little change them as I can change my body. I must myself live my own life, and I must myself alone meet death (and that very soon), and therefore I cannot believe otherwise than as I—preparing to go to that God from whom I came—do believe. I do not believe my faith to be the one indubitable truth for all time, but I see no other that is plainer, clearer, or answers better to all the demands of my reason and my heart ; should I find such a one, I shall at once accept it ; for God requires nothing but the truth. But I can no more return to

* ' And when ye pray, ye shall not be as the hypocrites : for they love to stand and pray in the synagogues and in the corners of the streets, that they may be seen of men. Verily I say unto you, They have received their reward. But thou, when thou prayest, enter into thine inner chamber, and having shut thy door, pray to thy Father which is in secret, and thy Father which seeth in secret shall recompense thee. And in praying use not vain repetitions, as the Gentiles do : for they think that they shall be heard for their much speaking. Be not therefore like unto them : for your Father knoweth what things ye have need of, before ye ask him. After this manner therefore pray ye : Our Father,' etc.—MATT. vi. 5-13.

that from which, with such suffering, I have escaped, than a flying bird can re-enter the eggshell from which it has emerged.

'He who begins by loving Christianity better than truth, will proceed by loving his own sect or church better than Christianity, and end in loving himself (his own peace) better than all,' said Coleridge.

I travelled the contrary way. I began by loving my Orthodox faith more than my peace, then I loved Christianity more than my Church, and now I love truth more than anything in the world. And up to now, truth, for me, corresponds with Christianity as I understand it. And I hold to this Christianity; and to the degree in which I hold to it I live peacefully and happily, and peacefully and happily approach death.

[April 4, o.s., 1901.]

# XXIII

## WHAT IS RELIGION, AND WHEREIN LIES ITS ESSENCE?

### I.

In all human societies, at certain periods of their existence, a time has come when religion has first swerved from its original purpose, then, diverging more and more, it has lost sight of that purpose, and has finally petrified into fixed forms, so that its influence on men's lives has become ever less and less.

At such times the educated minority cease to believe in the established religious teaching, and only pretend to hold it because they think it necessary to do so in order to keep the mass of the people to the established order of life ; but the mass of the people, though by inertia they keep to the established forms of religion, no longer guide their lives by its demands, but guide them only by custom and by the State laws.

That is what has repeatedly occurred in various human societies. But what is now happening in our Christian society has never happened before. It never before happened that the rich, ruling, and more educated minority, which has the most influence on the masses, not only disbelieved the existing religion, but was convinced that no religion at all is any longer needed, and, instead of influencing those who are doubtful of the truth of the generally professed religion to accept some religious teaching more rational and clear than the prevalent one, influenced them to regard religion in general as a thing that has outlived its day, and is now not merely a useless, but even a harmful, social organ, like the vermiform appendix in the human body.

Religion is regarded by such men, not as something known to us by inward experience, but as an external phenomenon—a disease, as it were, which overtakes certain people, and which we can only investigate by its external symptoms.

Religion, in the opinion of some of these men, arose from attributing a spirit to various aspects of Nature (animism); in the opinion of others, it arose from the supposed possibility of communicating with deceased ancestors; in the opinion of others, again, it arose from fear of the forces of Nature. But, say the learned men of our day, since science has now proved that trees and stones cannot be endowed with a spirit; that dead ancestors do not know what is done by the living; and that the aspects of Nature are explainable by natural causes—it follows that the need for religion has passed, as well as the need for all those restrictions with which, (in consequence of religious beliefs) people have hitherto hampered themselves. In the opinion of these learned men there was a period of ignorance: the religious period. That has long been outlived by humanity, though some occasional atavistic indications of it still remain. Then came the metaphysical period, which is now also outlived. But we, enlightened people, are living in a scientific period: a period of positive science which replaces religion and will bring humanity to a height of development it could never have reached while subject to the superstitious teachings of religion.

Early in 1901 the distinguished French savant Berthelot delivered a speech* in which he told his hearers that the day of religion has passed and religion must now be replaced by science. I refer to this speech because it is the first to my hand, and because it was delivered in the metropolis of the educated world by a universally recognised savant. But the same

* See the *Revue de Paris*, January, 1901.

T

thought is continually and ubiquitously expressed in every form, from philosophic treatises down to newspaper feuilletons.

M. Berthelot says in that speech, that there were formerly two motors moving humanity: Force and Religion; but that these motors have now become superfluous, for in their place we have *science*. By *science* M. Berthelot (like all devotees of science) evidently means a science embracing the whole range of things man knows, harmoniously united, co-ordinated, and in command of such methods that the data it obtains are unquestionably true. But as no such science really exists—and what is now called science consists of a collection of haphazard, disconnected scraps of knowledge, many of them quite useless, and such as, instead of supplying undoubted truth, very frequently supply the grossest delusions, exhibited as truth to-day, but refuted to-morrow—it is evident that the thing M. Berthelot thinks must replace religion is something non-existent. Consequently the assertion made by M. Berthelot and by those who agree with him, to the effect that science will replace religion, is quite arbitrary, and rests on a quite unjustifiable faith in the infallibility of science—a faith similar to the belief in an infallible Church.

Yet men who are said to be, and who consider themselves to be, educated, are quite convinced that a science already exists which should and can replace religion, and which even has already replaced it.

'Religion is obsolete: belief in anything but science is ignorance. Science will arrange all that is needful, and one must be guided in life by science alone.' This is what is thought and said both by scientists themselves and also by those men of the crowd who, though far from scientific, believe in the scientists and join them in asserting that religion is an obsolete superstition, and that we must be guided in life by science only: that is, in reality, by nothing at all; for science, by reason of its very aim (which is to study all that exists), can afford no guidance for the life of man.

## II.

The learned men of our times have decided that religion is not wanted, and that science will replace it, or has already done so; but the fact remains that, now as formerly, no human society and no rational man has existed or can exist without a religion. I use the term *rational* man because an irrational man may live, as the beasts do, without a religion. But a rational man cannot live without one; for only religion gives a rational man the guidance he needs, telling him what he should do, and what first and what next. A rational man cannot live without religion, precisely because reason is characteristic of his nature. Every animal is guided in its actions (apart from those to which it is impelled by the need to satisfy its immediate desires) by a consideration of the direct results of its actions. Having considered those results by such means of comprehension as it possesses, an animal makes its actions conform to those consequences, and it always unhesitatingly acts in one and the same way, in accord with those considerations. A bee, for instance, flies for honey and stores it in the hive because in winter it will need food for itself and for the young, and beyond these considerations it knows, and can know, nothing. So also a bird is influenced when it builds its nest, or migrates from the north to the south and back again. Every animal acts in a like way when it does anything not resulting from direct, immediate necessity, but prompted by considerations of anticipated results. With man, however, it is not so. The difference between a man and an animal lies in the fact that the perceptive capacities possessed by an animal are limited to what we call instinct, whereas man's fundamental perceptive capacity is reason. A bee, collecting honey, can have no doubts as to whether it is good or bad to collect honey; but a man gathering in his corn or fruit cannot but consider whether he is diminishing the prospects of obtaining future harvests, and whether he is not depriving his neighbour of food. Nor can he

T 2

help wondering what the children whom he now feeds will become like—and much else. The most important questions of conduct in life cannot be solved conclusively by a reasonable man, just because there is such a superabundance of possible consequences which he cannot but be aware of. Every rational man knows, or at least feels, that in the most important questions of life he can guide himself neither by personal impulses, nor by considerations of the immediate consequences of his activity—for the consequences he foresees are too numerous and too various, and are often contradictory one to another, being as likely to prove harmful as beneficial to himself and to other people. There is a legend which tells of an angel who descended to earth and, entering a devout family, slew a child in its cradle; when asked why he did so, he explained that the child would have become the greatest of malefactors, and would have destroyed the happiness of the family. But it is thus not only with the question, Which human lives are useful, useless, or harmful? None of the most important questions of life can a reasonable man decide by considerations of their immediate results and consequences. A reasonable man cannot be satisfied with the considerations that guide the actions of an animal. A man may regard himself as an animal among animals—living for the passing day; or he may consider himself as a member of a family, a society, or a nation, living for centuries; or he may, and even must necessarily (for reason irresistibly prompts him to this) consider himself as part of the whole infinite universe existing eternally. And therefore reasonable men should do, and always have done, in reference to the infinitely small affairs of life affecting their actions, what in mathematics is called *integrate*: that is to say, they must set up, besides their relation to the immediate facts of life, a relation to the whole immense Infinite in time and space, conceived as one whole. And such establishment of man's relation to that whole of which he feels himself to be a part, from which he draws guidance for his actions, is what has been called, and is called, Religion. And therefore religion always has been, and cannot cease to be, a necessary and an indispensable condition of the life of a reasonable man and of all reasonable humanity.

### III.

That is how religion has always been understood by men who were not devoid of the highest (that is, religious) consciousness, which distinguishes man from the beasts. The word religion itself comes either from *relegere*, *religens*, revering the Gods; or, as has been commonly supposed, from *religare*, to bind (in obligation to the higher powers). The oldest and most common definition of religion is that *religion is the link between man and God.* '*Les obligations de l'homme enver Dieu : voilà la religion*' (Man's obligations to God : that is religion) says Vauvenargues.* A similar meaning is given to religion by Schleiermacher[†] and by Feuerbach,[‡] who acknowledge *the basis of religion to be man's consciousness of his dependence on God.* '*La religion est une affaire entre chaque homme et Dieu*' (Religion is a matter between each man and God).—Bayle.[§] '*La religion est le résultat des besoins de l'âme et des effets de l'intelligence*' (Religion is the outcome of the needs of the soul and of the effects of intelligence).—B. Constant.[‖] '*Religion is a particular means by which man*

---

* Luc de Clapiers, Marquis de Vauvenargues (1715-1747), author of *Introduction à la Connaissance de l'Esprit humain*, and of *Réflexions* and *Maximes*.

† Friedrich E. D. Schleiermacher (1768-1834), author of *Der Christliche Glaube* and many other theological works.

‡ L. A. Feuerbach (1804-1872), author of *Das Wesen des Christenthums* (which was translated into English by George Eliot).

§ Pierre Bayle (1647-1706), author of the *Dictionnaire historique et critique*, which exercised a great influence, especially on the Continent, during the eighteenth century.

‖ Henri Benjamin Constant de Rebeque (1767-1830), politician, and author of *De la Religion*.

*realizes his relation with the superhuman and mysterious forces on which he considers himself dependent.'*—Goblet d'Alviella.* *' Religion is a definition of human life, based on the connection between the human soul and that mysterious spirit whose dominion over the world and over himself man recognises, and with which he feels himself united.'*—A. Réville.†

So that the essence of religion has always been understood—and is now understood by men not deprived of the highest human characteristic—to be the establishment by man of a relation between himself and the infinite Being or Beings, whose power he feels over him. And this relation—however different it may be for different nations and at different times—has always defined for men their destiny in the world; from which guidance for their conduct has naturally flowed. A Jew understood his relation to the Infinite to be, that he was a member of a nation chosen by God from among all nations, and that he had therefore to observe in the sight of God the agreement made by God with this people. A Greek understood his relation to be, that, being dependent on the representatives of eternity—*i.e.,* on the Gods—he ought to do what pleased them. A Brahman understands himself to be a manifestation of the infinite Brahma, and considers that he ought, by renunciation of life, to strive towards union with that highest being. A Buddhist considered, and considers, his relation to the Infinite to be: that, passing from one form of life to another, he inevitably suffers; and these sufferings proceed from passions and desires, and therefore his business is to strive to annihilate all passions and all desires, and so pass into Nirvana. Every religion is the setting up, between man and the infinite life to which he feels himself allied, of some relation from which he obtains guidance for his conduct. And, therefore, if a religion does not

* Eugène Goblet, Comte d'Alviella (1846-    ), author of *Evolution religieuse contemporaine* and other works.

† A. Réville (1826-    ), Protestant theologian of the advanced school, author of many works on religion.

establish any relation between man and the Infinite (as, for instance, is the case with idolatry or sorcery), then it is not a real religion, but only a degeneration. If, even, religion establishes some relation between man and God, but does this by means of assertions not accordant with reason and present-day knowledge, so that one cannot really believe the assertions—that also is not a religion, but only a counterfeit. If a religion does not unite the life of man with the infinite life, again it is not a religion. Nor does a belief in propositions from which no definite direction for human activity results constitute a religion.

*True religion is a relation, accordant with reason and knowledge, which man establishes with the infinite life surrounding him, and it is such as binds his life to that infinity, and guides his conduct.*

### IV.

Though there never was an age when, or a place where, men lived without a religion, yet the learned men of to-day say, like Molière's 'Involuntary Doctor' who asserted that the liver is on the left side : *Nous avons changé tout cela* (We have changed all that); and they think that we can and should live without any religion. But, nevertheless, religion remains what it has been in the past : the chief motor and heart of human societies ; and without it, as without a heart, human life is impossible. There have been, and there are, many different religions—for the expression of man's relation to the Infinite and to God, or to the Gods, differs at different times and in different places, according to the stages of development of different nations—but never in any society of men, since men first became rational creatures, could they live, or have they lived, without a religion.

It is true that there have been, and sometimes are, periods in the life of nations when the existing religion has been so perverted and has lagged so far behind life as to cease to guide it. But this cessation of its action on men's lives (occurring at times in all religions) has

been but temporary. It is characteristic of religion—
as of all that is really alive—that it is born, develops,
grows old, dies and again comes to life, and comes to
life ever in forms more perfect than before. After a
period of higher development in religion, a period
of decrepitude and lifelessness always follows, to be
usually succeeded in its turn by a period of regeneration, and the establishment of a religious doctrine
wiser and clearer than before. Such periods of development, decrepitude, and regeneration have occurred in
all religions. In the profound religion of Brahmanism,
as soon as it began to grow old and to petrify into
fixed and coarse forms not suited to its fundamental
meaning, came on one side a renascence of Brahmanism itself, and on the other the lofty teachings of
Buddhism, which advanced humanity's comprehension
of its relation to the Infinite. A similar decline
occurred in the Greek and Roman religions, and then,
following the lowest depths of that decline, appeared
Christianity. The same thing occurred again with
Church-Christianity, which in Byzantium degenerated
into idolatry and polytheism. To counterbalance this
perverted Christianity there arose, on one hand, the
Paulicians,* and on the other (in opposition to the doctrine of the Trinity and to Mariolatry) came strict
Mohammedanism with its fundamental dogma of One
God. The same thing happened again with Papal
Mediæval Christianity, which evoked the Reforma-
tion, so that periods when religion weakens in its
influence on the majority of men are a necessary condition of the life and development of all religious
teachings. This occurs because every religious teaching in its true meaning, however crude it may be,
always establishes a relation between man and the
Infinite, which is alike for all men. Every religion
regards men as equally insignificant compared to

* The Paulicians were a sect who played a great part in
the history of the Eastern Church (seventh to twelfth
centuries). They rejected the Church view of Christ's
teaching, and were cruelly persecuted.

Infinity ; and therefore every religion contains the conception of the equality of all men before that which it regards as God : whether that be lightning, wind, a tree, an animal, a hero, or a deceased—or even a living—king (as occurred in Rome). So that the admission of the equality of man, is an inevitable and fundamental characteristic of every religion. But as equality among men never has existed anywhere in actual life, and does not now exist, it has happened that as soon as a new religious teaching appeared (always including a confession of equality among all men*) then at once those people for whom inequality was profitable tried to hide this essential feature by perverting the teaching itself. So it has happened always, wherever a new religious teaching appeared. And this has been done for the most part not consciously, but merely because those to whom inequality was profitable—the rulers and the rich—in order to feel themselves justified by the teaching without having to alter their position, have tried by all means to fasten upon the religious teaching an interpretation sanctioning inequality. And, naturally, a religion so perverted that those who lorded it over others could consider themselves justified in so doing—when passed on to the common people, instilled into them also the idea that submission to those who exercise authority is demanded by the religion they profess.

### v.

All human activity is evoked by three motive causes : Feeling, Reason, and Suggestion, the last-named being the same thing that doctors call hypnotism. Sometimes man acts only under the influence of feeling—simply striving to get what he desires. Sometimes he acts solely under the influence of reason, which shows

---

* That is to say that all are equal in the sight of God : that human laws and customs should give them an equal right to life, liberty, and the pursuit of happiness ; and that men should treat one another as brothers.

him what he ought to do. Sometimes, and most frequently, man acts because he himself has, or other people have, suggested an activity to him, and he unconsciously submits to the suggestion. Under normal conditions of life all three influences play their part in prompting a man's activity. Feeling draws him towards a certain activity; reason judges of this activity in the light of present circumstances, as well as by past experience and future expectation; and suggestion causes a man, apart from feeling and reason, to carry out the actions evoked by feeling and approved by reason. Were there no feeling, man would undertake nothing; if reason did not exist, man would yield at once to many contradictory feelings, harmful to himself and to others; were there no capacity of yielding to one's own or other people's suggestion, man would have unceasingly to experience the feeling that prompted him to a particular activity, and to keep his reason continually intent on the verification of the expediency of that feeling. And, therefore, all these three influences are indispensable for even the simplest human activity. If a man walks from one place to another, this occurs because feeling has impelled him to move from one place to another; reason has approved of this intention and dictated means for its accomplishment (in this case—stepping along a certain road), and the muscles of the body obey, and the man moves along the road indicated. While he is going along, both his feeling and his reason are freed for other activity, which could not be the case but for his capacity to submit to suggestion. This is what happens with all human activities, and among the rest with the most important of them: religious activity. Feeling evokes the need to establish a man's relation to God; reason defines that relation; and suggestion impels man to the activity flowing from that relation. But this is so, only as long as religion remains unperverted. As soon as perversion commences, the part played by suggestion grows ever stronger and stronger, and the activity of feeling and of reason weakens. The methods of suggestion are

always and everywhere the same.    They consist in
taking advantage of man at times when he is most susceptible to suggestion (during childhood, and at important occurrences of life : deaths, births, or marriages),
and then acting on him by means of art : architecture,
sculpture, painting, music, and dramatic performances,
and, while he is in a condition of receptivity (com-
parable to that produced on individuals by semi-
hypnotization), instilling into him whatever the
suggestors wish.

This process may be observed in all ancient religions :
in the lofty religion of Brahmanism degenerating into
gross idolatry of multitudinous images in various
temples, accompanied by singing and the smoke of
incense ; in the ancient Hebrew religion preached by
the prophets, changing into a worship of God in a
gorgeous temple with ostentatious songs and proces-
sions ; in the lofty religion of Buddhism, transforming
itself—with its monasteries and images of Buddha and innumerable ostentatious rites—into impenetrable Lama-
ism ; and in Taoism with its sorcery and incantations.

Always, in all religious teachings when they began to
be perverted, their guardians, having brought men into
a state in which their reason acted but feebly, employed
every effort to suggest, and instil into men, whatever
they wished them to believe.    And in all religions it
was found necessary to suggest the same three things,
which serve as a basis for all the perversions to which a
degenerating religion is exposed.    First, it is suggested
that there are men of a particular kind, who alone can
act as intermediaries between man and God (or the
Gods) ; secondly, that miracles have been, and are, performed, proving and confirming the truth of what is
told by these intermediaries between man and God ;
and thirdly, that there are certain words—repeated
verbally, or written in books—which express the unalterable will of God (or of the Gods), and which are
therefore sacred and infallible.    And as soon as, under
the influence of hypnotism, these propositions are
accepted, then also all that the intermediaries between

man and God say, is also accepted as sacred truth, and
the chief aim of the perversion of religion is attained,
namely: the concealment of the law of human equality,
and even the establishment and assertion of the greatest
inequality ; the separation into castes, the separation
into chosen people and Gentiles, into orthodox and
heretics, saints and sinners.    This very thing has
occurred and is occurring in Christianity : complete
inequality among men has been admitted, and they are
divided, not only, with reference to their comprehension of the teaching, into clerics and laity, but, with
reference to social position, into those who have power
and those who ought to submit to power—which, in
accord with the teaching of Paul, is acknowledged as
having been ordained of God.

### VI.

Inequality among men, not only as clergy and laity,
but also as rich and poor, masters and slaves, is established by the Church-Christian religion as definitely
and glaringly as by other religions.   Yet, judging by
what we know of Christian teaching in its earliest form
in the Gospels, it would seem that the chief methods of
perversion made use of in other religions had been foreseen, and a clear warning against them had been uttered.
Against a priestly caste, it was plainly said that no
man may be the teacher of another ('Call no man your
father—neither be ye called masters').    Against
attributing sanctity to books it was said, that the spirit
is important, but not the letter, that man should not
believe in human traditions, and that all the law and
the prophets (that is, all the books regarded as sacred
writing) amount only to this, that we should do to
others as we wish them to do to us.   If nothing is said
against miracles, and if in the Gospels themselves
miracles are described which Jesus is supposed to have
performed, it is, nevertheless, evident from the whole
spirit of the teaching, that Jesus based the proof of the
validity of his doctrine, not on miracles, but on the

merits of the teaching itself. ('If any man willeth to do his will, he shall know of the teaching, whether it be of God, or whether I speak from myself.') And, above all, Christianity proclaims the equality of men, no longer merely as a deduction from man's relation to the infinite, but as a basic doctrine of the brotherhood of all men, resulting from their being acknowledged as sons of God.

It seems, therefore, as though it should have been impossible to pervert Christianity so as to destroy the consciousness of equality among men. But the human mind is subtle, and (perhaps unconsciously or semi-consciously) a quite new dodge was devised to make the warnings contained in the Gospels, and this plain pronouncement of equality among men, inoperative. This dodge consisted in attributing infallibility not only to certain writings, but also to a certain set of men called The Church, who have a right to hand on this infallibility to people they themselves select.

A slight addition to the Gospels was invented, telling how Christ, when about to go up into the sky, handed over to certain men the exclusive right—not merely to teach others divine truth (according to the literal text of the Gospel he bequeathed at the same time the right, not generally utilized, of being invulnerable by snakes, or poisons)*—but also to decide which people should be saved or the reverse, and, above all, to confer this power on others. And the result was that as soon as this idea of a Church was firmly established, all the Gospel warnings hindering the perversion of Christ's teaching became inoperative, for the Church was superior both to reason and to the writings esteemed sacred. Reason was acknowledged to be the source of errors, and the Gospels were explained not as common-sense demanded, but as suited those who constituted the Church.

* 'Go ye into all the world, and preach the Gospel. . . . And these signs shall follow them that believe; in my name . . . they shall take up serpents; and if they drink any deadly thing, it shall in no wise hurt them.'—MARK xvi. 15-18.

And so all the three former methods of perverting religion—a priesthood, miracles, and the infallibility of scriptures—were admitted in full force into Christianity. Intermediaries between God and man were admitted because the need and fitness of having such intermediaries was recognised by the Church; the validity of miracles was acknowledged because the infallible Church testified to them; and the sanctity of the Bible was acknowledged because it was acknowledged by the Church.

And Christianity was perverted as all other religions had been, but with this difference, that just because Christianity most clearly proclaimed its fundamental principle—the equality of all men as sons of God—it was necessary most forcibly to pervert its whole teaching, in order to hide this fundamental principle. And by the help of this conception of a Church, this has been done to a greater extent than in any other religion. So that really no religion has ever preached things so evidently incompatible with reason and with contemporary knowledge, or so immoral, as the doctrines preached by Church-Christianity. Not to speak of all the absurdities of the Old Testament, such as the creation of light before the sun, the creation of the world six thousand years ago, the housing of all the animals in the Ark; or of the many immoral horrors, such as injunctions to massacre children and whole populations at God's command; not to speak even of the absurd Sacrament of which Voltaire used to say, that though there have been and are many absurd religious doctrines, there never before was one in which the chief act of religion consisted in eating one's own God,—not to dwell on all that, what can be more absurd than that the Mother of God was both a mother and a virgin; that the sky opened and a voice spoke from up there; that Christ flew into the sky and sits somewhere up there at the right hand of his father; or that God is both One and Three, not three Gods like Brahma, Vishnu and Shiva, but One and yet Three? And what can be more immoral than the terrible doctrine that an angry and revengeful God punishes all men for Adam's sin, and sent his son on earth to save them, knowing beforehand that men would kill him and would therefore be damned; and that salvation from sin consists in being baptized, or in believing that all these things really happened, and that the son of God was killed by men that men might be saved, and that God will punish with eternal torments those who do not believe this?

So that, leaving aside things some people consider as additions to the chief dogmas of this religion—things such as various relics, icóns of various Mothers of God,* prayers asking for favours and addressed to saints each of whom has his own speciality—and not to speak also of the Protestant doctrine of predestination—the very foundations of this religion, admitted by all and formulated in the Nicene Creed, are so absurd and immoral, and run so counter to right feeling and to common-sense, that men cannot believe in them. Men may repeat any form of words with their lips, but they cannot believe things that have no meaning. It is possible to say with one's lips: 'I believe the world was created six thousand years ago'; or, 'I believe Christ flew up into the sky and sat down next to his Father'; or, 'God is One and at the same time Three' —but no one can believe these things, for the words have no sense. And therefore men of our modern world who profess this perverted form of Christianity really believe in nothing at all.

And that is the peculiar characteristic of our time.

### VII.

People in our time do not believe in anything, yet, using a false definition of faith which they take from the *Epistle to the Hebrews* (wrongly ascribed to Paul),

---

* The wonder-working icóns of the Kazán, Iberian, and many other 'Mothers of God,' are all paintings of Mary the mother of Jesus, to which various miraculous powers are attributed in Russia.

they imagine they have faith.    Faith according to that
definition is 'the substance of things hoped for, the
evidence of things not seen' (Heb. xi. 1).    But—not
to mention the fact that faith cannot be a 'substance,'
since it is a mental condition and not an objective
reality—faith is also not 'the evidence of things not
seen,' for the 'evidence' referred to in the Epistle, as
the context shows, is simply credulity, and credulity
and faith are two different things.*

Faith is neither hope nor credulity, but a special
state of the soul.    Faith is man's consciousness that
his position in the world is such as obliges him to do
certain things.    Man acts in accord with his faith not
because, as is said in our Russian Catechism, he believes
in the unseen as in the seen, nor because he hopes to
attain his expectation, but only because, having defined
his position in the universe, he naturally acts according
to that position.    An agriculturist cultivates the land,
and a navigator sets out to sea, not because, as the
Catechism says, they believe in the unseen, or hope to
receive a reward for their activity (such hope exists, but
it is not what guides them), but because they consider
that activity to be their calling.    So also a religiously-
believing man acts in a certain way, not because he
believes in the unseen or expects a reward for his
activity, but because, having understood his position in
the universe, he naturally acts in accord with that
position.    If a man has decided that his position in
society is that of a labourer, an artisan, an official, or a
merchant, then he considers it necessary to work ; and

* What is fundamental in the above argument is, that
the author of the *Epistle to the Hebrews* defines faith without
indicating that it relates man to God *rationally*, and *supplies
guidance for conduct;* while, in Tolstoy's apprehension, these
are just the essential characteristics of faith, as of religion.
The paragraph has been altered for the present edition
because, as Tolstoy first wrote it, it was aimed chiefly against
the Russian and Slavonic versions of *Hebrews* xi. 1, and
was therefore perplexing to English readers.    It has now
been worded to fit the English authorized version, and can,
with equal ease, be worded to fit the Greek text.

as a labourer, an artisan, an official, or a merchant, he does his work. Just so do men in general, who, one way or other, have defined their position in the world, necessarily and naturally act in accord with that definition (which sometimes is rather a dim consciousness than a definition). Thus, for instance, a man having defined his position in the world as that of a member of a nation chosen by God, which in order to enjoy God's protection must fulfil His demands, will live in such a way as to fulfil those demands ; another man, having defined his position on the supposition that he has passed and is passing through various forms of existence, and that on his actions more or less depends his better or worse future, will be guided in life by that definition ; and the conduct of a third man, who has defined his position as that of a chance combination of atoms, in which a consciousness has been temporarily kindled which must be extinguished for ever, will differ from that of the two first.

The conduct of these men will be quite different, because they have defined their positions differently— that is to say, they have different faiths. Faith is the same thing as religion, only with this difference : that by the word *religion* we imply something observed outside us, while what we call *faith* is the same thing, only experienced by man within himself. Faith is a relation man is conscious of towards the infinite universe, and from this relation the direction of his activity results. And, therefore, true faith is never irrational or incompatible with present-day knowledge, and it cannot be its characteristic to be supernatural or absurd, as people suppose, and as was expressed by a Father of the Church who said : ' *Credo quia absurdum* ' (I believe because it is absurd). On the contrary, the assertions of true faith, though they cannot be proved, never contain anything contrary to reason, or incompatible with human knowledge, but always explain that in life which, without the conception supplied by faith, would appear irrational and contradictory.

Thus, for instance, an ancient Hebrew, believing in

U

a Supreme, Eternal, All-powerful Being who created the universe, the world, the animals, man, etc., and who has promised to patronize His people if they will keep His law—did not believe in anything irrational or incompatible with his knowledge, but, on the contrary, this faith explained to him many things in life which without such a faith would have been inexplicable to him.

In the same way, a Hindu who believes that our souls have lived in animals, and that, according to the good or evil life led, they pass into higher or lower animals—by the help of this faith explains to himself many things that without it would be inexplicable to him.

It is the same with a man who considers life an evil, and the aim of life to be peace attainable by the annihilation of desire. He believes in nothing unreasonable, but, on the contrary, in something that makes his outlook on life more reasonable than it was without that faith.

It is the same with a true Christian who believes that God is the spiritual Father of all men, and that the highest human blessedness is attainable by man when he acknowledges his sonship to God and the brotherhood of all mankind.

All these faiths, if they cannot be demonstrated, are in themselves not irrational, but, on the contrary, give a more rational meaning to occurrences in life which without them seem irrational and contradictory. Moreover, all these beliefs, by defining man's position in the universe, inevitably demand conduct in accord with that position. And therefore, if a religious teaching asserts irrational propositions which explain nothing, but only help to confuse man's understanding of life—then it is not a faith, but only a perversion of faith, which has already lost the chief characteristic of true faith, and instead of demanding anything from men has become their pliant tool. One of the chief distinctions between true faith and its perversion, is that in a perverted faith man demands that God, in return for sacrifices and prayers, should fulfil his wishes and serve man. But, in a true faith, man feels that God demands from him the fulfilment of His will : demands that man should serve God.

And just this faith is lacking among the men of our time—they do not even understand what it is like, and by faith they mean, either repeating with their lips what is given to them as the essence of faith, or the performance of ceremonies which, as Church-Christianity teaches, help them to attain their desires.

### VIII.

People in our world live without any faith. One part, the educated, wealthy minority, having freed themselves from the Church hypnotism, believe in nothing at all, and look upon every faith as an absurdity, or as merely a useful means of keeping the masses in subjection. The immense, poor, uneducated majority—consisting of people who, with few exceptions, are really sincere—being still under the hypnotism of the Church, think they believe in what is suggested to them as a faith, although it is not really a faith, for instead of elucidating to man his position in the world it only darkens it.

This situation, and the relations of the non-believing, insincere minority to the hypnotized majority, are the conditions which shape the life of our so-called Christian world. And this life—both of the minority which holds in its hands the means of hypnotization, and of the hypnotized majority—is terrible, both on account of the cruelty and immorality of the ruling classes, and of the crushed and stupefied condition of the great working masses. Never at any period of religious decline has the neglect and forgetfulness of the chief characteristic of all religion, and of Christianity in particular—the principle of human equality—fallen to so low a level as it has descended to in our time.

A chief cause, in our time, of the terrible cruelty of man to man—besides the complete absence of religion—is the refined complexity of life, which hides from men the consequences of their actions.    However cruel the Attilas and Genghis-Khans and their followers may have been, the process of personally killing people face to face must have been unpleasant to them, and the consequences of the slaughter must have been still more unpleasant: the lamentations of the kindred of the slain, and the presence of the corpses.    So that the consequences of their cruelty tended to diminish it.    But to-day we kill people by so complex a transmission, and the consequences of our cruelty are so carefully removed and hidden from us, that there are no effects tending to restrain cruelty ; and the cruelty of one set of men towards another is ever increasing and increasing, till it has reached dimensions it never attained before.

I think that nowadays if—I do not say some prominent villain such as Nero, but—some most ordinary man of business wished to make a pond of human blood for diseased rich people to bathe in when ordered to do so by their learned medical advisers, he would not be prevented from arranging it, if only he observed the accepted and respectable forms : that is, did not use violence to make people shed their blood, but got them into such a position that they could not live without shedding it ; and if, also, he engaged priests and scientists : the former to consecrate the new pond as they consecrate cannons, ironclads, prisons and gallows ; and the latter to find proofs of the necessity and justifiability of such an institution, as they have found proofs of the necessity for wars and brothels.*

The fundamental principle of all religion — the equality of men—is so forgotten, neglected, and buried under all sorts of absurd dogmas, in the religion now professed ; and in science this same inequality (in the theory of the struggle for existence and survival of the fittest) is so acknowledged to be a necessary condition of life—that the destruction of millions of human lives for the convenience of a ruling

* Laws similar to our 'Contagious Diseases Prevention Act' of 1864 (supported by the Royal College of Physicians and Surgeons in 1866) still exist in Russia, as well as a regular system of licensing houses of ill-fame.

minority is considered a most usual and necessary event, and is continually going on.

Men of to-day do not know how to express sufficient delight over the splendid, unprecedented, colossal progress achieved by technical science during the nineteenth century.

There is no doubt that never in history was such material progress made in mastering the powers of Nature as during the nineteenth century. But, also, there is no doubt that never in history was there such an example of immoral life, freed from any force restraining man's animal inclinations, as that given by our ever-increasingly bestialized, Christian humanity. The material progress achieved in the nineteenth century has really been great; but that progress has been bought, and is being bought, by such neglect of the most elementary demands of morality, as humanity never before was guilty of, even in the days of Genghis-Khan, Attila, or Nero.

There is no doubt that the ironclads, railroads, printing-presses, tunnels, phonographs, Röntgen-rays, and so forth, are very good. They are all very good, but what are also good—good, as Ruskin says, beyond comparison with anything else—are human lives, such as those of which millions are now mercilessly ruined for the acquisition of ironclads, railways, and tunnels, which, instead of beautifying life, disfigure it. To this the usual reply is, that appliances are already being invented, and will with time be invented, to check such destruction of human life as is now going on—but this is untrue. As long as men do not consider all men their brothers, and do not consider human lives the most sacred of all things—on no account to be sacrificed; since to support them is the very first and most immediate of duties—that is, as long as men do not treat each other religiously, they will always, for the sake of personal advantage, ruin one another's lives. No one will be so silly as to agree to spend thousands of pounds, if he can attain the same end by spending a hundred pounds—with a few human lives that are at his disposal thrown in. On the railroad in Chicago, about the same number of people are crushed each year. And the owners of the railroads, quite naturally, do not adopt appliances which would prevent these people from being crushed, for they have calculated that the annual payments to the injured and to their families come to less than the interest on the cost of such appliances.

Very possibly these men who ruin human lives for their own profit may be shamed by public opinion, or otherwise compelled, to provide the appliances. But as long as men are not religious, and do their deeds to be seen of men and not as in the sight of God, they will, after providing appliances in one place to secure people's lives, in other matters again treat human lives as the best material out of which to make a profit.

It is easy to conquer Nature, and to build railways, steamers, museums, and so forth, if one does not spare human lives. The Egyptian Pharaohs were proud of their pyramids, and we are delighted with them, forgetting the millions of slaves' lives that were sacrificed for their erection. And in the same way we are delighted with our exhibition-palaces, ironclads, and transoceanic cables—forgetting with what we pay for these things. We should not feel proud of all this, till it is all done by free men, and not by slaves.

Christian nations have conquered and subdued the American Indians, Hindus, and Africans, and are now conquering and subduing the Chinese, and are proud of doing so. But, really, these conquests and subjugations do not result from the Christian nations being spiritually superior to those conquered, but, contrariwise, from their being spiritually far inferior to them. Leaving the Hindus and Chinese out of account, even among the Zulus there were, and still are, some sort of obligatory religious rules, prescribing certain actions and forbidding others ; but among our Christian nations there are none at all. Rome conquered the world just when Rome had freed itself from every religion. The same, only in a greater degree, is the case now with the Christian nations. They are all in one and the same condition of having rejected religion; and, therefore, notwithstanding dissensions among themselves, they are all united and form one confederate band of robbers, among whom theft, plunder, depravity and murder, individually or collectively, goes on without causing the least compunction of conscience, and even with the greatest self-complacency, as occurred the other day in China. Some believe in nothing, and are proud of it ; others pretend to believe in what they for their own advantage hypnotize the common folk into accepting as a faith ; while others, again—the great majority, the common people as a whole—accept as a faith the hypnotic suggestions to which they are subjected, and slavishly submit to all that is demanded of them by the dominant and unbelieving hypnotizers.

And what these hypnotizers demand is, what Nero and all like him, who have tried in some way to fill the emptiness of their lives, have always demanded : the satisfaction of their insane and superabounding luxury. Luxury is obtained in no other way than by enslaving men, and as soon as there is enslavement luxury increases ; and the increase of luxury inevitably drags after it an increase of slavery ; for only people who are cold and hungry, and bound down by want, will continue all their lives long doing not what *they* want, but what is wanted only for the pleasure of their masters.

## IX.

In chapter vi. of the Book of Genesis there is a profound passage in which the author says that God, before the Flood, having seen that the spirit He had given to men that they might serve Him was used by them only to serve their own desires, became so angry with men that He repented of having created them, and, before entirely destroying them, decided to shorten the life of man to 120 years. And the very thing that, according to the Bible, then so provoked God's anger that it caused Him to shorten man's life, is again going on among the people of our Christian world.

Reason is the power which enables men to define their relation to the universe, and as all men stand in one and the same relation to the universe, it follows that religion—which is the elucidation of that relation —unites men. And union among men affords them the highest attainable welfare, both physical and spiritual.

Complete union with the highest and most perfect reason, and therefore complete welfare, is the ideal towards which humanity strives ; and all religions unite people, by supplying identical answers to all men of any given society when they ask what the universe is, and what its inhabitants are ; and by uniting them it brings them nearer to the attainment of welfare. But when reason, diverging from its natural function (that of determining man's relation to God, and what his activity should be, conformably to that relation), is used in the service of the flesh, and for angry strife with other men and other fellow-creatures, and when it is even used to justify this evil life, so contrary to man's nature and to the purpose for which he is intended— then those terrible calamities result, under which the majority of men are now suffering, and a state is reached that makes any return to a reasonable and good life seem almost impossible.

Pagans united by the crudest religious teaching are far nearer the recognition of truth than the pseudo-Christian nations of our day, who live without any religion, and among whom the most advanced people are themselves convinced—and suggest to others—that religion is unnecessary, and that it is much better to live without any.

Among the pagans men may be found who, recognising the inconsistency of their faith with their increasing knowledge, and with the demands of their reason, produce or adopt a new religion more in accord with the spiritual condition of their nation, and acceptable to their compatriots and co-believers. But men of our world—some of whom regard religion as an instrument wherewith to keep common folk in subjection, while others consider all religion absurd, and yet others (the great majority of the nation), while living under the hypnotism of a gross deception, think they possess true religion—become impervious to any forward movement, and incapable of any approach towards truth.

Proud of their improvements in things that regard the bodily life, as well as of their refined, idle reasonings (in which they aim not only at justifying themselves, but also at proving their superiority to any other people of any age of history), they petrify in ignorance and immorality, while feeling fully assured that they stand on an elevation never before reached by humanity, and that every step forward along the path of ignorance and immorality raises them to yet greater heights of enlightenment and progress.

### x.

Man naturally wishes to bring his bodily (physical) and his rational (spiritual) activity into conformity. He cannot be at peace until, in one way or other, he has reached that conformity. But it is attainable in two different ways. One way is for a man to decide by the use of his reason on the necessity or desirability of a certain action or actions, and then to behave accordingly; the other way is for a man to commit actions under the influence of his feelings, and then to invent intellectual explanations or justifications for what he has done.

The first method of conforming one's actions with one's reason is characteristic of men who have some religion, and on the basis of its precepts decide what they ought and what they ought not to do. The second method is generally characteristic of men who are not religious, and have no general standard by which to judge the quality of actions, and who therefore always set up a conformity between their reason and their actions, not by subjecting the latter to their reason, but (after acting under the sway of feeling) by using reason to justify what they have done.

A religious man—knowing what is good and what is

bad in his own activity and in that of others, and
knowing also why one thing is good and another is
bad—when he sees a contradiction between the demands of reason and his own or other men's actions,
will employ the whole force of his reason to find means
to destroy these contradictions by learning how best to
bring his actions into agreement with the demands of
his reason. But a man without religion—who has no
standard whereby to judge the quality of actions apart
from the pleasure they afford him—yielding to the
sway of his feelings (which are most various and often
contradictory), involuntarily falls into contradictions;
and, having fallen into contradictions, tries to solve or
hide them by arguments more or less elaborate and
clever, but always untruthful. And therefore, while
the reasoning of truly religious men is always simple,
direct, and truthful, the mental activity of men who
lack religion becomes particularly subtle, complex, and
insincere.

I will take the most common example: that of a
man who is addicted to vice—that is, is not chaste, not
faithful to his wife, or, being unmarried, indulges in
vice. If he is a religious man, he knows that this is
wrong, and all the efforts of his reason are directed to
finding means to free himself from his vice: avoiding
intercourse with adulterers and adulteresses, increasing
the amount of his work, arranging a strict life for himself, not allowing himself to look on a woman as on an
object of desire, and so forth. And all this is very
simple, and everyone can understand it. But if the
incontinent man is not religious, he at once begins to
devise all sorts of explanations to prove that falling in
love with women is very good. And then we get all
sorts of most complex, cunning, and subtle considerations about the affinity of souls, about beauty, about the
freedom of love, etc.; and the more these spread, the
more they darken the question and hide the essential
truth.

Among those who lack religion, the same thing
happens in all spheres of activity and of thought. To

hide underlying contradictions, complex, subtle disquisitions are piled up, which, by filling the mind with all sorts of unnecessary rubbish, divert men's attention from what is important and essential, and make it possible for them to petrify in the deceit in which, without noticing it, the people of our world are living.

'Men loved the darkness rather than the light; for their works were evil,' says the Gospel. 'For every one that doeth ill hateth the light, and cometh not to the light, lest his works should be reproved.'

And therefore the men of our world, having, in consequence of their lack of religion, arranged a most cruel, animal, and immoral life, have also brought their complex, subtle, unprofitable activity of mind—hiding the evil of this kind of life—to such a degree of unnecessary intricacy and confusion, that the majority of them have quite lost the capacity to distinguish good from evil, or what is false from what is true.

There is not a single question the men of our world can approach directly and simply : all questions—economic, national, political (whether home or foreign), diplomatic or scientific, not to mention questions of philosophy and religion—are presented so artificially and incorrectly, and are swathed in such thick shrouds of complex, unnecessary disputations—such subtle perversions of meanings and words, such sophistries and disputes — that all arguments about such questions revolve on one spot, connected with nothing, and, like driving-wheels without a connecting strap, effect nothing except the one object for which they were produced : to hide from one's self and from others the evil in which men live and the evil they commit.

## XI.

In every domain of what is now called science, one and the same feature is encountered, baffling the mental efforts men direct to the investigation of various domains of knowledge. This feature is, that all these scientific investigations evade the essential question calling for an answer, and examine side-issues the investigation of which brings one to no definite result, but becomes more intricate the further one advances. Nor can this be otherwise in a science which selects the objects of its investigation haphazard, and not according to the demands of a religious conception of life, defining what should be studied and why ; what first and what after-wards. For instance, in the now fashionable subjects of Sociology and Political Economy, it would seem that there is really only one question : ' How is it, and why is it, that some people do nothing, while others are working for them?' (If there is another question : ' Why do people work separately, hindering one another, and not together in common, as would be more profitable?' that question is included in the first. For were there no inequality, there would be no strife.) It would seem that there ought to be only that one question, but science does not even think of pro-pounding and replying to it, but commences its discus-sions from afar off, and conducts them so that its conclusions can never either solve or assist the solution of the fundamental problem. Discussions are started concerning what used to be and what now is ; and the past and the present are regarded as something as unalterable as the course of the stars in the heavens ; and abstract conceptions are devised—value, capital, profit, and interest—and a complex play of wits results (which has now already continued for a hundred years) among the disputants. In reality the question can be settled very easily and simply.

Its solution lies in the fact that, as all men are brothers and equals, each should act towards others as he wishes them to act towards him ; and, therefore, the whole matter depends on the destruction of a false religious law, and the restoration of the true religious law. The advanced people of Christendom, however, not only refuse to accept that solution, but, on the con-trary, try to hide from men the possibility of such a solution, and therefore devote themselves to the idle play of intelligence which they call science.

The same thing takes place in the domain of Juris-prudence. There would seem to be only one essential question : 'How is it that there are men who allow themselves to perpetrate violence on others, to fleece them, confine them, execute them, send them to the wars, and so on?' The solution of that question is very simple, if it be examined from the only point of view suitable to the subject—the religious. From a religious point of view, man must not and should not subject his neighbour to violence, and therefore only one thing is needful for the solution of the question— namely, to destroy all superstitions and sophistries which allow of violence, and to instil into men religious principles clearly excluding the possibility of violence.

But the advanced men, instead of doing this, devote all their wits to the task of hiding from others the possibility and necessity of such a solution. They write mountains of books about all sorts of laws : civil, criminal, police, Church, commercial, etc., and ex-pound and dispute about these—fully assured that they are doing something not only useful but very impor-tant. To the question, 'Why, among men who are naturally equal, may some judge, coerce, fleece, and execute others?'—they give no reply, and do not even acknowledge the existence of such a question. Accord-ing to their doctrine, this violence is not committed by men, but by some abstraction called The State. And similarly, in all realms of knowledge, the learned men of to-day evade and are silent about the essential ques-tions, and hide the underlying contradictions.

In the realm of history, the only essential question is : 'How the workers (who form $\frac{999}{1000}$ths of the whole of humanity) lived ?' To this question we get nothing like an answer ; the question is ignored, while whole mountains of books are written by historians of one school to tell of the stomach-aches of Louis XI., the horrors committed by Elizabeth of England or Iván the Terrible of Russia, of who were their Ministers, and of what verses and comedies were written by literary men to amuse these Kings and their mistresses and Ministers.

Meanwhile, the historians of another school tell us
in what sort of country a people lived, what they ate,
what they sold, what clothes they wore—and in general
about things that could have no influence on the
people's true life, but were results of their religion,
which the historians of this class imagine to be itself
a result of the food the people ate and the clothes they
wore.

Yet an answer to the question : 'How did the
workers live?' cannot be given till we acknowledge
religion to be the essential condition of a people's life.
And the reply is, therefore, to be found in the study
of the religions believed in by the nations : for these
brought them to the position in which they lived.

In the study of Natural History one would think there
was little need to darken men's common-sense ; but
even here, following the bent of mind which contemporary science has adopted, instead of giving the most
natural replies to the questions : 'What is the world
of living things (plants and animals), and how is it
subdivided?' an idle, confused, and perfectly useless
chatter is started (directed chiefly against the Biblical
account of the creation of the world) as to how
organisms came into existence—which, really, one
neither needs to know nor can know, for this origin,
however we may explain it, always remains hidden
from us in endless time and space.    But on this theme,
theories and refutations and supplementary theories
are invented, filling millions of books, the unexpected
result arrived at being : That the law of life which man
should obey is—the struggle for existence.

More than that, the applied sciences—such as
Technology and Medicine—in consequence of the
absence of any guidance from religious principle,
inevitably diverge from their reasonable purpose and
take a false direction.    Thus, Technology is directed
not to lightening the toil of the people, but to
achieving improvements needed only by the rich, and
which therefore will yet more widely separate the rich
from the poor, the masters from their slaves.    If some

advantage from these inventions and improvements—
some crumbs—do reach the working classes, this is not
at all because they were intended for the people, but
only because by their nature they could not be kept
from the people.

It is the same with medical science, which has advanced in its false direction till it has reached a stage
at which only the rich can command it; while from
their manner of life and their poverty (and as a
result of the fact that the questions relating to the
amelioration of the life of the poor have been neglected)
the mass of the people can only avail themselves of it
under conditions that most clearly show how medical
science has diverged from its true purpose.

But this avoidance and perversion of essential questions is most strikingly seen in what is now called
Philosophy. There would seem to be one essential
question for philosophy to answer : ' What must I do ?'
And in the philosophy of the Christian nations answers
to this question—though combined with very much
that is unnecessary and confused, as in the case of
Spinoza, Kant (in his *Critique of Practical Reason*),
Schopenhauer, and particularly Rousseau—have at any
rate been given. But latterly, since Hegel (who
taught that whatever exists is reasonable) the question :
' What must we do ?' has been pushed into the back-
ground, and philosophy directs its whole attention to
the investigation of things as they are, and to making
them fit into a prearranged theory. That was the first
downward step. The next step, leading human thought
to a yet lower level, was the acknowledgment of the
law of the struggle for existence as fundamental,
merely because that struggle can be observed among
plants and animals. Under the influence of that
theory, it is assumed that the destruction of the
weakest is a law which should not be checked. Finally
came the third step, when the semi-sane Nietzsche's
puerile efforts at originality, which do not even present
anything complete or coherent, but are as it were
immoral, offhand jottings of utterly baseless thoughts,

were accepted by advanced people as the last word of philosophic science. In reply to the question : 'What must we do ?' the advice is now plainly offered : 'Live as you please, paying no attention to the lives of others.'

If anyone doubted the terrible state of stupefaction and bestiality to which our Christian humanity has descended—without speaking of the crimes recently committed in South Africa and China, and which were defended by priests and accepted as achievements by all the great ones of the earth—the extraordinary success of the writings of Nietzsche would alone suffice to supply an unanswerable proof. Some disjointed writings—aiming most obtrusively at effect—appear, written by a man suffering from megalomania, a bold but limited and abnormal German. Neither in talent nor by their validity have these writings any claim on public attention. In the days of Kant, Leibnitz, or Hume, or even fifty years ago, such writings, far from attracting attention, could not even have appeared. But in our days all the so-called educated classes of humanity are delighted with the ravings of Mr. Nietzsche ; they dispute about him and explain him, and innumerable copies of his works are printed in all languages.

Tourgénef humorously says that there are such things as 'reversed platitudes,' and that they are often used by people lacking in talent, but desirous of attracting attention. Everyone knows, for instance, that water is wet: but suddenly someone seriously asserts that water is dry—not ice, but water is dry ; and such an opinion, if confidently expressed, attracts attention.

In the same way, the whole world knows that virtue consists in subduing one's passions, and in self-renunciation. This is known not by Christians only (with whom Nietzsche imagines he is fighting), but it is an eternal and supreme law which all humanity has recognised—in Brahmanism, Buddhism, Confucianism, and in the ancient Persian religion. And suddenly a man appears who announces his discovery that self-renunciation, mildness, meekness, love—that all these are vices, which are ruining humanity (he refers to Christianity, forgetting all the other religions). It is comprehensible that such an assertion should, at first, perplex people. But, after thinking a little and failing to find in his writings any proofs supporting this vague assertion, every rational man ought to reject such books, and only be surprised that nowadays there is no nonsense too arrant to find a publisher. With the works of Nietzsche that course has not been adopted. The majority of pseudo-enlightened people seriously discuss the theory of 'Superhumanity,' and acclaim its author as a great philosopher: a successor to Descartes, Leibnitz and Kant.

And all this has happened because the majority of pseudo-enlightened men of to-day dislike anything reminding them of virtue, or of its chief basis: self-renunciation and love—things that restrain and condemn the animal life they lead; and they gladly welcome a doctrine of egotism and cruelty—however poorly, unintelligibly and disjointedly expressed—which justifies the system of founding one's own happiness and greatness upon the lives of others: the system in which they live.

### XII.

Christ reproached the scribes and Pharisees, because they took the keys of the Kingdom of Heaven, but neither themselves entered in nor let others enter.

The learned scribes of to-day do the same: they have now taken the keys, not of the Kingdom of Heaven but of enlightenment, and neither enter in nor let others enter.

The hierophants, the priests, by all sorts of deception and hypnotism, have instilled into people an idea that Christianity is not a teaching proclaiming the equality of all men, and therefore destructive of the whole present system of life; but that, on the contrary,

x

it supports the existing order of things and bids us differentiate people, like the stars, and regard them as belonging to different orders—acknowledging any existing authority as ordained of God, and obeying it absolutely; in fact, suggesting to the oppressed that their position is what God wishes it to be, and that they ought to put up with it meekly and humbly, submitting to their oppressors, who need not be meek or humble, but should—as Emperors, Kings, Popes, Bishops, and secular or spiritual magnates of various kinds—correct others by teaching and punishing them, while themselves living in splendour and luxury which it is the duty of those in subjection to supply. And the ruling classes, thanks to this false teaching which they strongly support, rule over the people, obliging them to furnish means of support for their rulers' idleness, luxury and vices. And the only men who have freed themselves from this hypnotism—the scientific people : those, therefore, who alone are able to free the people from their oppression—do not do it, though they say they wish to ; but, instead of doing what might attain that end, they do just the opposite, imagining that they thereby serve the people.

One would think these men—even from casually observing what it is that those who hold the masses in subjection are most afraid of—might see what really moves men, and what really keeps them down in the places they now occupy ; and would direct their whole force to that source of power. They not only do not do this, however, but they consider such action quite useless.

It is as if these men did not wish to see the facts. They assiduously, and sincerely, do all sorts of different things for the people, but they do not do the one thing primarily needful ; and their activity is like the activity of a man trying to move a train by exerting his muscles, when he need only get upon the engine and do what he constantly sees the engine-driver do : move a lever to let steam into the cylinders. That steam is men's religious conception of life. And they need only notice the eagerness with which those in authority retain control of that motive power—by means of which the rulers lord it over the masses—and the advanced men will understand to what they must direct their efforts in order to free the people from its slavery.

What does the Sultan of Turkey guard, and to what does he cling for support? And why does the Russian Emperor, on arriving at a town, go first thing to kiss an icón or the relics of some saint? And why, in spite of all the varnish of culture he so prides himself on, does the German Emperor in all his speeches—seasonably or unseasonably—speak of God, of Christ, of the sanctity of religion, of oaths, etc.? Simply because they all know that their power rests on the army, and that the army—the very possibility of such a thing as an army existing—rests on religion. And if wealthy people are generally particularly devout: making a show of believing, going to Church, and observing the Sabbath—it is all done chiefly because an instinct of self-preservation warns them that their exceptionally advantageous position in the community is bound up with the religion they profess.

These people often do not know in what way their privileges rest on religious deception, but their instinct of self-preservation warns them of the weak spot in that on which their power rests, and they first of all defend that place. Within certain limits these people always allow, and have allowed, socialistic and even revolutionary propaganda; but the foundations of religion they never allow to be touched.

And therefore, if history and psychology do not suffice to enable the advanced men of to-day—the learned, the Liberals, the Socialists, the Revolutionists and Anarchists—to discover what it is that moves the people, this visible indication should suffice to convince them that the motive power lies, not in material conditions, but only in religion.

Yet, strange to say, the learned, advanced people of to-day, who understand and discuss the conditions of life of various nations very acutely, do not see what is

x 2

so obvious that it strikes one's eye. If these men intentionally leave the people in their religious ignorance for the sake of retaining their own profitable position among the minority,—this is a terrible, a revolting fraud. Men who act so are the very hypocrites Christ especially denounced—the only people He did in fact denounce—and He denounced them because no monsters or malefactors ever brought so much evil into human life as is brought by these men.

But if they are sincere, the only explanation of so strange an eclipse of reason is, that just as the masses are hypnotized by a false religion, so also are the pseudo-enlightened men of to-day hypnotized by a false science which has decided that the chief motor-nerve, that now as heretofore actuates humanity, has become altogether useless, and can be replaced by something else.


### XIII.

This delusion or deceit of the scribes—the educated men of our world—is the peculiarity of our times, and in this lies the cause of the miserable condition in which Christian humanity now lives, as well as of the brutalization into which it is sinking deeper and deeper.

It is usual for the advanced, educated classes of our world to assert that the false religious beliefs held by the masses are of no special importance, and that it is not worth while, and is unnecessary, to struggle against them directly, as was done by Hume, Voltaire, Rousseau and others. Science, they think—that is to say, the disconnected, casual information they disseminate among the people—will of itself attain that end, and man, having learned how many million miles it is from the earth to the sun, and what metals exist in the sun and the stars, will cease to believe in Church doctrines.

This sincere, or insincere, assertion or assumption covers either a great delusion or a terrible deception. From the very earliest years of childhood—the years most susceptible to suggestion, when those who train children cannot be sufficiently careful what they transmit to them—a child is hypnotized with the absurd, immoral dogmas of so-called Christian religion, irreconcilable with our reason and knowledge. He is taught the dogma of the Trinity, which healthy reason cannot hold ; the coming of one of the three Gods to earth for the salvation of the human race, and his resurrection and ascent into heaven ; is taught to expect a second coming, and punishment in eternal torments for disbelief in these dogmas ; also he is taught to pray for what he wants ; and many other things. And when all this (incompatible as it is with reason, contemporary knowledge, and man's conscience) is indelibly stamped on the child's impressionable mind, he is left to himself to find his way as he can amid the contradictions which flow from these dogmas he has accepted and assimilated as unquestionable truths. No one tells him how he may or should reconcile these contradictions ; or if the theologians do try to reconcile them, their attempts only confuse the matter more than before. So, little by little, the man becomes accustomed to suppose (and the theologians strongly support this notion) that reason cannot be trusted, and therefore anything is possible, and that there is no capacity in man by means of which he can himself distinguish good from evil, or falsehood from truth ; and that in what is most important for him —his actions—he should be guided not by his reason, but by what others tell him. It is evident what a terrible perversion of man's spiritual world such an education must produce, reinforced as it is in adult life by all the means of hypnotization which, by the aid of the priests, is continually exercised upon the people.

If a man of strong spirit, with great labour and suffering, does succeed in freeing himself from the hypnotism in which he has been educated in childhood and held in mature life, the perversion of his mind, produced by the persuasion that he must distrust his own reason, can still not pass without leaving traces—just as in the physical world the poisoning of an organism with some powerful virus cannot pass without leaving its trace. It is natural for such a man, having freed himself from the hypnotism of this deceit, and hating the falsehood from which he has just escaped, to adopt the view advocated by advanced men, and to regard every religion as an obstacle in the path along which humanity is progressing. And having adopted that opinion, such a man becomes, like his teachers, devoid of principle—that is, devoid of conscience, and guided in life merely by his desires. Nor does he condemn himself for this, but he considers that it places him on the highest plane of mental development attainable by man.

That is what may happen with men of strong minds. The less strong, though they may be roused to doubts, will never completely free themselves from the deception in which they were brought up ; but adopting or inventing various cunningly-devised, cloudy theories to justify the absurd dogmas they have accepted, and living in a sphere of doubts, mist, sophistries and self-deception, they will co-operate in the mystification of the masses and oppose their enlightenment.

But the majority of men, having neither the strength nor the opportunity to struggle against the hypnotism exercised over them, will live and die generation after generation, as they now do—deprived of man's highest welfare, which is a truly religious understanding of life —and will remain docile tools of the classes that rule over them and deceive them.

And it is this terrible deception that advanced and learned men consider unimportant, and not worth directly attacking. The only explanation of such an assertion, if those who make it are sincere, is, that they are themselves under the hypnotism of a false science ; but if they are not sincere, then their conduct is explained by the fact that an attack on established beliefs is unprofitable and often dangerous. In any case, one way or another, the assertion that the profession of a false religion does no harm—or though harmful is unimportant—and that one can therefore disseminate enlightenment without destroying religious deception, is quite untrue.

Mankind can be saved from its ills only by being freed both from the hypnotism in which the priests are holding it, and from that into which the learned are leading it. To pour anything into a full bottle one must first empty out what it contains. And similarly it is necessary to free men from the deception of their false faith, in order that they may be able to adopt a true religion : that is, a correct relation (in accord with the development humanity has attained) towards the Source of all—towards God ; and that from this relation, they may obtain guidance for their actions.

## XIV.

'But is there any true religion? Religions are endlessly various, and we have no right to call one of them true, just because it most nearly suits our own taste,'—is what people say who look at the external forms of religion as at some disease from which they feel themselves free, but from which other people still suffer. But this is a mistake ; religions differ in their external forms, but they are all alike in their fundamental principles. And it is these principles, that are fundamental to all religions, that form the true religion which alone at the present time is suitable for us all, and the adoption of which alone can save men from their ills.

Mankind has lived long, and just as it has produced and improved its practical inventions through successive generations, so also it could not fail to produce and improve those spiritual principles which have formed the bases of its life, as well as the rules of conduct that resulted from those principles. If blind men do not see these, that does not prove that they do not exist.

This religion of our times, common to all men, exists —not as some sect with all its peculiarities and perversions, but as a religion consisting of those principles which are alike in all the widespread religions known to us, and professed by more than nine-tenths of the human race; and that men are not yet completely brutalized is due to the fact that the best men of all nations hold to this religion and profess it, even if unconsciously, and only the hypnotic deception practised /on men by the aid of the priests and scientists now hinders men from consciously adopting it.

The principles of this true religion are so natural to men, that as soon as they are put before them they are accepted as something quite familiar and self-evident. For us the true religion is Christianity in those of its principles in which it agrees, not with the external forms, but with the basic principles of Brahmanism, Confucianism, Taoism, Hebraism, Buddhism, and even Mohammedanism. And just in the same way, for those who profess Brahmanism, Confucianism, etc.—true religion is that of which the basic principles agree with those of all other religions. And these principles are very simple, intelligible and clear.

These principles are: that there is a God, the origin of all things; that in man dwells a spark from that Divine Origin, which man, by his way of living, can increase or decrease in himself; that to increase this divine spark man must suppress his passions and increase love in himself; and that the practical means to attain this result is to do to others as you would they should do to you. All these principles are common to Brahmanism, Hebraism, Confucianism, and Mohammedanism. (If Buddhism supplies no definition of God, it nevertheless acknowledges That with which man commingles, and into Which he is absorbed when he attains to Nirvana. So, That with which man commingles, or into Which he is absorbed in Nirvana, is the same Origin that is called God in Hebraism, Christianity, and Mohammedanism.)

'But that is not religion,' is what men of to-day will say, who are accustomed to consider that the supernatural, i.e., the unmeaning, is the chief sign of religion. 'That is anything you like: philosophy, ethics, ratiocination — but not religion.' Religion, according to them, must be absurd and unintelligible

(*Credo quia absurdum*). Yet it was only from these very principles, or rather in consequence of their being preached as religious doctrines, that—by a long process of perversion—all those absurd miracles and supernatural occurrences were elaborated, which are now considered to be the fundamental signs of every religion. To assert that the supernatural and irrational form the essential characteristic of religion is like observing only rotten apples, and then asserting that a flabby bitterness and a harmful effect on the stomach are the prime characteristics of the fruit called Apple.

Religion is the definition of man's relation to the Source of all things, and of man's purpose in life which results from that relation; and it supplies rules of conduct resulting from that purpose. And the universal religion whose first principles are alike in all the faiths, fully meets the demands of this understanding of religion. It defines the relation of man to God, as being that of a part to the whole; from this relation it deduces man's purpose, which is to increase the divine element in himself; and this purpose involves practical demands on man, in accord with the rule: Do to others as you wish them to do to you.

People often doubt, and I myself at one time doubted, whether such an abstract rule as, Do to others as you wish them to do to you, can be as obligatory a rule and guide for action as the simpler rules: to fast, pray, and take communion, etc. But an irrefutable reply to that doubt is supplied, for instance, by the spiritual condition of a Russian peasant who would rather die than spit out the Sacrament on to a manure-heap, but who yet, at the command of men, is ready to kill his brothers.

Why should demands flowing from the rule of doing to others as you wish them to do to you—such, for instance, as: not killing one's brother man, not reviling, not committing adultery, not revenging one's self, not taking advantage of the need of one's brethren to satisfy one's own caprice, and many others,—why should not they be instilled as forcibly, and become as binding and inviolable, as the belief in the sanctity of the Sacraments, or of images, etc., now is to men whose faith is founded more on credulity than on any clear inward consciousness.

## xv.

The truths of the religion common to all men of our time are so simple, so intelligible, and so near the heart of each man, that it would seem only necessary for parents, rulers and teachers to instil into children and adults—instead of the obsolete and absurd doctrines, in which they themselves often do not believe: about Trinities, virgin-mothers, redemptions, Indras, Trimurti, and about Buddhas and Mohammeds who fly away into the sky—those clear and simple truths, the metaphysical essence of which is, that the spirit of God dwells in man; and the practical rule of which is, that man should do to others as he wishes them to do to him—for the whole life of humanity to change. If only—in the same way that the belief is now instilled into children and confirmed in adults, that God sent His son to redeem Adam's sin, and that He established His Church which must be obeyed; as well as rules deduced from these beliefs: telling when and where to pray and make offerings, when to refrain from such and such food, and on what days to abstain from work—if only it were instilled and confirmed that God is a spirit whose manifestation is present in us, the strength of which we can increase by our lives: if only this and all that naturally flows from this, were instilled in the same way that quite useless stories of impossible occurrences, and rules of meaningless ceremonies deduced from those stories, are now instilled—then, instead of purposeless strife and discord, we should very soon (without the aid of diplomatists, international law, peace-congresses, political economists, and Socialists in all their various subdivisions) see humanity living a peaceful, united, and happy life guided by the one religion.

But nothing of the kind is done: not only is the deception of false religion not destroyed, and the true one not preached, but, on the contrary, men depart further and further away from the possibility of accepting the truth.

The chief cause of people not doing what is so natural, necessary, and possible, is that men to-day, in consequence of having lived long without religion, are so accustomed to establish and defend their existence by violence, by bayonets, bullets, prisons, and gallows, that it seems to them as if such an arrangement of life were not only normal, but were the only one possible. Not only do those who profit by the existing order think so, but those even who suffer from it are so stupefied by the hypnotism exercised upon them, that they also consider violence to be the only means of securing good order in human society. Yet it is just this arrangement and maintenance of the commonweal by violence, that does most to hinder people from comprehending the causes of their sufferings, and consequently from being able to establish a true order.

The results of it are such as might be produced by a bad or malicious doctor who should drive a malignant eruption inwards, thereby cheating the sick man, and making the disease worse and its cure impossible.

To people of the ruling classes, who enslave the masses and think and say : ' *Après nous le déluge*,'* it seems very convenient by means of the army, the priesthood, the soldiers, and the police, as well as by threats of bayonets, bullets, prisons, workhouses, and gallows, to compel the enslaved people to remain in stupefaction and enslavement, and not to hinder the rulers from exploiting them. And the ruling men do this, calling it the maintenance of good order, but there is nothing that so hinders the establishment of a good social order as this does. In reality, far from being

* Madame de Pompadour's remark, 'After me (us) the deluge.'

the establishment of good order, it is the establishment of evil.

If men of our Christian nations, still possessing some remnants of those religious principles which in spite of everything yet live in the people, had not before them the continual example of crime committed by those who have assumed the duty of guarding order and morality among men—the wars, executions, prisons, taxation, sale of intoxicants and of opium—they would never have thought of committing one one-hundredth of the evil deeds—the frauds, violence and murders—which they now commit in full confidence that such deeds are good and natural for men to commit.

The law of human life is such, that the only way to improve it, whether for the individual or for a society of men, is by means of inward, moral growth towards perfection. All attempts of men to better their lives by external action—by violence—serve as the most efficacious propaganda and example of evil, and therefore not only do not improve life, but, on the contrary, increase the evil which, like a snowball, grows larger and larger, and removes men more and more from the only possible way of truly bettering their lives.

In proportion as the practice of violence and crime, committed in the name of the law by the guardians of order and morality, becomes more and more frequent and cruel, and is more and more justified by the hypnotism of falsehood presented as religion, men will be more and more confirmed in the belief that the law of their life is not one of love and service to their fellows, but is one demanding that they should strive with, and devour, one another.

And the more they are confirmed in that thought, which degrades them to the plane of the beasts, the harder will it be to shake off the hypnotic trance in which they are living, and to accept as the basis of their life the true religion of our time, common to all humanity.

A vicious circle has been established : the absence of religion makes possible an animal life based on violence ;

an animal life based on violence makes emancipation
from hypnotism and an adoption of true religion more
and more impossible. And, therefore, men do not do
what is natural, possible and necessary in our times :
do not destroy the deception and simulacrum of
religion, and do not assimilate and preach the true
religion.

### XVI.

Is any issue from this enchanted circle possible, and
if so, what is it?

At first it seems as if the Governments, which have
taken on themselves the duty of guiding the life of the
people for their benefit, should lead us out of this
circle. That is what men who have tried to alter the
arrangements of life founded on violence, and to replace
them by a reasonable arrangement based on mutual
service and love, have always supposed. So thought
the Christian reformers, and the founders of various
theories of European Communism, and so also thought
the celebrated Chinese reformer Mo Tî,* who for the
welfare of the people proposed to the Government not
to teach school-children military sciences and exercises,
and not to give rewards to adults for military achievements, but to teach children and adults the rules of
esteem and love, and give rewards and encouragement
for feats of love. So also thought, and think, many
religious peasant-reformers, of whom I have known and
now know several, beginning with Soutáyef and ending
with an old man who has now five times presented a
petition to the Emperor, asking him to decree the
abrogation of false religion, and to order that true
Christianity be preached.

It seems to men natural that the Government—which
justifies its existence on the score of its care for the
welfare of the people—must, to secure that welfare,
wish to use the only means which can never do people

* Mo Tî (or Mih Teih) lived a little before Mencius (about
372-289 B.C.), who wrote against the former's doctrine of
universal love.

any harm, and can only produce the most fruitful results. Government, however, has not only never taken upon itself this duty, but, on the contrary, has always and everywhere maintained with the greatest jealousy any false, effete religion prevalent at the period, and has in every way persecuted those who have tried to inform the people of the principles of true religion. In reality this cannot be otherwise ; for Governments to expose the falsity of the present religions, and to preach the true one, would be as if a man were to cut down the branch on which he is sitting.

But if Government will not do this work, it would seem certain that those learned men—who, having freed themselves from the deception of false religion, say they wish to serve the common people whose labour has provided for their education and support—are bound to do it. But these men, like the Government, do not do it : first, because they consider it inexpedient to risk unpleasantness and to suffer the danger of persecution at the hands of the ruling classes for exposing a fraud which Government protects, and which, in their opinion, will disappear of itself ; secondly, because, considering all religion to be an effete error, they have nothing to offer the people in place of the deception they are expected to destroy.

There remain those great masses of unlearned men who are under the hypnotic influence of Church and Government deception, and who therefore believe that the simulacrum of religion which has been instilled into them is the one true religion, and that there is and can be no other. These masses are under a constant and intense hypnotic influence. Generation after generation they are born and live and die in the stupefied condition in which they are kept by the clergy and the Government ; and if they free themselves from that influence, they are sure to fall into the school of the scientists who deny religion—when their influence becomes as useless and harmful as the influence of their teachers.

So that for some men the work is unprofitable, while for others it is impossible.

### XVII.

It looks as if no issue were possible.

And indeed for irreligious men there is not, and cannot be, any issue from this position ; those who belong to the higher, governing classes, even if they pretend to be concerned for the welfare of the masses, will never seriously attempt (guided by worldly aims, they cannot do it) to destroy the stupefaction and servitude in which these masses live, and which make it possible for the upper classes to rule over them.  In the same way, men belonging to the enslaved masses cannot, while guided by worldly motives, wish to make their own hard position harder by entering on a struggle against the upper classes, to expose a false teaching and to preach a true one.   Neither of these sets of men have any motive to do this, and if they are intelligent they will never attempt it.

But it is otherwise for religious people : men such as those who—however perverted a society may be—are always to be found guarding with their lives the sacred fire of religion, without which human life could not exist. There are times (and our time is such) when these men are unnoticed, when—as among us in Russia—despised and derided by all, their lives pass unrecorded—in exile, in prisons, and in penal battalions—yet they live, and on them depends the rational life of humanity. And it is just these religious men—however few they may be—who alone can and will rend asunder that enchanted circle which keeps men bound.   They can do it, because all the disadvantages and dangers which hinder a worldly man from opposing the existing order of society, not only do not impede a religious man, but rather increase his zeal in the struggle against falsehood, and impel him to confess by word and deed what he holds to be divine truth.   If he belongs to the ruling classes he will not only not wish to hide the truth out of regard for his own advantageous position, but, on the contrary, having come to hate such advantages, he will exert his whole strength to free himself from them, and to preach the truth, for he will no longer have any other aim in life than to serve God. If he belongs to the enslaved, then in the same way, unbiassed by the wish, common among those of his position, to improve the conditions of his physical life, such a man will have no aim but to fulfil the will of God by exposing false-hood and confessing truth ; and no sufferings or threats will make him cease to live in accord with that purpose which he has recognised in his life. They will both act thus, as naturally as a worldly man exerts himself and puts up with privations to obtain riches, or to please a ruler from whom he expects to receive advan-tages. Every religious man acts thus, because a human soul enlightened by religion no longer lives merely by the life of this world, as irreligious people do, but lives an eternal, infinite life, for which suffering and death in this life are as insignificant as are blisters on his hands, or weariness of limbs, to a ploughman when he is ploughing a field.

These are the men who will rend asunder the enchanted circle in which people are now confined. However few such men there may be, however humble their social position, however poor in education or ability, as surely as fire lights the dry steppe, so surely will these people set the whole world aflame, and kindle all the hearts of men, withered by long lack of religion, and now thirsting for a renewal of life.

Religion is not a belief, settled once for all, in certain supernatural occurrences supposed to have taken place once upon a time, nor in the necessity for certain prayers and ceremonies; nor is it, as the scientists suppose, a survival of the superstitions of ancient ignorance, which in our time has no meaning or application to life ; but religion is a certain relation of man to eternal life and to God, a relation accordant with reason and contemporary knowledge, and it is the one thing that alone moves humanity forward towards its destined aim.

A wise Hebrew proverb says, ' The soul of man is the lamp of God.' Man is a weak and miserable animal until the light of God burns in his soul. But when that light burns (and it burns only in souls enlightened by religion) man becomes the most powerful being in the world. Nor can this be otherwise, for what then acts in him is no longer *his* strength, but is the strength of God.

So this is what religion is, and in what its essence consists.

[February, 1902.]

## XXIV

## LETTER ON EDUCATION

Dear S.,

I was very glad to have a serious conversation with X. about the education of children. What he and I quite agree about, but what is only negative, is that children should be taught *as little as possible.** That children should grow up without having learnt certain subjects is not nearly so bad as what happens to nearly all children, especially those whose education is directed by mothers who do not know the subjects their children learn—viz., they get educational *indigestion* and come to detest education. A child, or a man, can learn when he has an appetite for what he studies. Without appetite, instruction is an evil—a terrible evil causing people to become mentally crippled. For Heaven's sake, dear S., if you do not quite agree with me, take my word for it, that were it not a matter of such enormous importance I would not write to you about it. Above all, believe your husband, who sees the thing quite reasonably.

But then comes the customary reply: If children are not taught, how are they to be occupied? Are they to play knuckle-bones with the village children, and learn all sorts of stupidities and nastiness? With our squirely way of life, this reply has some reasonable ground. But is it really necessary to accustom children to a squirely way of life, and to make them feel that all their requirements are satisfied by someone, somehow, without their having to take any part in the

* This is meant to be taken comparatively and not absolutely. Elsewhere Tolstoy has expressed the opinion that a child may reasonably do lessons for eight hours a day; though he should not be compelled to learn what he does not wish to learn.

work? I think the first condition of a good education is that the child should know that all he uses does not fall from heaven ready-made, but is produced by other people's labour. To understand that all he lives on comes from the labour of other people who neither know nor love him, is too much for a child (God grant he may understand it when he is grown up); but to understand that the chamber-pot he uses is emptied and wiped, without any pleasure, by a nurse or a house-maid, and that the boots and goloshes he always puts on clean are cleaned in the same way—not out of love for him, but for some other reason quite unintelligible to him—is something he can and should understand, and of which he should be ashamed. If he is not ashamed and if he continues to use them, that is the very worst commencement of an education, and leaves the deepest traces for his whole life. To avoid that, however, is very simple, and is just what (to use poetic language), standing on the threshold of the grave, I beseech you to do for your children. Let them do all they can for themselves: carry out their own slops, fill their own jugs, wash up, arrange their rooms, clean their boots and clothes, lay the table, etc. Believe me that, un-important as these things may seem, they are a hundred times more important for your children's happiness than a knowledge of French, or of history, etc. It is true that here the chief difficulty crops up: children do willingly only what their parents do, and therefore I beg of you, do these things. This will effect two objects at once: it makes it possible to learn less, by filling the time in the most useful and natural way, and it trains the children to simplicity, to work, and to self-dependence. Please do this. You will be gratified from the first month, and the children yet more so. If to this you can add work on the land, if it be but a kitchen-garden, that will be well; though it too often becomes a mere pastime. The necessity of attending to one's own needs and carrying out one's own slops is admitted by all the best schools, such as Bedale, where the director of the school himself takes a share in such work. Believe me, that without that condition there is no possibility of a moral education, a Christian education, or a consciousness of the fact that all men are brothers and equals. A child may yet understand that a grown-up man, his father—a banker or turner, an artist or an overseer, who by his work feeds the whole family—may free himself from occupations which prevent his giving all his time to his profitable work. But how can a child—as yet untried and unable to do anything—explain to himself that others do for him what he naturally should do for himself?

The only explanation for him is that people are divided into two classes—masters and slaves; and however much we may talk to him in words about equality and the brotherhood of man, all the conditions of his life, from his getting up, to his evening meal, show him the contrary.

Not only does he cease to believe what his elders tell him about morality, he sees in the depth of his soul that all these teachings are mendacious, and he ceases to believe his parents and teachers, and ceases even to believe in the need for any kind of morality whatever.

Yet one more consideration. If it is not possible to do all that I have mentioned, at least one must set children to do things the disadvantage of not doing which would be at once felt by them—*e.g.*, if one's clothes and boots for going out in are not cleaned, one must not go out; if water has not been fetched and the crockery washed up, there is nothing to drink. Above all, in this matter do not be afraid of *ridicule*. Nine-tenths of all the bad things in the world are done because not to do them would be held ridiculous.

[1902.]

This letter was written to a near relation, belonging to the upper class of Russian society, in which the children are generally sent to the high schools (gymnasia), where they are crammed with much knowledge, chiefly in order to pass examinations and to obtain certain privileges (*e.g.*, diminution of military service). The 'X.' mentioned is the husband of the lady addressed.

## XXV

## AN APPEAL TO THE CLERGY

### I.

WHOEVER you may be: popes, cardinals, bishops, superintendents, priests, or pastors, of whatever Church, forego for a while your assurance that you—you in particular—are the only true disciples of the God Christ, appointed to preach his only true teaching; and remember that before being popes, cardinals, bishops, or superintendents, etc., you are first of all men: that is, according to your own teaching, beings sent into this world by God to fulfil His will; remember this, and ask yourselves what you are doing. Your whole life is devoted to preaching, maintaining, and spreading among men a teaching which you say was revealed to you by God Himself, and is, therefore, the only one that is true and brings redemption.

In what, then, does this one true and redeeming doctrine that you preach, consist? To whichever one of the so-called Christian Churches—Roman Catholic, Russo-Greek, Lutheran, or Anglican—you may belong, you acknowledge that your teaching is quite accurately expressed in the articles of belief formulated at the Council of Nicæa sixteen hundred years ago. Those articles of belief are as follows:

*First*: There is a God the father (the first person of a Trinity), who has created the sky and the earth, and all the angels who live in the sky.

*Second*: There is an only son of God the father, not

created, but born (the second person of the Trinity). Through this son the world was made.

*Third :* This son, to save people from sin and death (by which they were all punished for the disobedience of their forefather Adam), came down to the earth, was made flesh by the Holy Ghost and the virgin Mary, and became a man.

*Fourth :* This son was crucified for the sins of men.

*Fifth :* He suffered and was buried, and rose on the third day, as had been foretold in Hebrew books.

*Sixth :* Having gone up into the sky, this son seated himself at his father's right side.

*Seventh :* This son of God will, in due time, come again to the earth to judge the living and the dead.

*Eighth :* There is a Holy Ghost (the third person of the Trinity), who is equal to the father, and who spoke through the prophets.

*Ninth* (held by some of the largest Churches) : There is one holy, infallible Church (or, more exactly, the Church to which he who makes the confession belongs is held to be unique, holy, and infallible. This Church consists of all who believe in it, living or dead.

*Tenth* (also for some of the largest Churches) : There exists a Sacrament of Baptism, by means of which the power of the Holy Ghost is communicated to those who are baptized.

*Eleventh :* At the second coming of Christ, the souls of the dead will re-enter their bodies, and these bodies will be immortal ; and

*Twelfth :* After the second coming, the just will have eternal life in paradise on a new earth under a new sky, and sinners will have eternal life in the torments of hell.

Not to speak of things taught by some of your largest Churches (the Roman Catholic and Russo-Greek Orthodox)—such as the belief in saints, and in the good effects of bowing to their bodily remains, and to representations of them as well as of Jesus and the mother of God—the above twelve points embrace the fundamental positions of that truth which you say has been revealed to you by God Himself for the redemption of man. Some of you preach these doctrines simply as they are expressed; others try to give them an allegorical meaning more or less in accord with present-day knowledge and common-sense; but you all alike are bound to confess, and do confess, these statements to be the exact expression of that unique truth which God Himself has revealed to you, and which you preach to men for their salvation.

## II.

Very well. You have had the one truth capable of saving mankind revealed to you by God Himself. It is natural for men to strive towards truth, and when it is clearly presented to them they are always glad to accept it, and to be guided by it.

And, therefore, to impart this saving truth revealed to you by God Himself, it would seem sufficient, plainly and simply, verbally and through the Press, to communicate it with reasonable persuasion to those capable of receiving it.

But how have you preached this truth?

From the time a society calling itself the Church was formed, your predecessors taught this truth chiefly by violence. They laid down the truth, and punished those who did not accept it. (Millions and millions of people have been tortured, killed, and burnt for not wishing to accept it.) This method of persecution, which was evidently not suited to its purpose, came in course of time to be less and less employed, and is now, of all the Christian Churches, used, I think, only in Russia.

Another means was through external action on people's feelings—by solemnity of setting: with pictures, statues, singing, music, even dramatic performances, and oratorical art. In time this method, also, began to be less and less used. In Protestant countries —except the orator's art—it is now but little used (though the Salvation Army, which has devised new methods of external action on the feelings, supplies an exception).

But all the strength of the clergy is now directed to a third and most powerful method, which has always been used, and is now with special jealousy retained by the clergy in their own hands. This method is that of instilling Church doctrine into people who are not in a position to judge of what is given them : for instance, into quite uneducated working people who have no time for thought, and chiefly into children, who accept indiscriminately what is imparted to them and on whose minds it remains permanently impressed.

III.

So that in our day your chief method of imparting to men the truth God has revealed to you, consists in teaching this truth to uneducated adults, and to children who do not reason, but accept everything.

This teaching generally begins with what is called Scripture History : that is to say, with selected passages from the Bible : the Hebrew books of the Old Testament ; which according to your teaching are the work of the Holy Ghost, and are therefore not only unquestionably true, but also holy. From this history your pupil draws his first notions of the world, of the life of man, of good and evil, and of God.

This Scripture History begins with a description of how God, the ever-living, created the sky and the earth 6,000 years ago out of nothing ; how He afterwards created beasts, fishes, plants, and finally man : Adam, and Adam's wife, who was made of one of Adam's ribs. Then it describes how, fearing lest the man and his wife should eat an apple which had the magic quality of giving knowledge, He forbade them to eat that apple ; how, notwithstanding this prohibition, the first people ate the apple, and were therefore expelled from Paradise ; and how all their descendants were therefore cursed, and the earth was cursed also, so that since then it has grown weeds. Then the life of Adam's descendants is described: how they became so perverted that God not only drowned them all, but drowned all the animals with them, and left alive only Noah and his family and the animals he took into the ark. Then it describes how God chose Abraham alone of all people, and made an agreement with him; which agreement was that Abraham was to consider God to be God, and, as a sign of this, was to be circumcised. On His side God undertook to give Abraham a numerous progeny, and to patronize him and all his offspring. Then it tells how God, patronizing Abraham and his descendants, performed on their behalf most unnatural actions called miracles, and most terrible cruelties. So that the whole of this history—excepting certain stories, which are sometimes naïve (as the visit of God with two angels to Abraham, the marriage of Isaac, and others), and are sometimes innocent, but are often immoral (as the swindles of God's favourite, Jacob, the cruelties of Samson, and the cunning of Joseph)—the whole of this history, from the plagues Moses called down upon the Egyptians, and the murder by an angel of all their firstborn, to the fire that destroyed 250 conspirators, the tumbling into the ground of Korah, Dathan, and Abiram, and the destruction of 14,700 men in a few minutes, and on to the sawing of enemies with saws,* and the execution of the priests who did not agree with him by Elijah (who rode up into the sky), and to the story of Elisha, who cursed the boys that laughed at him, so that they were torn in pieces and eaten by two bears—all this history is a series of miraculous occurrences and of terrible crimes, committed by the Hebrew people, by their leaders, and by God Himself.

* Father John of Kronstadt having published an article in which he says that this passage shows Tolstoy's ignorance of the Bible, it may be well here to quote 1 Chron. xx. 3: 'And he brought forth the people that were therein, and cut them with saws, and with harrows of iron, and with axes. And thus did David unto all the cities of the children of Ammon.'

But your teaching of the history you call sacred is not limited to that. Besides the history of the Old Testament, you also impart the New Testament to children and to ignorant people, in a way that makes the importance of the New Testament consist not in its moral teaching, not in the Sermon on the Mount, but in the conformity of the Gospels with the stories of the Old Testament, in the fulfilment of prophecies, and in miracles, the movement of a star, songs from the sky, talks with the devil, the turning of water into wine, walking on the water, healings, calling people back to life, and, finally, the resurrection of Jesus himself, and his flying up into the sky.

If all these stories, both from the Old and New Testaments, were taught as a series of fairy-tales, even then hardly any teacher would decide to tell them to children and adults he desired to enlighten. But these tales are imparted to people unable to reason, as though they were the most trustworthy description of the world and its laws, as if they gave the truest information about the lives of those who lived in former times, of what should be considered good and evil, of the existence and nature of God, and of the duties of man.

People talk of harmful books! But is there in Christendom a book that has done more harm to mankind than this terrible book, called 'Scripture History from the Old and New Testaments'?* And all the men and women of Christendom have to pass through a course of this Scripture History during their childhood, and this same history is also taught to ignorant adults as the first and most essential foundation of knowledge —as the one, eternal, truth of God.

### IV.

You cannot introduce a foreign substance into a living organism without the organism suffering, and

---

* The reference here is not to the Old and New Testaments in their entirety (the extreme value of many parts of which Tolstoy does not question), but to a compilation for school use, which is largely used in place of the Bible.

sometimes perishing, from its efforts to rid itself of this foreign substance.   What terrible evil to a man's mind must, then, result from this rendering of the teaching of the Old and New Testaments—foreign alike to present-day knowledge, and to common-sense, and to moral feeling—and instilled into him at a time when he is unable to judge, but accepts all that is given him !

For a man—into whose mind has been introduced as sacred truths a belief in the creation of the world out of nothing 6,000 years ago ; in the flood, and Noah's ark which accommodated all the animals; in a Trinity; in Adam's fall ; in an immaculate conception ; in Christ's miracles, and in salvation for men by the sacrifice of his death—for such a man the demands of reason are no longer obligatory, and such a man cannot be sure of any truth.   If the Trinity, and an immaculate conception, and the salvation of mankind by the blood of Jesus, are possible—then anything is possible, and the demands of reason are not obligatory.

Drive a wedge between the floor-boards of a granary, and no matter how much grain you may pour into the granary, it will not stay there.   Just so a head into which the wedge has been driven of a Trinity, or of a God who became man and redeemed the human race by his sufferings and then flew up into the sky, can no longer grasp any reasonable or firm understanding of life.

However much you may put into the granary which has cracks in its floor, all will run out.   Whatever you may put into a mind which has accepted nonsense as a matter of faith, nothing will remain in it.

Such a man, if he values his beliefs, will inevitably, all his life long, either be on his guard (as against something harmful) against all that might enlighten him and destroy his superstitions ; or—having once for all assumed (and the preachers of Church doctrine will always encourage him in this) that reason is the source of error—he will repudiate the only light given to man to enable him to find his path of life ; or, most terrible of all, he will, by cunning argumentation, try to demonstrate the reasonableness of what is unreasonable, and, worst of all, will discard, together with the superstitions that were instilled into him, all consciousness of the necessity for any faith whatever.

In either of these three cases, a man into whom, during childhood, meaningless and contradictory assertions have been instilled as religious truth—unless with much effort and suffering he free himself from them—is a man mentally diseased. Such a man, seeing around him the constantly moving and changing facts of life, cannot without a feeling of desperation watch this movement destroying his conception of life, and cannot but experience (openly or secretly) an unkindly feeling towards those who co-operate in this reasonable progress. Nor can he help being a conscious partisan of obscurity and lies against light and truth.

And such the majority of people in Christendom—by the inculcation of nonsensical beliefs deprived from childhood of the capacity to think clearly and firmly—actually are.

v.

Such is the evil done to man's mind by having it impregnated with Church doctrines. But much worse than this is the moral perversion which that impregnation produces in man's soul. Every man comes into the world with a consciousness of his dependence on a mysterious, all-powerful Source which has given him life, and consciousness of his equality with all men, the equality of all men with one another, a desire to love and be loved, and a consciousness of the need of striving towards perfection. But what do you instil into him?

Instead of the mysterious Source of which he thinks with reverence, you tell him of an angry, unjust God, who executes and torments people.

Instead of the equality of all men, which the child and the simple man recognise with all their being, you tell them that not only people, but nations, are unequal;

that some of them are loved, and others are not loved, by God; and that some people are called by God to rule, others to submit.

Instead of that wish to love and to be loved, which forms the strongest desire in the soul of every unperverted man, you teach him that the relations between men can only be based on violence, on threats, on executions; and you tell him that judicial and military murders are committed not only with the sanction but at the command of God.

In place of the need of self-improvement, you tell him that man's salvation lies in belief in the Redemption, and that by improving himself by his own powers, without the aid of prayers, sacraments and belief in the Redemption, man is guilty of sinful pride, and that for his salvation man must trust, not to his own reason but to the commands of the Church, and must do what she decrees.

It is terrible to think of the perversion of thought and feeling produced in the soul of a child or an ignorant adult by such teaching.

### VI.

Only to think of the things I know of, that have been done in Russia during the sixty years of my conscious life, and that are still being done!

In the theological colleges, and among the bishops, learned monks and missionaries, hair-splitting discussions of intricate theological problems are carried on— they talk of reconciling moral and dogmatic teaching, they dispute about the development or immutability of dogmas, and discuss similar religious subtleties. But to the hundred million populace all that is preached is a belief in Iberian or Kazán icons of the Mother of God, a belief in relics, in devils, in the redemptive efficacy of having bread blessed and placing candles, and having prayers for the dead, etc.; and not only is this all preached and practised, but the inviolability of these popular superstitions is guarded with particular jealousy from any infringement. A peasant has but to omit to observe the name's day of the local saint, or to omit to invite to his house a wonder-working icón when it makes the round of his village, or he has only to work on the Friday before St. Elias's day—and he will be denounced, and prosecuted, and exiled. Not to speak of sectarians being punished for not observing the ceremonies of the Church, they are tried for even meeting together to read the Gospels, and are punished for that. And the result of all this activity is that tens of millions of people, including nearly all the peasant women, are not only ignorant of Jesus, but have never even heard who he was, or that he existed. This is hard to believe, but it is a fact which anyone can easily verify for himself.

Listen to what is said by the bishops and academicians at their conferences, read their magazines, and you would think that the Russian priesthood preaches a faith which, even if it be backward, is still a Christian faith, in which the Gospel truths find a place and are taught to the people. But watch the activity of the clergy among the people, and you will see that what *is* preached, and energetically inculcated, is simply idolatry : the elevation of icóns, blessing of water, the carrying from house to house of miracle-working icóns, the glorification of relics, the wearing of crosses, and so forth; while every attempt to understand the real meaning of Christianity is energetically persecuted.

Within my recollection the Russian labouring classes have, in a great measure, lost the traits of true Christianity which they formerly possessed, but which are now carefully banished by the clergy.

Among the people there formerly existed (but now only in out-of-the-way districts) Christian legends and proverbs, verbally handed down from generation to generation, and these legends—such as the legend of Christ wandering in the guise of a beggar, of the angel who doubted God's mercy, of the crazy man who danced at a drum-shop ; and such sayings as : ' Without God one can't reach the threshold,' ' God is not in

might, but in right,' 'Live till eve, live for ever,' etc.
—these legends and proverbs formed the spiritual food
of the people.

Besides these, there were Christian customs : to
have pity on a criminal or a wanderer, to give of one's
last resources to a beggar, and to ask forgiveness of a
man one has offended.

All this is now forgotten and discarded.  It is now
all replaced by learning by rote the Catechism, the
triune composition of the Trinity, prayers before
lessons, and prayers for teachers and for the Tsar, etc.
So, within my recollection, the people have grown ever
religiously coarser and more coarse.

One part—most of the women—remain as superstitious as they were 600 years ago, but without
that Christian spirit which formerly permeated their
lives ; the other part, which knows the Catechism by
heart, are absolute atheists.  And all this is consciously
brought about by the clergy.

'But that applies to Russia,' is what Western
Europeans—Catholics and Protestants—will say.  But
I think that the same, if not worse, is happening in
Catholicism, with its prohibition of the Gospels and its
Notre-Dames ; and in Protestantism, with its holy
idleness on the Sabbath day, and its bibliolatry—that
is, its blind belief in the letter of the Bible.  I think,
in one form or another, it is the same throughout the
quasi-Christian world.

In proof of this, it is sufficient to remember the age-
old fraud of the flame that kindles in Jerusalem on the
day of the Resurrection, and which no one of the
Church people exposes ; or the faith in the Redemption,
which is preached with peculiar energy in the very
latest phases of Christian Protestantism.

## VII.

But not only is the Church teaching harmful by its
irrationality and immorality, it is specially harmful
because people professing this teaching, while living

without any moral demands to restrain them, feel quite convinced they are living a really Christian life.

People live in insensate luxury, obtaining their wealth by the labour of the humble poor, and defending themselves and their riches by policemen, law-courts and executions—and the clergy, in the name of Christ, approve, sanctify, and bless this way of life, merely advising the rich to allot a small part of what they have stolen to the service of those from whom they continue to steal. (When slavery existed, the clergy always and everywhere justified it, and did not consider it inconsistent with Christianity.)

People strive by force of arms, by murder, to attain their covetous aims, personal or public, and the clergy approve, and in Christ's name bless preparations for war, and war itself, and not only approve, but often encourage these things ; holding war—that is, murder—not to be contrary to Christianity.

People who believe in such teaching are not merely led by it into an evil way of life, but are fully persuaded that their evil life is a good one, which there is no need for them to alter.

Nor is that all : the chief evil of this teaching is, that it is so skilfully interwoven with the external forms of Christianity, that, while professing it, people think your doctrine is the one true Christianity, and that there is no other ! It is not only that you have diverted from men the spring of living water—were that all, people might still find it—but you have poisoned it with your teachings, so that people cannot find any Christianity but this one poisoned by your interpretations.

The Christianity preached by you is an inoculation of false Christianity, resembling the inoculation for small-pox or diphtheria, and has the effect of making those who are inoculated immune to true Christianity.

People having for many generations built their lives on foundations irreconcilable with true Christianity, feel fully persuaded that they are living Christian lives, and thus they are unable to return to true Christianity.

### VIII.

Thus it is with those who profess your doctrines; but there are others, who have emancipated themselves from those doctrines: the so-called unbelievers.

They (though in most cases more moral in their lives than the majority of those who profess Church doctrines), as a result of the spiritual taint to which they were exposed in their childhood, have an influence on their neighbours which is worse even than that of those who profess your teachings. They are specially harmful because, having in childhood shared the misfortune of the rest of the inhabitants of Christendom and been trained in the Church frauds, they have so identified Church teachings with Christianity in their own perception, that they now cannot distinguish the one from the other, and in rejecting the false Church teaching throw away with it that true Christian teaching which it has hidden.

These people, detesting the fraud that has caused them so much suffering, preach not only the uselessness but the harmfulness of Christianity, and not of Christianity only, but of any religion whatever.

Religion, in their perception, is a remnant of superstition, which may have been of use to people once, but now is simply harmful. And so their doctrine is, that the quicker and more completely people free themselves from every trace of religious consciousness, the better it will be.

And preaching this emancipation from all religion, they—including among them most educated and learned men, who, therefore, have the greatest authority with people searching for the truth—consciously or unconsciously become most harmful preachers of moral laxity.

By suggesting to people that the most important mental characteristic of rational creatures—that of ascertaining their relation to the Source of all things,

z

from which alone any firm moral laws can be deduced —is something man has outlived, the deniers of religion involuntarily postulate as the basis of human activity simply self-love, and the bodily appetites that flow therefrom.

And among these people sprang up that teaching of egotism, evil and hatred, which (though it was always present in hidden, latent form in the life-conception of the materialists) at first showed itself timidly, but has latterly been so vividly and deliberately expressed in the doctrines of Nietzsche, and is now spreading so rapidly, evoking the most coarsely animal and cruel instincts in mankind.

So that, on the one hand, the so-called believers find complete approval of their evil way of life in your teaching, which recognises as compatible with Christianity those actions and conditions which are most contrary to it ; while, on the other hand, unbelievers —arriving at the denial of all religion, as a consequence of your teaching—wipe out all distinction between good and evil, preach a doctrine of inequality among men, of egotism, of strife, and of the oppression of the weak by the strong—and preach this as the highest truth attainable by man.

### IX.

You, and none but you, by your teaching forcibly instilled into people, are the cause of this dreadful evil from which they suffer so cruelly.

Most terrible of all is the fact that, while causing this evil, you do not believe the teaching you preach ; not only do not believe all the assertions of which it is composed, but often do not believe a single one of them.

I know that, repeating the celebrated *credo quia absurdum*, many of you think that, in spite of everything, you do believe all that you preach. But the fact that you *say* you believe that God is a Trinity, or that the heavens opened and the voice of God spoke from up there, or that Jesus rose up into the heavens and will come from there to judge all mankind in their bodies, does not prove that you really believe that the things mentioned have occurred, or will occur. You believe you ought to say that you believe these things happened. But you do not believe them; for the assertions that God is One and Three; that Jesus flew up into the sky and will come back from there to judge those who will rise in their bodies—have, for you, no meaning. One may utter words that have no sense, but one cannot *believe* what has no sense. It is possible to believe that the souls of the dead will pass into other forms of life, pass into animals, or that the annihilation of the passions, or the attainment of love, is the destiny of man; or it is possible to believe simply that God has forbidden us to kill men, or even that He forbids us to eat—and many other things may be believed that do not involve self-contradiction: but one cannot believe that God is, at the same time, both One and also Three, or that the sky—which for us is no longer a thing that exists—opened, etc.

The people of former ages, who framed these dogmas, could believe in them, but you can no longer do so. If you say you have faith in them, you say so only because you use the word 'faith' in one sense, while you apply to it another. One meaning of the word 'faith' refers to a relation adopted by man towards God, which enables him to define the meaning of his whole life, and guides all his conscious actions. Another meaning of the word 'faith' is the credulous acceptance of assertions made by a certain person or persons.

In the first sense, the objects of faith—though the definition of man's relation to God and to the world is generally accepted as framed by those who lived previously—are verified and accepted by reason.

But in the second sense, the objects of faith are not only accepted independently of reason, but are accepted on the absolute condition that reason is not to be allowed to question what is asserted.

On this double meaning of the word 'faith' is founded that misunderstanding which enables people to say they believe, or have 'faith,' in propositions devoid of sense or involving a contradiction in terms. And the fact that you are blindly credulous towards your teachers is no proof that you have faith in what—being senseless and, therefore, supplying no meaning either to your imagination or your reason—cannot be an object of faith.

The well-known preacher, Père Didon, in the introduction to his *Vie de Jésus-Christ*, announces that he believes, not in some allegorical sense but plainly, without explanations, that Christ, having risen, was carried up into the sky, and sits there at the right hand of his father.

An illiterate Samára peasant of my acquaintance, in reply to the question whether he believed in God, simply and firmly replied, as his priest told me : 'No, sinner that I am, I don't believe.' His disbelief in God the peasant explained by saying that one could not live as he was living if one believed in God : 'One scolds, and grudges help to a beggar, and envies, and over-eats, and drinks strong drinks. Could one do such things if one believed in God ?'

Père Didon affirms that he has faith both in God and in the ascension of Jesus, while the Samára peasant says he does not believe in God, since he does not obey His commandments.

Evidently Père Didon does not even know what faith is, and only says he believes : while the Samára peasant knows what faith is, and, though he says he does not believe in God, really believes in Him in the very way that is true faith.

## x.

But I know that arguments addressed to the intellect do not persuade—only feeling persuades, and therefore, leaving arguments aside, I appeal to you—whoever you may be : popes, bishops, archdeacons, priests, or what not—I appeal to your feelings and to your conscience.

For you know that what you teach about the creation of the world, about the inspiration of the Bible by God, and much else, is not true; how then can you teach it to little children and to ignorant adults, who look to you for true enlightenment?

Ask yourself, with your hand on your heart, do you believe what you preach? If you really ask yourself that question, not before men but before God, remembering the approaching hour of death, you cannot but answer, 'No, I do not believe it.' You do not believe in the inspiration by God of the whole of those writings which you call sacred: you do not believe all the horrors and wonders of the Old Testament, you do not believe in hell, you do not believe in an immaculate conception, in the resurrection and ascension of Christ, you do not believe in the physical resurrection of the dead, and in the triune personality of God—not only do you not believe all the articles of the creed which expresses the essence of your faith, but many of you do not even believe a single one of them.

Disbelief, if but in a single dogma, involves disbelief in the infallibility of the Church which has set up the dogma you do not believe. But if you have not faith in the Church, you will not believe in the dogmas she set up.

If you do not believe, if even you have any doubts, think what you are doing in preaching as divine, unquestionable truth—what you do not yourselves believe: and in preaching it by methods which are exceptional and unfair: methods such as you employ. And do not say you cannot take on yourselves the responsibility of depriving people of intimate union with the great or small number of your co-religionists. That is not fair. By instilling into them your special faith, you are doing just what you say you do not wish to do: you are depriving people of their natural union with all mankind, and are confining them within the narrow limits of your single sect, thereby involuntarily and inevitably placing them, if not in a hostile, at least in an alien attitude towards everyone else.

I know that you do not consciously do this terrible thing. I know that you yourselves, for the most part, are entangled, hypnotized, and often so situated that for you to confess the truth would mean to condemn all your former activity, the activity sometimes of several decades. I know how difficult, just for you, with the training you have had, and especially with the assurance common among you, that you are the infallible successors of the God-Christ—I know how difficult it will be for you to face sober realities and to confess yourselves wandering sinners, engaged in one of the worst activities a man can possibly pursue.

I know all the difficulties of your position ; but remembering the words of the Gospels you acknowledge as divine—that God rejoices more over one sinner that repenteth than over a hundred righteous persons—I think that for each one of you, whatever his position may be, it should be easier to repent, and to cease to take part in what you are doing, than, not believing, to continue to do it.

Whoever you may be : popes, cardinals, metropolitans, archbishops, bishops, superintendents, priests, or pastors—think of this.

If you belong to those of the clergy—of whom there are unfortunately in our days very many (and continually more and more)—who see clearly how obsolete, irrational, and immoral is the Church teaching, but who, without believing in it, still from personal motives (for their salaries as priests or bishops) continue to preach it, do not console yourself with the supposition that your activity is justified by any utility it has for the masses of the people, who do not yet understand what you understand.

Falsehood cannot be useful to anyone. What you know—that falsehoods are falsehoods—could be known equally by the common man whom you have indoctrinated, and are indoctrinating, with them, and he might be free from them. Not only might he, but for you, free himself from these falsehoods—he might find the truth which Christ has shown, and which by your doctrines you—standing between the common man and his God—have hidden away. What you are doing, you are doing not to serve man, but only from ambition or covetousness.

Therefore, however magnificent may be the palaces in which you live, the churches in which you officiate and preach, and the vestments in which you adorn yourselves, your occupation is not made better by these things. 'That which is highly esteemed among men is an abomination in the sight of God.'

So it is with those who, not believing, continue to preach what is false, and to strengthen men in it.

But there are among you those also—and their number is continually increasing—who, though they see the bankrupt position of the Church creeds in our day, cannot make up their minds to examine them critically. Belief has been so instilled into them in childhood, and is so strongly supported by their environment and by the influence of the crowd, that they (without even trying to free themselves from it) devote all the strength of their minds and education to justify, by cunning allegories and false and confused reasonings, the incompatibilities and contradictions of the creed they profess.

If you belong to this class of clergy, which though less guilty is even more harmful than the class previously mentioned, do not imagine that your reasonings will quiet your conscience or justify you before God. In the depth of your soul you cannot but know that all you can devise and invent will not make the immoral stories of Scripture history—which are nowadays in opposition to man's knowledge and understanding—or the archaic affirmations of the Nicene Creed, either moral, reasonable, clear, or accordant with contemporary knowledge and common-sense.

You know that you cannot by your arguments convince anyone of the truth of your faith, and that no fresh, grown-up, educated man, not trained from childhood to your belief, can believe you; but that such a man will either laugh, or will suppose you to be mentally afflicted, when he hears your account of the commencement of the world, of the first man, of Adam's sin, and of the redemption of man by the death of the son of God.

All you can effect by your false, pseudo-scientific argumentations, and (what counts for more) by your authority, will be temporarily to retain in hypnotic submission to a false faith, those who are awakening from its influence and preparing to free themselves from it.

That is what you are doing; and it is a very evil work. Instead of employing your mental powers to free yourselves and others from the fraud you and they are involved in, and which causes you and them to suffer, you use your powers yet further to entangle yourselves and them.

You, the clergy of this class, should not entangle yourselves and others by obscure argumentation, should not try to demonstrate that truth is what you call truth; but, on the contrary, making an effort, you should try to verify the beliefs you have accepted as truth—by comparing them with what you and everyone else accept as sure knowledge, and also by the simple demands of common-sense. You need only sincerely set yourselves that task, and you will at once awake from the hypnotic sleep in which you now are—and the terrible delusion in which you have lived will become clear to you.

So it is with this second class, the philosophizing clergy, who in our day are very numerous and most harmful.

But there is also a third, most numerous, class of simple-minded clergy who have never doubted the truth of the faith they profess and preach. These men have either never thought about the sense and meaning of the affirmations taught them in their childhood as sacred divine truth; or, if they have thought, were so unaccustomed to independent thinking, that they did not see the incompatibilities and contradictions involved in those affirmations, or, seeing them, were yet so overpowered by the authority of the Church tradition that they have not dared to think otherwise than

as former and present ecclesiastics have thought.
These men generally console themselves with the
thought that Church doctrine probably has some satis-
factory explanation of the incompatibilities which (as
they suppose) only appear incompatibilities to them
owing to their own deficiency in theological erudition.

If you belong to that class of men—sincerely and
naïvely believing, or who, though they do not believe
are yet willing to believe, and are oblivious of the
obstacles to so doing—whether you are an already
ordained priest, or a young man only preparing for the
priesthood, pause for a while in your activity or in your
preparations for that activity, and consider what you
are doing or are about to do.

You are preaching, or are preparing to preach, a
teaching which will define for men the meaning of their
life, will define its aim, will indicate the features of
good and evil, and will give direction to all their
activity.   And this teaching you preach not as any
other human doctrine—imperfect and open to question
—but as a teaching revealed by God Himself, and
therefore not to be questioned ; and you preach it not
in a book or ordinary conversation, but either to children—at an age when they cannot understand the
meaning of what is conveyed to them, but when it all
stamps itself indelibly on their consciousness—or you
preach it to ignorant adults unable to weigh the instruction you give them.

Such is your activity, or for such activity you are
preparing.

But what if this that you teach, or are preparing to
teach, be untrue?

Is it possible that this cannot be, or must not be, considered ?   If you consider it and compare this teaching
with other teachings claiming to be equally unique and
infallible, and compare it with what you yourselves
know, and with common-sense ; if, in a word, you
consider it, not in a spirit of blind credulity, but freely
—you cannot fail to see that what has been given to
you as sacred truth, is not only not sacred truth, but is

simply an obsolete and superstitious belief, which, like other similar beliefs, is maintained and preached by men not for the benefit of their brother-men but for some other object. And as soon as you have understood that, all those of you who look on life seriously and attend to the voice of conscience, will be unable to continue to preach this doctrine, or to prepare to preach it.

### XI.

But I hear the usual reply : 'What will become of men if they cease to believe the Church doctrines? Won't things be worse than they now are?'

What will happen if the people of Christendom cease to believe in Church doctrine? The result will be—that not the Hebrew legends alone, but the religious wisdom of the whole world, will become accessible and intelligible to them. People will grow up and develop with unperverted understandings and feelings. Having discarded a teaching accepted credulously, people will order their relation towards God reasonably, in conformity with their knowledge ; and will recognise the moral obligations flowing from that relation.

'But will not the results be worse?'

If the Church doctrine is not true—how can it be worse for men not to have falsehood preached to them as truth, especially in a way so unfair as is now adopted for the purpose?

'But,' some people say, 'the common folk are coarse and uneducated ; and what we, educated people, do not require, may yet be useful and even indispensable for the masses.'

If all men are made alike, then all must travel one and the same path from darkness to light, from ignorance to knowledge, from falsehood to truth. You have travelled that road and have attained consciousness of the unreliability of the belief in which you were trained. By what right, then, will you check others from making the same advance?

You say, that though you do not need such food, it

is needed by the masses. But no wise man undertakes to decide the physical food another must eat; how, then, can it be decided—and who can decide—what spiritual food the masses of the people must have?

The fact that you notice among the people a demand for this doctrine, in no way proves that the demand ought to be supplied. There exists a demand for intoxicants and tobacco—and other yet worse demands. And the fact is that you yourselves, by complex methods of hypnotization, evoke this very demand, by the existence of which you try to justify your own occupation. Only cease to evoke the demand, and it will not exist; for, as in your own case so with everyone else, there can be no demand for lies, but all men have moved and still move from darkness to light; and you, who stand nearer to the light, should try to make it accessible to others, and not to hide it from them.

'But,' I hear a last objection, 'will the result not be worse if we—educated, moral men, who desire to do good to the people—abandon our posts because of the doubts that have arisen in our souls, and let our places be taken by coarse, immoral men, indifferent to the people's good?'

Undoubtedly the abandonment of the clerical profession by the best men, will have the effect that the ecclesiastical business passing into coarse, immoral hands, will more and more disintegrate, and expose its own falseness and harmfulness. But the result will not be worse, for the disintegration of ecclesiastical establishments is now going on, and is one of the means by which people are being liberated from the fraud in which they have been held. And, therefore, the quicker this emancipation is accomplished, by enlightened and good men abandoning the clerical profession, the better it will be. And so, the greater the number of enlightened and good men who leave the clerical profession, the better.

So from whichever side you look at your activity, that activity remains harmful, and therefore all those among you who still fear God and have not quite stifled the voice of conscience, cannot do otherwise than exert all your strength to release yourselves from the false position in which you are placed.

I know that many of you are encumbered with families, or are dependent on parents who require you to follow the course you have begun; I know how difficult it is to abandon a post that brings honour or wealth, or even gives a competence and enables you and your families to continue a life to which you are accustomed, and I know how painful it is to go against relations one loves. But anything is better than to do what destroys your own soul and injures your fellow men.

Therefore, the sooner and more definitely you repent of your sin and cease your activity, the better it will be not only for others, but for yourselves.

That is what I—standing now on the brink of my grave, and clearly seeing the chief source of human ills —wished to say to you; and to say, not in order to expose or condemn you (I know how imperceptibly you were yourselves led into the snare which has made you what you are), but I wished to say it in order to co-operate in the emancipation of men from the terrible evil which the preaching of your doctrine produces by obscuring the truth: and at the same time I wished to help you to rouse yourselves from the hypnotic sleep in which now you often fail to understand all the wickedness of your own actions.

May God, who sees your hearts, help you in the effort.

[November 1, o.s., 1902.]

## XXVI

## THOUGHTS SELECTED FROM PRIVATE
## LETTERS

### Two Views of Life.

THERE are only two strictly logical views of life : one, a false one, which understands life to mean those visible phenomena that occur in our bodies from the time of birth to the time of death ; the other, a true one, which understands life to be the invisible consciousness which dwells within us. One view is false, the other true, but both are logical.

The first of these views, the false one, which understands life to mean the phenomena visible in our bodies from birth till death, is as old as the world. It is not, as many people suppose, a view of life produced by the materialistic science and philosophy of our day ; our science and philosophy have only carried that conception to its furthest limits, making more obvious than ever the incompatibility of that view of life with the fundamental demands of human nature, but it is a very old and primitive view, held by men on the lowest level of development. It was expressed by Chinese, by Buddhists, and by Jews, and in the Book of Job.

This view is now expressed as follows : Life is an accidental play of the forces in matter, showing itself in time and space. What we call our consciousness is not life, but is a delusion of the senses, which makes it seem as if life lay in that consciousness. Consciousness is a spark which, under certain conditions, is ignited in matter, burns up to a flame, dies down, and at last goes out altogether. This flame (*i.e.*, consciousness) attendant upon matter for a certain time between two infinities of time, is—nothing. And *though consciousness perceives itself and the whole universe, and sits in judgment on itself and on the universe, and sees the play of chance in this universe, and, above all, calls it a play of chance, in contradistinction to something which is not chance*—this consciousness itself is only an outcome of lifeless matter—a phantom, appearing and vanishing without meaning or result. Everything is the outcome of ever-changing matter ; and what we call life is but a condition of dead matter.

That is one view of life. It is a perfectly logical view. According to this view, man's reasonable consciousness is but an accident incidental to a certain state of matter, and, therefore, what we in our consciousness call life, is but a phantom. Only dead matter exists. What we call life, is the play of death.

The other view of life is this. Life is only what I am conscious of in myself. And I am always conscious of my life, not as something that has been or will be (that is how I *reflect* on my life), but when I am *conscious* of it, I feel that—I *am*—never beginning anywhere, never ending anywhere. With the consciousness of my life, conceptions of time and space do not blend. My life manifests itself in time and space, but that is only its *manifestation*. Life itself, as I am conscious of it, is something I perceive apart from time and space. So that, in this view of life, we get just the contrary result : not that consciousness of life is a phantom, but that everything relating to time and space is of the nature of a phantom.

Therefore, in this view, the cessation of my physical existence in time and space has no reality, and cannot end, or even hinder, my true life. And, according to this view, death does not exist.

### MATTER IS THE LIMIT OF SPIRIT.

The material form in which the awakening of our consciousness of true life finds us in this world, is, so to speak, the boundary limiting the free development of our spirit.

Matter is the limit of spirit. But true life is the destruction of this limitation.

In this understanding of life lies the very essence of the understanding of truth—that essence which gives man the consciousness of eternal life.

Materialists mistake that which limits life, for life itself.

## THE SCAFFOLDING.

We must remind ourselves as often as possible that our true life is not this external, material life that passes before our eyes here on earth, but that it is the inner life of our spirit, for which the visible life serves only as a scaffolding—a necessary aid to our spiritual growth. The scaffolding itself is only of temporary importance, and, after it has served its purpose, is no longer wanted, but even becomes a hindrance.

Seeing before him an enormously high and elaborately constructed scaffolding, while the building itself only just shows above its foundations, man is apt to make the mistake of attaching more importance to the scaffolding than to the building for the sake of which, alone, this temporary scaffolding has been put up.

We must remind ourselves and one another, that the scaffolding has no meaning or importance, except to make possible the erection of the building itself.

## THE LIFE OF THE SPIRIT.

There are moments when one ceases to believe in spiritual life.

This is not unbelief, but rather periods of belief in physical life.

A man suddenly begins to be afraid of death. This always happens when something has befogged him, and he once more begins to believe that bodily life is real life, just as in a theatre you may forget yourself, and think that what you see on the stage is actually happening, and so may be frightened by what is done there.

That is what happens in life.

After a man has understood that his life is not on the stage, but in the stalls—that is, not in his personality, but outside it—it sometimes happens that, from old habit, he suddenly succumbs again to the seduction of illusion, and feels frightened.

But these moments of illusion are not enough to convince me that what goes on before me (in my physical life) is really happening.

At times when one's spirit sinks, one must treat one's self as one treats an invalid—and keep quiet !

## THE FEAR OF DEATH.

It is generally supposed that there is something mystical in our view of life and death. But there is nothing of the kind.

I like my garden, I like reading a book, I like caressing a child. By dying I lose all this, and therefore I do not wish to die, and I fear death.

It may be that my whole life consists of such temporary worldly desires and their gratification. If so, I cannot help being afraid of what will end these desires. But if these desires and their gratification have given way and been replaced in me by another desire—the desire to do the will of God, to give myself to Him in my present state, and in any possible future state—then the more my desires have changed, the less I fear death, and the less does death exist for me. And if my desires be completely transformed, then nothing but life remains, and there is no death. To replace what is earthly and temporary by what is eternal is the way of life, and along it we must travel. But in what state his own soul is—each one knows for himself.

## THE WAY TO KNOW GOD AND THE SOUL.

God and the Soul are known by me in the same way that I know infinity : not by means of definitions, but in quite another way. Definitions only destroy for me that knowledge. Just as I know assuredly that there is an infinity of numbers, so do I know that there is a God, and that I have a soul. For me this knowledge is indubitable, simply because I am led to it unavoidably.

To the certainty of the infinity of numbers, I am led by addition.

To the certain knowledge of God I am led by the question, 'Whence come I?'

To the knowledge of the soul I am led by the question, 'What am I?'

And I know surely of the infinity of numbers, and of the existence of God, and of my soul, when I am led to the knowledge of them by these most simple questions.

To one I add one, and one more, and another one, and another one; or I break a stick in two, and again in two, and again, and again—and I cannot help knowing that number is infinite.

I was born of my mother, and she of my grandmother, and she of my great-grandmother, but the very first—of whom? And I inevitably arrive at God.

My legs are not I, my arms are not I, my head is not I, my feelings are not I, even my thoughts are not I: then what am I? I am I, I am my soul.

From whatever side I approach God, it will always be the same. The origin of my thoughts, my reason, is God. The origin of my love, is also He. The origin of matter, is He too.

It is the same with the conception of the soul. If I consider my striving after truth, I know that this striving after truth is my immaterial basis—my soul. If I turn to my feelings of love for goodness, I know that it is my soul which loves.

These 'Thoughts' are taken from the 1903 Moscow edition of Tolstoy's works, and (except 'Two Views,' which compare with chapter xvii. of 'On Life') are new in English.

# INDEX

370

THE END

BILLING AND SONS, LTD., PRINTERS, GUILDFORD.